D0755317

PRACTICAL PHONETICS AND PHONOLOGY

Routledge English Language Introductions cover core areas of language study and are one-stop resources for students.

Assuming no prior knowledge, books in the series offer an accessible overview of the subject, with activities, study questions, sample analyses, commentaries and key readings – all in the same volume. The innovative and flexible 'two-dimensional' structure is built around four sections – introductions, development, exploration and extension – which offer self-contained stages for study.

Practical Phonetics and Phonology:

- ❑ provides a wide-ranging survey of many practical aspects of English phonetics and phonology
- ❑ introduces step-by-step the core concepts of speech science such as: the phoneme, syllable structure, production of speech, vowel and consonant possibilities, glottal settings, stress, rhythm, intonation and the surprises of connected speech
- ❑ features a discussion of regional and social accent variation, backed up by an accompanying audio CD containing a collection of samples provided by genuine speakers of 20 accent varieties from Britain, Ireland, the USA, Canada, Australia, New Zealand, South Africa, India, Singapore and West Africa
- ❑ outlines pronunciation change in the past and indicates the significance of the widespread changes now in progress
- ❑ applies phonetic insights to the practical problems of learning the pronunciation of foreign languages and teaching English to non-native speakers
- ❑ places the study of speech science in a wider linguistic and social setting through classic readings from key names in the discipline including David Abercrombie, David Crystal, Dennis Fry, Daniel Jones, Peter Ladefoged and Steven Pinker

The accompanying website to this book can be found at
http://www.routledge.com/textbooks/0415261341

Written by experienced teachers and researchers this accessible textbook is an essential resource for all students of English language and linguistics.

Beverley Collins is Lecturer in English Linguistics at the University of Leiden in the Netherlands. **Inger M. Mees** is Associate Professor in the Department of English at Copenhagen Business School, Denmark. Their joint publications include pronunciation courses for Danish and Dutch learners of English, *The Real Professor Higgins* (a biography of the phonetician Daniel Jones), together with numerous articles on sociophonetics, contrastive phonetics and the historiography of phonetics.

ROUTLEDGE ENGLISH LANGUAGE INTRODUCTIONS

SERIES EDITOR: PETER STOCKWELL

Peter Stockwell is Senior Lecturer in the School of English Studies at the University of Nottingham, UK, where his interests include sociolinguistics, stylistics and cognitive poetics. His recent publications include *Cognitive Poetics: An Introduction* (Routledge, 2002), *The Poetics of Science Fiction, Investigating English Language* (with Howard Jackson), and *Contextualized Stylistics* (edited with Tony Bex and Michael Burke).

SERIES CONSULTANT: RONALD CARTER

Ronald Carter is Professor of Modern English Language in the School of English Studies at the University of Nottingham, UK. He is the co-series editor of the forthcoming *Routledge Applied Linguistics* series, series editor of *Interface*, and was co-founder of the Routledge *Intertext* series.

OTHER TITLES IN THE SERIES:

Sociolinguistics
Peter Stockwell

Pragmatics and Discourse
Joan Cutting

Grammar and Vocabulary
Howard Jackson

Psycholinguistics
John Field

World Englishes
Jennifer Jenkins

FORTHCOMING:

Child Language
Jean Stilwell Peccei

Stylistics
Paul Simpson

PRACTICAL PHONETICS AND PHONOLOGY

A resource book for students

A
B
C
D

BEVERLEY COLLINS AND INGER M. MEES

Routledge
Taylor & Francis Group

LONDON AND NEW YORK

First published 2003 by Routledge
2 Park Square, Milton Park, Abingdon, Oxon, OX14 4RN

Simultaneously published in the USA and Canada
by Routledge
270 Madison Ave, New York, NY 10016

Reprinted 2005

Routledge is an imprint of the Taylor & Francis Group

Typeset in 10/12.5 pt Minion by Graphicraft Limited, Hong Kong
Printed and bound in Great Britain by TJ International Ltd, Padstow, Cornwall

British Library Cataloguing in Publication Data
A catalogue record for this book is available from the British Library

Library of Congress Cataloging in Publication Data
Has been applied for

ISBN 0-415-26133-3 (hbk)
ISBN 0-415-26134-1 (pbk)

For the 2004-reprinted edition, in response to readers' suggestions a number of corrections and changes
have been made. In particular, there has been a complete revision of the table on p. 189.

In addition, we have a minor correction to the website. In the file 'Keys to activities', one change should be
made to Activity 65 where '*silipa slipper*' should be INSERTED so that the final three lines should now
read:

Kalapu	*club*
Silipa	*slipper*
Parakarafa	*paragraph*

HOW TO USE THIS BOOK

The Routledge English Language Introductions offer key information and a set of resources that you can use to suit your own style of study. The books are divided into four sections:

A   **Introduction** – sets out the key concepts for the area of study.
B   **Development** – adds to your knowledge and builds on the key ideas already introduced.
C   **Exploration** – provides examples of language data and guides you through your own investigation of the field.
D   **Extension** – offers you the chance to compare your expertise with key readings in the area. These are taken from the work of important writers, and are provided with guidance and questions for your further thought.

Most books in the Routledge English Language Introductions series are designed to be read either straight through (like a traditional textbook), or across the numbered units to allow you to follow a thread in depth quickly. For *Practical Phonetics and Phonology* we have retained the four-section structure. However, the nature of phonetics requires a cumulative build-up of knowledge; so you first need to read all the units in Sections A and B fully and in sequence before going on to the accent samples in Section C, and the extension readings in Section D.

The glossary/index at the end, together with the suggestions for further reading, will help to keep you orientated. Each textbook has a supporting website with extra commentary, suggestions, additional material and support for teachers and students.

PRACTICAL PHONETICS AND PHONOLOGY

One word in the title above is all-important: note that this book concentrates on *practical* rather than theoretical aspects of phonetics and phonology. It has been our aim to present the subject in the kind of down-to-earth way that readers will find easy to follow, enabling them to absorb the most significant basic principles and terminology. Exercise activities are provided at regular intervals to reinforce and extend what has been learnt.

We emphasise throughout how phonetics and phonology can supply insights to help you understand those aspects of speech and pronunciation that most people seem to find interesting. These include such matters as the ways in which regional accents differ from each other, how over the centuries English pronunciation has changed (and is still changing), and how phonetic knowledge can help you to pronounce foreign languages more effectively. Incidentally, we must state at the outset that this is not a book on elocution or speech training. We believe that the way you speak your *native* language is your own concern, and it isn't any of our business to tell native English speakers that certain types of accent are better or worse than others. (For non-natives we do provide some hints and guidance on making your English pronunciation more convincing.)

The practical emphasis also explains why we include a free audio CD with this book. Not only does this provide you with spoken examples as you read along, but it also enables you to listen to nearly forty-five minutes of samples of English drawn from all over the world. A final practical resource is the website with extra information, questions, keys to exercise activities and links to many other Internet pages. By accessing this material, you can go on to expand your knowledge by investigating areas of speech science beyond what we can deal with in an introductory textbook.

Section A introduces some basic concepts and leads you on to absorb the ideas and terminology needed for the all-round study of human speech (i.e. general phonetics). It introduces the phoneme and teaches you how to use phonemic transcription to write down the sounds of English with greater accuracy than ordinary spelling would ever allow.

Building on this foundation, Section B develops your expertise through a closer study of the phonetics of English – including not just the vowels and consonants, but also many of the interesting features of connected speech such as stress and intonation.

Section C explores English in a selection of its many varieties. The audio CD includes English spoken by twenty genuine speakers of different English accents worldwide – ranging from Dublin to Delhi, and from Scotland to Singapore. For each accent there is a full transcript plus a brief description of the salient phonetic features. You'll also find out how English has developed over the centuries and how its pronunciation is changing even now in our own time. This section is rounded off with guidelines showing you how practical phonetics can be used both as an aid for English-speakers learning foreign languages, and also as an effective way of teaching English pronunciation to non-natives.

Section D extends your knowledge further by means of a selection of writings about phonetics by well-known experts in the field. These take in a wide range – including attitudes to regional accents, computer speech synthesis and speech recognition, the ways in which forensic phonetics can be used to fight crime, and how children learn the significance of intonation patterns. Our hope is that through reading these authors you'll be inspired to go on to discover much more about that most complex and fascinating of human activities – speech.

CONTENTS

CONTENTS **CROSS-REFERENCED**

CONTENTS **CROSS-REFERENCED**

LIST OF FIGURES

LIST OF TABLES

LIST OF TRACKS ON AUDIO CD

ACKNOWLEDGEMENTS

In the course of writing this book we have been helped in many different ways by colleagues, students, friends and family. Our thanks go out to them all, but especially to those mentioned below.

Ron Carter gave us much wise advice at the planning stage, and the series editor Peter Stockwell has provided us with valuable guidance from then on. Crucial help and support has come all along the way from the editorial staff at Routledge, successively from Louisa Semlyen, Christy Kirkpatrick, Kate Parker and Ruth Jeavons; a special note of gratitude for her efficiency, patience and cheerfulness under pressure goes to Margaret Aherne.

We want to thank all those colleagues who offered perceptive critical comments on preliminary drafts and the final manuscript. Most (though not all) of their suggestions have been acted upon, and we have ended up with a greatly improved book as a consequence. In this regard, we must make special mention of Philip Carr, Rias van den Doel, Jack Windsor Lewis, Robert Phillipson and Gilda Suárez de Nielsen. We also gained much from the detailed criticism contained in Paul Tench's review of the penultimate version of the manuscript. Colin Ewen not only read and commented on the book in draft form, but also aided us in a very practical way by constructing and digitising all the vowel diagrams and intonation representations. Help with providing and checking language materials was given by Sarah Branci, Rolf Bremmer, Inès Carr, Robert Druce, Gyde Hansen, Arnt Lykke Jakobsen, María Pilar Lorenzo, Vincent Phillips, Klaske van Leyden and Carol Williams. Useful feedback on many matters came from students at the Copenhagen Business School who allowed us to expose them to earlier versions of the text. We are also grateful to Jennifer Jenkins, who used portions of the material with her students at King's College London. Finally, mention must be made of Arnold Warthog, who was constantly on hand to assist us in every aspect of our work.

For the audio CD, we benefited greatly from the technical expertise of Steve Hitchins, who assembled and edited the final version of the disc. In this connection, we also want to thank Vincent van Heuven for the use of recording facilities at Leiden University, and John Wells for permission to use a portion of the recording of the cardinal vowels made for University College London by the late A. C. Gimson. For the provision of recorded materials used in the collection of English accent varieties we are much indebted to Alastair Hamilton, Mia Overlade Hansen, Jen Hay, Gerry Knowles, Lesley Milroy, Debi Molnar, Tine Ditlev Nielsen, Kitt Spangbjerg Petersen, Yvonne Spuijbroek, Karen Stetting and Maria Vanlaeken-Kester. Finally, our thanks go out to all the anonymous recorded speakers for their time, trouble and goodwill.

Naturally, we do not wish to saddle any of those mentioned above with blame for whatever defects and errors remain in the book. That responsibility is ours alone.

This book is dedicated to the memory of I.M.'s mother, Birthe Mees, and B.C.'s sister, Beryl Adams.

Beverley Collins and Inger M. Mees
Leiden and Copenhagen, March 2003

The authors and publishers wish to thank all mentioned below for permission to reproduce copyright materials.

Blackwell Publishers for the extract from Peter Ladefoged's *Vowels and Consonants* (2001).

Cambridge University Press for the extract from Dennis Fry's *Homo Loquens* (1977).

Edinburgh University Press for the extract from David Abercrombie's *Fifty Years in Phonetics* (1991).

English Today for the extract from Barbara Bradford's 'Upspeak in British English' (1997) and Maurice Varney's 'Forensic linguistics' (1997).

Penguin Books for the extracts from David Crystal's *The English Language* (1988) and *Listen to Your Child* (1986) and the extract from Stephen Pinker's *The Language Instinct* (1994).

Paul Evans, Bernadette Evans and *The Oldie* for the poem used in Activity 114.

Mrs Michelle Stanbury for the extract from Daniel Jones's 'Speech training: the phonetic aspect' reprinted from *British Journal of Educational Psychology* (1935).

The International Phonetic Association for the IPA Chart (to contact the IPA, visit its website on http://www.arts.gla.ac.uk/IPA/ipa.html).

While every effort has been made to find the copyright holders of materials used in this volume, the publishers would be happy to hear from any they have been unable to contact and will make any necessary amendment at the earliest opportunity.

LIST OF PHONETIC SYMBOLS

The following list used in this book does not include (1) the symbols employed for English phonemic transcription (see p. 13) or (2) the symbols for the cardinal vowels (see pp. 61 and 63). A more comprehensive set of symbols is to be found on the IPA chart, p. 258.

ṭ   voiced medial /t/, American English *better*

ɹ   post-alveolar approximant, English *rural*

r   voiced alveolar trill, Spanish *parra* 'grapevine'

ɾ   voiced alveolar tap, Spanish *para* 'for'

ʀ   voiced uvular trill, old-fashioned French *rue* 'street'

ʋ   labio-dental approximant, so-called 'defective' English /r/: *merry* ['meʋi]

ç   voiceless palatal fricative, German *nicht* 'not'

x   voiceless velar fricative, German *Nacht* 'night'

ʍ   voiceless labial-velar fricative, Scottish English *which*

ɸ   voiceless bilabial fricative, allophone of English /f/, *helpful*

β   voiced bilabial fricative, Spanish *aviso* 'warning'

ɮ   voiced lateral fricative, Zulu *dlala* 'play!' (imp.)

ɫ   velarised alveolar lateral approximant ('dark *l*'), English *still*

ɬ   voiceless alveolar lateral fricative, Welsh *Llangollen* (place-name)

ʔ   glottal stop, Cockney *hutter*

ˀ   pre-glottalised, English *crackdown* [kræˀkdaʊn]

~   (through symbol) velarised, English *still* [stɪɫ]

˜   (above symbol) nasalised, English *man* [mæ̃n]

ʷ   labialised, English *dwell* [dʷwel]

̪   dental (applied to alveolars), English *hid them* [hɪḓ ðəm]

ʲ   palatalised, English *tube* [tʲjuːb]

̥   (below symbol, but above for descending symbols) devoiced, English *tweed* [tw̥iːd̥], *big* [b̥ɪg̊]

ʰ   aspirated, English *cat* [kʰæt]

ˌ   (above or beneath the symbol) syllabic consonant, English *button* ['bʌtn̩]

ː   length mark, English *green* [griːn]

+   (after or below symbol) advanced, English *key* [k₊iː],[ki̟ː]

-     (after or below symbol) retracted, English *core* [k-ɔː],[k̠ɔː]

ˈ   stressed, English *potato* [pəˈteɪtəʊ]

/ /   enclosing phonemic transcription

[ ]   enclosing phonetic transcription

*   unacceptable or non-existent form

Section A
INTRODUCTION

A1 ENGLISH WORLDWIDE

Introduction

If you've picked up this book and are reading it, we can assume one or two things about you. Firstly, you're a human being – not a dolphin, not a parrot, not a chimpanzee. No matter how intelligent such creatures may appear to be at communicating in their different ways, they simply do not have the innate capacity for language that makes humans unique in the animal world.

Then, we can assume that you speak English. You are either a **native speaker**, which means that you speak English as your mother tongue; or you're a **non-native speaker** using English as your second language, or a learner of English as a foreign language. Whichever applies to you, we can also assume, since you are reading this, that you are literate and are aware of the conventions of the written language – like spelling and punctuation. So far, so good. Now, what can a book on English phonetics and phonology do for you?

In fact, the study of both **phonetics** (the science of speech sound) and **phonology** (how sounds pattern and function in a given language) are going to help you to learn more about language in general and English in particular. If you're an English native speaker, you'll be likely to discover much about your mother tongue of which you were previously unaware. If you're a non-native learner, it will also assist in improving your pronunciation and listening abilities. In either case, you will end up better able to teach English pronunciation to others and possibly find it easier to learn how to speak other languages better yourself. You'll also discover some things about the pronunciation of English in the past, and about the great diversity of accents and dialects that go to make up the English that's spoken at present. Let's take this last aspect as a starting point as we survey briefly some of the many types of English pronunciation that we can hear around us in the modern world.

Accent and dialect in English

You may well already have some idea of what the terms 'accent' and 'dialect' mean, but we shall now try to define these concepts more precisely. All languages typically exist in a number of different forms. For example, there may be several ways in which the language can be pronounced; these are termed **accents**. To cover variation in grammar and vocabulary we use the term **dialect**. If you want to take in all these aspects of language variation – pronunciation together with grammar and vocabulary – then you can simply use the term **variety**.

We can make two further distinctions in language variation, namely between **regional variation**, which involves differences between one place and another; and **social variation**, which reflects differences between one social group and another (this can cover such matters as gender, ethnicity, religion, age and, very significantly, social class). Regional variation is accepted by everyone without question. It is common knowledge that people from London do not speak English in the same way as those from Bristol, Edinburgh or Cardiff; nor, on a global scale, in the same way as the citizens of New York, Sydney, Johannesburg or Auckland. What is more controversial is the question of social variation in language, especially where the link with social class is concerned. Some people may take offence when it is pointed out that accent and dialect are closely connected with class differences, but it would be very difficult to deny this fact.

In considering variation we can take account of a range of possibilities. The broadest local accents are termed **basilects** (adjective: **basilectal**). These are associated with working-class occupations and persons less privileged in terms of education and other social factors. The most prestigious forms of speech are termed **acrolects** (adjective: **acrolectal**). These, by contrast, are generally found in persons with more advantages in terms of wealth, education and other social factors. In England, at least, there is great variation regionally amongst the basilectal varieties. On the other hand, the acrolectal varieties exhibit very few differences from one area to another.

In the British Isles it is fair to say that one variety of English pronunciation has traditionally been connected with the more privileged section of the population. As a result, it became what is termed a **prestige accent**, namely, a variety regarded highly even by those who do not speak it, and associated with status, education and wealth. This type of English is variously referred to as 'Oxford English', 'BBC English' and even 'the Queen's English', but none of these names can be considered at all accurate. For a long time, phoneticians have called it **RP** – short for **Received Pronunciation**; in the Victorian era, one meaning of 'received' was 'socially acceptable'. Recently the term 'Received Pronunciation' (in the full form rather than the abbreviation favoured by phoneticians) seems to have caught on with the media, and has begun to have wider currency with the general public.

Traditional RP could be regarded as the classic example of a prestige accent, since although it was spoken only by a small percentage of the population it had high status everywhere in Britain and, to an extent, the world. RP was not a regional but a social accent; it was to be heard all over England (though only from a minority of speakers). Although to some extent associated with the London area, this probably only reflected the greater wealth of the south-east of England as compared with the rest of the country. RP continues to be much used in the theatre and at one time was virtually the only speech employed by national BBC radio and television announcers – hence the term 'BBC English'. Nowadays, the BBC has a declared policy of employing a number of announcers with (modified) regional accents on its national TV and radio networks. On the BBC World Service and BBC World TV there are in addition announcers and presenters who use other global varieties. Traditional RP also happens to be the kind of pronunciation still heard from older members of the British Royal Family; hence the term 'the Queen's English'.

Within RP itself, it was possible to distinguish a number of different types (see Wells 1982: 279–95 for a detailed discussion). The original narrow definition included only persons who had been educated at one of what in Britain are called 'public schools' (actually very expensive boarding schools) like Eton, Harrow and Winchester. It was always true, however, that – for whatever reason – many English people from less exclusive social backgrounds either lost, or considerably modified, their distinctive regional speech and ended up speaking RP or something very similar to it. In this book, because of the dated – and to some people objectionable – social connotations, we shall not normally use the label RP (except consciously to refer to the upper-class speech of the twentieth century). Rather than dealing with what is now regarded by many of the younger generation as a quaint minority accent, we shall instead endeavour to describe a more encompassing neutral type of modern English but one which nevertheless lacks obvious local accent features. To refer to this variety we shall employ the term **non-regional pronunciation** (abbreviated to **NRP**). We shall thus be able to allow for the present-day range of variation to be heard from educated middle and younger generation speakers in England who have a pronunciation which cannot be pinned down to a specific area.

Traditional Received Pronunciation (RP) ☺ Track 1

Jeremy: yes what put *me* off Eton was the importance attached to games because I wasn't sporty – I was very bad at games – I was of a rather sort of cowardly dis-position – and the idea to have to run around in the mud and get kicked in the face – by a lot of larger boys three times a week – I found terribly terribly depressing – fortunately this only really happened one time a year – at the most two – because in the summer one could go rowing – and then one was just alone with one's enormous blisters – in the stream –

Interviewer: which games did you play though – or did you have to play –

Jeremy: well you had to play – I mean I liked – I was – the only thing I was any good at was fencing and I liked rather solitary things like fencing or squash and things like that – but you had to play – Eton had its own ghastly combination of rugger and soccer which was called the 'field game' – and that was for the so-called Oppidans *[fee-paying pupils who form the overwhelming majority at Eton]* like myself – and then there was the Wall Game – which was even worse – and that was for the college – in other words the non-paying students known as 'tugs' –

Interviewer: known as –

Jeremy: tugs –

Interviewer: ah right –

Jeremy: they were called tugs –

Interviewer: there was a lot of slang I suppose

Jeremy: there was a *lot* of slang – I wonder how much it's still understood – and I don't know if it still exists at Eton – whether it's changed

Jeremy, a university professor, was born in the early 1940s. His speech is a very con-servative variety, by which we mean that he retains many old-fashioned forms in his pronunciation. Jeremy, in fact, preserves many of the features of traditional Received Pronunciation (as described in numerous books on phonetics written in the twentieth century) which have since been abandoned by most younger speakers.

Modern non-regional pronunciation (NRP) ☺ Track 2

Daniel: last time I went to France I got bitten – thirty-seven times by mosquitoes – it was really cool – I had them all up my leg – and I got one on the sole of my foot – that was the worst place ever – it's really actually quite interesting – that's really big – and we didn't have like any – any mosquito bite stuff – so I just itched all week

Interviewer: what are you going to do this summer – except for going to France

Daniel: go to France – and then come back here for about – ten days – I'm supposed to get a job to pay my Dad back all the money that I owe him – except no one wants to give me a job – so – I'm going to have to be a prostitute or something – I don't know – well – I'm here for ten days after I come from France anyway – and then we go to Orlando on the 1st of August – for two weeks – come back and then I get my results – and if they're good then – I'm happy – and if they're not good – then – I spend – the next six weeks working – to do resits – and then end of September – go to university

You'll notice straightaway that this speaker, Daniel, whose non-regionally defined speech is not atypical of the younger generation of educated British speakers, sounds different from Jeremy in many ways. Daniel grew up in the 1980s (the recording dates from 1996) indicating that well before the end of the twentieth century non-regional pronunciation (NRP) was effectively largely replacing traditional RP.

Just recently, there's been talk of a 'new' variety of British accent which has been dubbed **Estuary English** – a term originally coined by David Rosewarne (1984) and later enthusiastically embraced by the media. The estuary in question is that of the Thames, and the name has been given to the speech of those whose accents are a compromise between traditional RP and popular London speech (or Cockney, see Section C2). Claims have been made that Estuary English will in the future become the new prestige British accent – but perhaps it's too soon to make predictions. What does seem certain, however, is that change is in progress, and that one can no longer delimit a prestige accent of British English as easily as one could in the early twentieth century. The speech of young educated speakers in the south of England indeed appears to show a considerable degree of London influence and we shall take account of these changes in our description of NRP.

World Englishes

A British model of English is what is most commonly taught to students learning English as a second language in Europe, Africa, India and much of Asia. In this book, NRP is the accent we assume non-native speakers will choose. Our main reason for selecting NRP is that English of this kind is easily understood not only all over Britain but also elsewhere in the world.

In Scotland, Ireland and Wales, notwithstanding the fact that there never were very many speakers of RP in those countries, the accent was formerly held in high regard (certainly this is less so nowadays). This was also true of more distant English-speaking countries such as Australia, New Zealand and South Africa. Today scarcely any Australians, New Zealanders or South Africans consciously imitate traditional RP as was once the case, even though the speech of radio and television announcers in these countries clearly shows close relationships with British English. In the USA, surprisingly, there was also many years ago a tradition of using a special artificial type of English, based on RP, for the stage – especially for Shakespeare and other classic drama. Even today, the 'British accent' (by which Americans essentially mean traditional RP) retains a degree of prestige in the United States; this is especially so in the acting profession – although increasingly in the modern cinema it seems to be the villains rather than the heroes who speak in this manner!

But in the twenty-first century any kind of British English is in reality a minority form. Most English is spoken outside the British Isles – notably in the USA, where it is the first language of more than 220 million people. It is also used in several other countries as a first language, e.g. Canada, Australia, New Zealand, South Africa and the countries of the Caribbean. English is used widely as a second language for official purposes, again by millions of speakers, in southern Asia, e.g. India, Pakistan, Sri Lanka, and in many countries across Africa. In addition, there are large second language English-speaking populations in, for example, Hong Kong, Malaysia and Singapore.

Let's now look a little more closely at two regions of the world where English is used as a first language – North America (USA and Canada) and Australasia (Australia and New Zealand). In the United States, over the course of the last century, an accent of English developed which today goes under the name of **General American** (often abbreviated to GA). This variety is an amalgam of the educated speech of the northern USA, having otherwise no recognisably local features. It is said to be in origin the educated English of the Midwest of America; it certainly lacks the characteristic accent forms of East Coast cities such as New York and Boston. Canadian English bears a strong family resemblance to GA – although it has one or two features which set it firmly apart. On the other hand, the accents of the southern states of America are clearly quite different from GA in very many respects.

GA is to be heard very widely from announcers and presenters on television and radio networks all over the USA, and for this reason it is popularly known by another name, 'Network American'. General American is also used as a model by millions of students learning English as a second language – notably in Latin America and Japan, but nowadays increasingly elsewhere. We shall return to this variety in Section C1.

Other varieties of English which are now of global significance are those spoken in Australia and New Zealand. Once again there is an obvious relationship between these two varieties, although they also have clear differences from each other. New Zealand English has distinct 'South Island' types of pronunciation – but there is surprisingly little regional variation across the huge continent of Australia. On the other hand, there is considerable social variation between what are traditionally termed 'Broad Australian', 'General Australian' and 'Cultivated Australian English'. The first is the kind which most vigorously exhibits distinctive Australian features and is the everyday speech of perhaps a third of the population. The last is the term used for the most prestigious variety (in all respects much closer to British NRP); this minority accent is not only to be heard from television and radio presenters but is also, in Australia itself, taught as a model to foreign learners. General Australian, used by the majority of Australians, falls between these two extremes.

Finally, we have to remember that while there are so many different world varieties of English, they are essentially (at least in their standard forms) very similar. In fact, although the differences are interesting, it's the degree of similarity characterising these widely dispersed varieties of English which is really far more striking. English as used by educated speakers is readily understood all over the world. In fact, it is unquestionably the most widespread form of international communication that has ever existed.

A

PHONEME AND ALLOPHONE

Introduction

At this point, let's sort out some basic terminology. The study of sound in general is the science of **acoustics**. We'll remind you that **phonetics** is the term used for the study of sound in human language. The study of the selection and patterns of sounds in a single language is called **phonology**. To get a full idea of the way the sounds of a language work, we need to study not only the phonetics of the language concerned but also its phonological system. Both phonetics and phonology are important components of **linguistics**, which is the science that deals with the general study of language. A specialist in linguistics is technically termed a **linguist**. Note that this is different from the general use of *linguist* to mean someone who can speak a number of languages. **Phonetician** and **phonologist** are the terms used for linguists who study phonetics and phonology respectively.

We can examine speech in various ways, corresponding to the stages of the transmission of the speech signal from a speaker to a listener. The movements of the tongue, lips and other speech organs are called **articulations** – hence this area of phonetics is termed **articulatory phonetics**. The physical nature of the speech signal is the concern of **acoustic phonetics** (you can find some more information about these matters on the recommended websites, p. 255). The study of how the ear receives the speech signal we call **auditory phonetics**. The formulation of the speech message in the brain of the speaker and the interpretation of it in the brain of the listener are branches of **psycholinguistics**. In this book, our emphasis will be on articulatory phonetics, this being in many ways the most accessible branch of the subject, and the one with most applications for the beginner.

In our view, phonetics should be a matter of practice as well as theory. We want you to produce sounds as well as read about them. Let's start as we mean to go on: say the English word *mime*. We are going to examine the sound at the beginning and end of the word: [m].

⭐ **Activity**

1

Say the English word *mime* several times. Use a mirror to look at your mouth as you pronounce the word. Now cut out the vowel and just say a long [m]. Keep it going for five seconds or so.

There's a tremendous amount to say just about this single sound [m]. Firstly, it can be short, or we can make it go on for quite a long period of time. Secondly, you can see and feel that the lips are closed.

2

Produce a long [m]. Now pinch your nostrils tightly, blocking the escape of air. What happens? (The sound suddenly ceases, thus implying that when you say [m], there must be an escape of air from the nose.)

3

Once again, say a long [m]. This time put your fingers in your ears. Now you'll be able to hear a buzz inside your head: this effect is called **voice**. Try alternating [m] with silence [m . . . m . . . m . . . m . . .]. Note how the voice is switched on and off.

Consequently, we now know that [m] is a sound which:

❑ is made with the lips (bilabial)
❑ is said with air escaping from the nose (nasal)
❑ is said with voice (voiced).

Do the same for a different sound – [t] as in *tight*.

4

Say [t] looking in a mirror. Can you prolong the sound? If you put your fingers in your ears, is there any buzz? If you pinch your nostrils, does this have any effect on the sound? (The answer is 'no' in each case.)

So [t] is a sound which:

❑ is made with the tongue-tip against the teeth-ridge (alveolar)
❑ has air escaping not from the nose but from the mouth (oral)
❑ is said without voice (voiceless).

A word now about the use of different kinds of brackets. The symbols between square brackets [ ] indicate that we are concerned with a sound and are called phonetic symbols. The letters of ordinary spelling, technically termed **orthographic** symbols, can either be placed between angled brackets <m> – or, as in this book, they can be printed in bold, thus **m**.

How languages pick and pattern sounds

Human beings are able to produce a huge variety of sounds with their vocal apparatus and a surprisingly large number of these are actually part of human speech. Noises like clicks, or lip trills – which may seem weird to speakers of European languages – may be simply part of everyday speech in languages spoken in, for example, Africa, the Amazon or the Arctic regions. No language uses more than a small number of the available possibilities but even European languages may contain quite a few sounds unfamiliar to native English speakers. To give some idea of the possible cross-linguistic variation, let's now compare English to some of its European neighbours.

For example, English lacks a sound similar to the 'scrapy' Spanish consonant **j**, as in *jefe* 'boss'. This sound does exist in Scottish English (spelt **ch**), e.g. *loch*, and is used by some English speakers in loanwords and names from other languages. A similar sound also occurs in German *Dach* 'roof', Welsh *bach* 'little' and Dutch *schip* 'ship', but not in French or Italian. German has no sound like that represented by **th** in English *think*. French and Italian also have a gap here but a similar sound does exist in Spanish *cinco* 'five' and in Welsh *byth* 'ever'. English has no equivalent to the French vowel in the word *nu* 'naked'. Similar vowels can be heard in German *Bücher* 'books', Dutch *museum* 'museum' and Danish *typisk* 'typical', although not in Spanish, Italian or Welsh. We could go on, but these examples are enough to illustrate that each language selects a limited range of sounds from the total possibilities of human speech.

In addition we need to consider how sounds are *patterned* in languages. Here are just a few examples.

❑ Neither English nor French has words beginning with the sound sequence [kn], like German *Knabe* 'boy' or Dutch *knie* 'knee'. Many centuries ago English did indeed have this sequence, which is why spellings like *knee* and *knot* still exist.
❑ Both French and Spanish have initial [fw], as in French *foi* 'faith' and Spanish *fuente* 'fountain'; this initial sequence does not occur in English, Dutch or Welsh.
❑ English has many words ending in [d], contrasting with others ending in [t], e.g. *bed* and *bet*. This is not true of German where, although words like *Rad* 'wheel' and *Rat* 'advice' are spelt differently, the final **d** and **t** are both pronounced as [t]. Dutch is similar to German in this respect, so that Dutch *bot* 'bone' and *bod* 'bid' are said exactly the same. The same holds true for Russian and Polish, whereas French, Spanish and Welsh are like English and contrast final [t] and [d].

Phonemes

Speech is a continuous flow of sound with interruptions only when necessary to take in air to breathe, or to organise our thoughts. The first task when analysing speech is to divide up this continuous flow into smaller chunks that are easier to deal with. We call this process **segmentation**, and the resulting smaller sound units are termed **segments** (these correspond very roughly to vowels and consonants). There is a good degree of agreement among native speakers on what constitutes a speech segment. If English speakers are asked how many speech sounds there are in *man*, they will almost certainly say 'three', and will state them to be [m], [æ] and [n] (see p. 13 for symbols).

Segments do not operate in isolation, but combine to form words. In *man*, the segments [m], [æ] and [n] have no meaning of their own and only become meaningful if they form part of a word. In all languages, there are certain variations in sound which are significant because they can change the meanings of words. For example, if we take the word *man*, and replace the first sound by [p], we get a new word *pan*. Two words of this kind distinguished by a single sound are called a **minimal pair**.

Activity

5

Make minimal pairs in English by changing the initial consonant in these words: *hate, pen, kick, sea, down, lane, feet.*

Let's take this process further. In addition to *pan*, we could also produce, for example, *ban, tan, ran* etc. A set of words distinguished in this way is termed a **minimal set**.

Instead of changing the initial consonant, we can change the vowel, e.g. *mean, moan, men, mine, moon*, etc. which provides us with another minimal set. We can also change the final consonant, giving yet a third minimal set: *man, mat, mad*. Through such processes, we can eventually determine those speech sounds which are phonologically significant in a given language. The contrastive units of sound which can be used to change meaning are termed **phonemes**. We can therefore say that the word *man* consists of the three phonemes /m/, /æ/ and /n/. Note that from now on, to distinguish them as such, we shall place phonemic symbols between slant brackets / /. We can also establish a **phonemic inventory** for NRP English, giving us 20 vowels and 24 consonants (see 'Phonemes in English and Other Languages' below).

But not every small difference that can be heard between one sound and another is enough to change the meaning of words. There is a certain degree of variation in each phoneme which is sometimes very easy to hear and can be quite striking. English /t/ is a good example. It can range from a sound made by the tip of the tongue pressed against the roof of the mouth to types of articulation involving a 'catch in the throat' (technically termed a **glottal stop**). Compare /t/ in *tea* (tongue-tip **t**) and /t/ in *button* (usually made with a glottal stop).

Activity

6

Ask a number of your friends to say the word *button*. Try to describe what you hear. Is there an obvious t-sound articulated by the tongue-tip against the roof of the mouth? Or is the /t/ produced with glottal stop? Is there a little vowel between /t/ and /n/? Or does the speaker move directly from the /t/ to /n/ without any break? And is it the same with similar words, like *kitten, cotton*, and *Britain*? Now try the same thing with final /l/, as in *bottle, rattle, brittle*. Do you notice any difference in people's reactions to the use of glottal stop in these two groups of words?

Each phoneme is therefore really composed of a number of different sounds which are interpreted as one meaningful unit by a native speaker of the language. This range is termed **allophonic variation,** and the variants themselves are called **allophones.**

Only the allophones of a phoneme can exist in reality as *concrete* entities. Allophones are real – they can be recorded, stored and reproduced, and analysed in acoustic or articulatory terms. Phonemes are *abstract* units and exist only in the mind of the speaker/listener. It is, in fact, impossible to 'pronounce a phoneme' (although this phrasing is often loosely employed); one can only in fact produce an *allophone* of the phoneme in question. As the phoneme is an abstraction, we instead refer to its being **realised** (in the sense of 'made real') as a particular allophone.

Although each phoneme includes a range of variation, the allophones of any single phoneme generally have considerable **phonetic similarity** in both acoustic and articulatory terms; that is to say, the allophones of any given phoneme:

❑   usually sound fairly similar to each other
❑   are usually (although not invariably) articulated in a somewhat similar way.

We can now proceed to a working definition of the phoneme as: *a member of a set of abstract units which together form the sound system of a given language and through which contrasts of meaning are produced.*

Phonemes in English and other languages

A single individual's speech is termed an **idiolect.** Generally speaking, it is easy for native speakers to interpret the phoneme system of another native speaker's idiolect, even if they speak a different variety of the language. Problems may sometimes arise, but they are typically few, since broadly the phoneme systems will be largely similar. Difficulties occur for the non-native learner, however, because there are always important differences between the phoneme system of one language and that of another. Take the example of an English native speaker learning French. French people are often surprised when they discover that an English native speaker has difficulty in hearing (let alone producing) the difference between words like French *tu* 'you' and *tout* 'all'. The French vowel phonemes in these words, /y/ and /u/, seem alike to an English ear, sounding similar to the allophones of the English vowel phoneme /uː/ as in *two*. This effect can be represented as follows (using the symbol [–] to mean **contrasts with**):

French *tu* /ty/ – *tout* /tu/
   English *two* /tuː/

On the other hand, French learners of English also have their problems. The English words *sit* and *seat* sound alike to French ears, the English vowel phonemes /ɪ/ and /iː/ being heard as if they were allophones of French /i/ as in French *site* 'site':

English *seat* /siːt/ – *sit* /sɪt/
   French *site* /sit/

Another similar example is the contrast /ʊ – uː/ as in the words *pull* and *pool* as compared with French /u/ in *poule* 'hen':

English *pull* /ʊ/ – *pool* /uː/
   French *poule* /u/

Of course, we need not confine this to vowel sounds. Learners often have trouble with some of the consonants of English, for instance /θ/ as in *mouth*. German students of English have to learn to make a contrast between *mouth* and *mouse*. German has no /θ/, and German speakers are likely to interpret /θ/ as /s/ as in the final sound of *Maus* 'mouse' – this being what to a German seems closest to /θ/.

English *mouth* /maʊθ/ – *mouse* /maʊs/
German *Maus* /mɑʊs/

From the moment children start learning to talk they begin to recognise and appreciate those sound contrasts which are important for their own language; they learn to ignore those which are insignificant. We all interpret the sounds of language we hear in terms of the phonemes of our mother tongue and there are many rather surprising examples of this. For instance, the Japanese at first hear no difference between the contrasting phonemes /r/ and /l/ of English, e.g. *royal – loyal*; Greek learners cannot distinguish /s/ and /ʃ/ as in *same* and *shame*; Cantonese Chinese students of English may confuse /l/ not only with /r/ but also with /n/, so finding it difficult to hear the contrast between *light*, *right* and *night*. So non-natives must learn to interpret the sound system of English as heard by English native speakers and ignore the perceptions imposed by years of speaking and listening to their own language. Any English person learning a foreign language will have to undertake the same process in reverse.

Overview of the English phonemic system ☺ Track 3

The consonants of English
Certain of the English consonants function in pairs – being in most respects similar, but differing in the *energy* used in their production. For instance, /p/ and /b/ are produced in the same manner, but /p/ is a strong voiceless articulation, termed **fortis**; whereas /b/ is a weak potentially voiced articulation, termed **lenis**. With other English consonants, there is no fortis/lenis opposition. Table A2.1 shows the English consonant phonemes.

The vowels of English
The vowels of English fall into three groups. We'll classify these in very basic terms at the moment, but shall elaborate on this in Section B3, 'Overview of the English Vowel System'. For steady-state/diphthong distinction, see p. 64.

- ❏ **Checked steady-state** vowels: these are short and are represented by a single symbol, e.g. /ɪ/
- ❏ **Free steady-state** vowels: these are long and are represented by a symbol plus a length mark ː, e.g. /iː/.
- ❏ **Free diphthongs**: these are long with tongue and/or lip movement, and are represented by two symbols, e.g. /eɪ/.

In Table A2.2 we have provided keywords (adapted from Wells 2000) as a convenient way of referring to each of the English vowel phonemes. Keywords are shown in small capitals thus: KIT.

Table A2.1 The consonant system of English

Fortis	Example	Lenis	Example
p	*pip*	b	*babe*
t	*taught*	d	*dead*
k	*kick*	g	*gig*
tʃ	*church*	dʒ	*judge*
f	*fluff*	v	*verve*
θ	*thirtieth*	ð	*they breathe*
s	*socks*	z	*zoos*
ʃ	*shortish*	ʒ	*measure*

Consonant	Example
h	*hay*
m	*maim*
n	*nine*
ŋ	*sinking*
l	*level*
r	*rarest*
w	*witch*
j	*yellow*

Table A2.2 The vowels of English NRP

Checked steady-state	Keyword	Free steady-state	Keyword	Free diphthongs	Keyword
ɪ	KIT	iː	FLEECE	eɪ	FACE
e	DRESS	ɛː	SQUARE	aɪ	PRICE
æ	TRAP	ɑː	PALM	ɔɪ	CHOICE
ɒ	LOT	ɔː	THOUGHT	əʊ	GOAT
ʊ	FOOT	uː	GOOSE	aʊ	MOUTH
ʌ	STRUT	ɜː	NURSE	ɪə	NEAR
ə	*bonus*			ʊə	CURE

The syllable

The **syllable** is a unit difficult to define, though native speakers of a language generally have a good intuitive feeling for the concept, and are usually able to state how many syllables there are in a particular word. For instance, if native speakers of English are asked how many syllables there are in the word *potato* they usually have little doubt

PHONEMES	əneləfəntnevəfəgets
SYLLABLES	ən e lə fənt ne və fə gets
WORDS	An elephant never forgets

Figure A2.1 Phoneme, syllable and word

that there are three (even if for certain words, e.g. *extract*, they might find it difficult to say just where one syllable ends and another begins).

A syllable can be defined very loosely as *a unit potentially larger than the phoneme but smaller than the word*. Phonemes can be regarded as the basic phonological elements. Above the phoneme, we can consider units larger in extent, namely the syllable and the word.

Syllabic consonants

Typically, every syllable contains a vowel at its **nucleus**, and may have one or more consonants either side of this vowel at its margins. If we take the syllable *cats* as an example, the vowel acting as the nucleus is /æ/, and the consonants at the margins /k/ and /ts/. However, certain consonants are also able to act as the nuclear elements of syllables. In English, /n m l/ (and occasionally /ŋ/) can function in this way, as in *bitten* /ˈbɪtn̩/, *rhythm* /ˈrɪðm̩/, *subtle* /ˈsʌtl̩/. Here the syllabic element is not formed by a vowel, but by one of the consonants /m n ŋ l/, which are in this case longer and more prominent than normal. Such consonants are termed **syllabic consonants**, and are shown by a little vertical mark [ˌ] placed beneath the symbol concerned. In many cases, alternative pronunciations with /ə/ are also possible, e.g. /ˈrɪðəm/. In certain types of English, such as General American, Scottish and West Country, /r/ can also be syllabic: *hiker* /ˈhaɪkɹ̩/.

Phonemic and phonetic transcription

One of the most useful applications of phonetics is to provide transcription to indicate pronunciation. It is especially useful for languages like English (or French) which have inconsistent spellings. For instance, in English, the sound /iː/ can be represented as **e** (*be*), **ea** (*dream*), **ee** (*seen*), **ie** (*believe*), **ei** (*receive*), etc. See Section C6 for the same phenomenon in French.

Activity

7

Find a number of different spellings for (1) the vowel sounds of FACE, PRICE, THOUGHT and NURSE (in NRP /eɪ aɪ ɔː ɜː/) and (2) the consonant sounds /dʒ ʃ s k/.

Now try doing the same thing in reverse. See if you can find a number of different pronunciations for (1) the vowel *letters* **o** and **a** and (2) the consonant *letters* **c** and **g**.

Finally, a rather tougher question. One of the English vowel sounds is virtually always represented by the same single letter in spelling. Can you work out which sound it is?

We can distinguish between **phonetic** and **phonemic transcription**. A phonetic transcription can indicate minute details of the articulation of any particular sound by the use of differently shaped symbols, e.g. [ʔ ɹ], or by adding little marks (known as **diacritics**) to a symbol, e.g. [ā ṭ]. In contrast, a phonemic transcription shows only the phoneme contrasts and does not tell us precisely what the realisation of the phoneme is. We can illustrate this difference by returning to our example of English /t/. Typically, a word-initial /t/ is realised with a little puff of air, an effect termed **aspiration**, which we indicate by [ʰ], e.g. *tea* [tʰiː]. In many word-final contexts, as in *eat this*, we are more likely to have [t] with an accompanying glottal stop, symbolised thus: [iːˀt ðɪs]. In a phonemic transcription we would simply show either as /t/, since the replacement of one kind of /t/ by another does not result in a word with a different meaning (whereas replacing /t/ by /s/ would change *tea* into *see*).

Both the phonetic and phonemic forms of transcription have their own specific uses. Phonemic transcription may at first sight appear less complex, but it is in reality a far more sophisticated system, since it requires from the reader a good knowledge of the language concerned; it eliminates superfluous detail and retains only the information essential to meaning. Even in a phonetic transcription, however, we generally show only a very small proportion of the phonetic variation that occurs, often only the most significant phonetic feature of a particular context. For instance, the difference in the pronunciation of the two **r**-sounds in *retreat* could be shown thus: [ɹəˈtɹ̥iːt]. Once we introduce a single phonetic symbol or diacritic then the whole transcription needs to be enclosed in square and not slant brackets.

Transcription is not only used to represent words in isolation but can also be employed for whole stretches of speech. In all languages, the pronunciation of words in isolation is very different from the way they appear in connected speech (see 'A Sample of Phonemic Transcription', pp. 20–1). Phonemic transcription allows us to indicate these features with a degree of precision that is impossible to capture with traditional spelling. As such, it is an essential skill for phoneticians. In the next section of this chapter (after learning about some features of connected speech) you too will get to acquire this very useful ability.

CONNECTED SPEECH AND PHONEMIC TRANSCRIPTION A3

Stress

A word of more than one syllable is termed a **polysyllable**. When an English polysyllabic word is said in its **citation form** (i.e. pronounced in isolation) one strongly **stressed** syllable will stand out from the rest. This can be indicated by a **stress mark** ['] placed *before* the syllable concerned, e.g. *'yesterday* /ˈjestədeɪ/, *to'morrow* /təˈmɒrəʊ/, *to'day* /təˈdeɪ/.

> **8**
>
> Say these English words in citation form. Which syllable is the most strongly stressed? Mark it appropriately: *manage, final, finality, resolute, resolution, electric, electricity.*

Stress in the isolated word is termed **word stress**. But we can also analyse stress in connected speech, termed **sentence stress**, where both polysyllables and **monosyllables** (single-syllable words) can carry strong stress while other words may be completely unstressed. We shall come back to examine English stress in more detail in Section B5. At this point we just need to note that the words most likely to receive sentence stress are those termed **content words** (also called 'lexical words'), namely nouns, adjectives, adverbs and main verbs. These are the words that normally carry a high information load. We can contrast these with **function words** (also called 'grammar words' or 'form words'), namely determiners (e.g. *the, a*), conjunctions (e.g. *and, but*), pronouns (e.g. *she, them*), prepositions (e.g. *at, from*), auxiliary verbs (e.g. *do, be, can*). Function words carry relatively little information; their role is holding the sentence together. If we compare language to a brick wall, then content words are like 'bricks of information' while function words act like 'grammatical cement' keeping the whole structure intact. Unlike content words, function words for the most part carry little or no stress. Only two types of function words are regularly stressed: the demonstratives (e.g. *this, that, those*) and *wh*-interrogatives (e.g. **wh**ere, **wh**o, **wh**ich, **h**ow). Note, however, that when *wh*-words and *that* are used as relatives they are unstressed, e.g. *the girl who lent me the yellow hat that I wore to your wedding.*

Strong, weak and contracted forms

Certain function words are pronounced differently according to whether they are stressed or unstressed. Although few in number, they are of very high frequency. Look at this example:

> *Megan had decided to fetch them from the hospital*
> /ˈmeɡən əd dəˈsaɪdɪd tə ˈfetʃ ðəm frəm ðə ˈhɒspɪtl̩/

Here the words *had, to, them, from, the* are all unstressed and reduced to /əd tə ðəm frəm ðə/. When in citation form, or stressed, these would instead be /hæd tuː ðem frɒm ðiː/. The reduced, unstressed pronunciation is termed the **weak form** (often abbreviated to **WF**); while the full pronunciation characteristic of stressed contexts is called the **strong form** (often abbreviated to **SF**). A select list of the commonest weak forms is given in Table A3.1 (we have restricted it to those that are necessary for native-speaker English).

Many function words can combine with other function words, so producing **contracted forms** (often abbreviated to **CF**, also called 'contractions'), e.g. *he + will →* *he'll, do + not → don't.* Unlike weak forms, contracted forms can be stressed – and indeed frequently are. All contracted forms have orthographic representations including

Table A3.1 Essential weak forms

Class	Word	Weak forms	Comments
Determiners	a	/ə/	Not before vowels
	an	/ən, n̩/	Only before vowels
	the	/ðə, ði/	/ði/ before vowels
Conjunctions	and	/ənd, ən, n̩/	
	as	/əz/	
	than	/ðən/	SF /ðæn/ is hardly ever used
	that	/ðət/	
Prepositions	at	/ət/	
	for	/fə/	/fər/ before vowels
	from	/frəm/	
	of	/əv, ə/	/ə/ is often used before *the* /ðə/
	to	/tə, tu/	/tu/ used before vowels
Verb *be*	am ('m)	/əm, m̩/	/m̩/. See Contracted Forms (CFs)
	are ('re)	/ə/	/ər/ before vowels. See CFs
	is ('s)	/s, z/	See CFs
	was	/wəz/	
	were	/wə/	/wər/ before vowels
Auxiliary verb	has ('s)	/əz, s, z/	See Section A3, pp. 19–20
have	have ('ve)	/əv, v/	See CFs
	had ('d)	/əd, d/	See CFs
Other auxiliary	do	/də, du/	
verbs	can	/kən/	
	will ('ll)	/əl, l/	See CFs
	shall ('ll)	/ʃəl/	See CFs
	would ('d)	/əd, d/	See CFs
	should ('d)	/əd, d/	See CFs
Pronouns	that	/ðət/	If a *relative*. See Section A3, p. 19
	them	/ðəm, ðm̩/	/ɑː/ is also used in stressed contexts
	our	/ɑː/	
Negative particle	n't	/nt/	See CFs

an apostrophe. These spellings are regularly used in dialogue, and often in informal writing, but only sporadically in other kinds of written English. You may have noticed that we use them quite a lot in this book. Table A3.2 provides a list of the most common English contracted forms.

If you're a non-native learner of English, remember that weak and contracted forms are necessary for anyone with the goal of approaching fluent native-speaker English.

Table A3.2 Contracted forms

	Full form	Written CF	Spoken CF	Comments
be	I am	I'm	/aɪm/	
	you are	you're	/jɔː/	/jɔːr/ before vowels
	he is	he's	/hiz/	
	she is	she's	/ʃiz/	
	it is	it's	/ɪts/	
	we are	we're	/wiə/	/wiər/ before vowels
	they are	they're	/ðɛː/	/ðɛːr/ before vowels
have	I have	I've	/aɪv/	Not necessarily used if *have* is
	you have	you've	/juv/	a main verb.
	he has	he's	/hiz/	Cannot be used if *have* is a
	she has	she's	/ʃiz/	main verb.
	it has	it's	/ɪts/	
	we have	we've	/wiv/	Not necessarily used if *have* is
	they have	they've	/ðeɪv/	a main verb.
shall/	I shall/will	I'll	/aɪl/	
will	you will	you'll	/jul/	
	he will	he'll	/hil/	
	she will	she'll	/ʃil/	
	it will	it'll	/ɪtl̩/	
	we shall/will	we'll	/wil/	
	they will	they'll	/ðeɪl/	
had/	I had/would	I'd	/aɪd/	There is no way of telling
would	you had/would	you'd	/jud/	whether *had* or *would* is
	he had/would	he'd	/hid/	meant from pronunciation.
	she had/would	she'd	/ʃid/	Context usually makes the
	it had/would	it'd	/ɪtəd/	underlying form clear.
	we had/would	we'd	/wid/	
	they had/would	they'd	/ðeɪd/	
not	are not	aren't	/ɑːnt/[1]	Also used in *aren't I?* All
	were not	weren't	/wɜːnt/	auxiliaries may combine with
	do not	don't	/dəʊnt/	n't to form CFs and only the
	shall not	shan't	/ʃɑːnt/	most significant and/or
	will not	won't	/wəʊnt/	irregular are given here. There
	cannot	can't	/kɑːnt/	are many more, such as *isn't*,
	must not	mustn't	/ˈmʌsn̩t/	*wasn't, couldn't, shouldn't*
	dare not	daren't	/dɛːnt/	/ˈɪzn̩t, ˈwɒzn̩t, ˈkʊdn̩t, ˈʃʊdn̩t/
let	let us	let's	/lets/	
there	there is	there's	/ðɛːz, ðəz/	
	there are	there're	/ˈðɛːrə, ðərə/	/ˈðɛːrər, ðərər/ before vowels
	there will	there'll	/ðɛːl, ðəl/	
	there would	there'd	/ðɛːd, ðəd/	

1 The older CF of *aren't* and *isn't* was *ain't* – a form now heard only in regional varieties.

It's certainly fair to argue that they are of less significance to a person learning English as a 'lingua franca' (see Jenkins 2000) – namely a basic form of communication. But we assume that people reading this book will either be native speakers (in which case you'll want to know about these features of your language), or if you are a non-native you'll be aiming at more than bare intelligibility.

Among the languages of the world, English is remarkable for the number of its weak and contracted forms and the frequency of their occurrence. Using them appropriately doesn't come easily to non-native learners. Even if a language does have weak forms (like Dutch, for instance) it's unlikely that the system will be as complex or extensive as in English.

Note that, in English, weak and contracted forms are in no way confined to very informal contexts, nor are they 'slang' or 'lazy speech', as some people mistakenly believe. Avoidance of contracted forms is perhaps even more immediately noticeable than not using weak forms. Again, as a non-native, you will usually not be misunderstood, but it will certainly make your English sound less effective.

The use of weak/strong/contracted forms

Remember that WFs and CFs are far more frequent than SFs. Bearing that in mind, look at this summary of their usage.

1   WFs are used only if the function word is unstressed. Otherwise SFs must be used, e.g.

> *It turned out that it* **was** *possible* /ɪt tɜːnd 'aʊt ðət ɪt 'wɒz pɒsəbl̩/

2   SFs are used at the end of the intonation group (see B6, 'The Structure of Intonation Patterns in English'), even if the word is unstressed.

> *What was she getting at?* /'wɒt wəz ʃi 'getɪŋ æt/

Pronouns form an exception in this respect, retaining the WF even in final position.

> *Jenny collected them* /'dʒeni kə'lektɪd ðəm/

3   Remember that demonstrative *that* invariably has SF (even if unstressed).

> *That's the best approach to the problem* /ðæts ðə 'best ə'prəʊtʃ tə ðə 'prɒbləm/

Relative pronoun *that* and conjunction *that* always have WFs, e.g.

> *The furniture that we ordered hasn't arrived* /ðə 'fɜːnɪtʃə ðət wi 'ɔːdəd hæznt ə'raɪvd/
> *Christopher told me that he'd written two books* /'krɪstəfə 'təʊld mi ðət id 'rɪtn̩ 'tuː 'bʊks/

4   WFs ending in /ə/, e.g. *to, for* /tə fə/, take on different forms before vowels (see Table A3.1).

5   In WFs of words spelt with initial **h**, i.e. verb forms *have, has, had*, pronouns *he, his, him, her*, pronouncing /h/ is variable. The /h/ forms occur without exception at the beginning of an utterance but in other contexts both /h/ and /h/-less forms can be heard; see Section B4. (The use of a great many /h/ forms in colloquial English tends to sound somewhat over-careful.)

Activity

9

In which of the following auxiliary verbs and pronouns (all spelt with **h**) would you actually pronounce /h/?

Jack's handed him the money.
Tom's handed her the money.
He's handed Jack the money.
Has he handed her the money?
Would he have handed her the money?
Would she have told him about having been handed the money?
I haven't handed her any of his money
He hasn't had any of her money.

Discuss your responses with the other members of your class. Does everybody have the same patterning? If there are any differences, where are they to be found?

6 *Have/has* when used as a main verb implying possession usually retains SF, e.g. *I have an interesting bit of news* /aɪ ˈhæv ən ˈɪntrəstɪŋ ˈbɪt əv ˈnjuːz/. While *have* occasionally enters into CFs (e.g. *I've an interesting bit of news* /aɪv ən ˈɪntrəstɪŋ ˈbɪt əv ˈnjuːz/), this is never the case with *has*; compare the inappropriate: **She's an interesting piece of news* – which would mean something quite different! (Note, incidentally, that the asterisk * is used in linguistic work to indicate unacceptable forms.) *Do/does* behaves in a similar manner. When used as a main verb, the strong form is used, e.g. *What are they going to do about it?* /ˈwɒt ə ðeɪ ˈɡəʊɪŋ tə ˈduː əˈbaʊt ɪt/.

See the 'Brief Transcription Guide' below for the regular pronunciation patterns of **'s** in weak forms of *has* and *is*.

7 Notice that a few common function words have no regular WF. These include: *if, in, on, one, then, up, when, what, with*.

A sample of phonemic transcription

Now that you know something about stress, and also have a knowledge of the crucial matter of weak/contracted forms, you're ready to move on from transcribing isolated words to doing a phonemic transcription of a short passage of English. This will enable us to show features of real connected speech such as sentence stress and also all the WFs and CFs. For further detail on other features of connected speech, e.g. assimilation and elision, see Section B4.

Here's a short extract (slightly adapted) from Lewis Carroll's *Alice in Wonderland* (Ch. 6), shown first of all in an orthographic version (i.e. in ordinary spelling) and then in phonemic transcription. Note that our transcription is only *one* possible version – there can be quite a lot of freedom in such matters as stressing, the choice of alternative pronunciations, and much else besides.

Orthographic version

'How do you know I'm mad?' said Alice.

'You must be,' said the cat, 'or you wouldn't have come here.'

Alice didn't think that proved it at all. However, she went on, 'And how do you know that you're mad?'

'To begin with,' said the cat, 'a dog's not mad. You grant that?'

'I suppose so,' said Alice.

'Well, then,' the cat went on, 'you see a dog growls when it's angry, and wags its tail when it's pleased. Now I growl when I'm pleased, and wag my tail when I'm angry. Therefore I'm mad.'

'*I* call it purring, not growling,' said Alice.

'Call it what you like,' said the cat.

Phonemic transcription of the same passage ☺ Track 4

'haʊ dʒu¹ 'nəʊ aɪm 'mæd | sed 'ælɪs ||

ju 'mʌs² bi | sed ðə 'kæt | ɔː ju 'wʊdn̩t əv 'kʌm hɪə ||

'ælɪs 'dɪdn̩t θɪŋk ðæt 'pruːvd ɪt ə 'tɔːl³ || haʊ'evə | ʃi went 'ɒn | ən 'haʊ dʒu¹ 'nəʊ ðətʃɔː¹ 'mæd ||

tə bə'gɪn wɪð | sed ðə 'kæt | ə 'dɒgz nɒt 'mæd || ju 'grɑːnt 'ðæt ||

aɪ sə'pəʊz 'səʊ | sed 'ælɪs ||

'wel ðen | ðə 'kæt went 'ɒn | ju 'siː | ə 'dɒg 'graʊlz wen ɪts 'æŋgri | ən 'wægz ɪts 'teɪl wen ɪts 'pliːzd || naʊ aɪ 'graʊl wen aɪm 'pliːzd | ən 'wæg maɪ 'teɪl wen aɪm 'æŋgri || 'ðɛːfɔː r⁴ aɪm 'mæd ||

'aɪ kɔːl ɪt 'pɜːrɪŋ | nɒt 'graʊlɪŋ | sed 'ælɪs ||

'kɔːl ɪt wɒtʃu¹ 'laɪk | sed ðə 'kæt ||

Notes

1   See Section B4, 'Patterns of Assimilation in English', for information on these assimilations.

2   See Section B4, 'Elision' and 'Patterns of Elision in English', for information on elision.

3   This phrase has a fixed pronunciation with stress as shown.

4   See Section B4, 'Liaison', for information on linking *r*.

Brief transcription guide

This simplified survey is intended to start you off doing transcription and deals with some frequent beginners' problems. Several of the points mentioned in passing here are discussed at greater length later on in the book.

1 Transcription from a written text

Transcription may be from a text in conventional orthography.

1 Read the passage *aloud* to yourself a number of times.

2 In transcribing, you must always remember that you are dealing with connected speech and not a string of isolated words. First, mark off with a single vertical bar the breaks between intonation groups (see Section B6, 'The Structure of Intonation

Patterns in English'). These normally occur where in reading it would be possible to make a brief pause. Sentence breaks are shown by a double bar.

> A most important thing to remember | is to clean the filter frequently. || This will ensure | that the machine runs efficiently at all times. ||

Note that for any written text, there are usually several different possibilities for division into intonation groups. See Section B6 for more detail.

3 Using the orthographic text, mark the stressed syllables as found in connected speech (i.e. *sentence stress*). This is different from stress in the isolated word as indicated in the dictionary (*word stress*). Sentence stress is most likely to fall on a syllable of content words (i.e. nouns, main verbs, adjectives, most adverbs). Function words (except for demonstratives, e.g. *this*, *those*, and *wh*-words used in questions, e.g. *what*, *where*, *who*) are typically unstressed. Mark sentence stress thus ['] *before* the stressed syllable, e.g.

> A 'most im'portant 'thing to re'member | is to 'clean the 'filter 'frequently. || This will en'sure | that the ma'chine 'runs e'fficiently | at 'all 'times. ||

4 Now begin transcribing into phonemic symbols. If in doubt about a difficult word, make an attempt at it but go back later and check in any dictionary showing pronunciation in phonemic transcription (e.g. the *Longman Pronunciation Dictionary*: Wells 2000). Note that there may be minor differences between the transcription system used in your dictionary and the one in this book. Your dictionary may also show alternative pronunciations, possibly by superscript or italic letters. Don't indicate all these variants; just choose *one* of the possibilities.

2 Transcription from speech

For phonemic transcription of actual speech, e.g. dictation from your instructor, or an audio recording, you must bear the following points in mind.

1 Listen to the whole passage several times. Mark intonation group boundaries. Then concentrating on one intonation group at a time, mark sentence stress.

2 Remember that in transcribing a passage of spoken language, you cannot (as you can with a written text) choose between a variety of interpretations. You must try to render faithfully in phonemic transcription *exactly* what the speaker has uttered. Bearing this point in mind, proceed as for a written text.

3 Writing the symbols

1 Always use the letter shapes of print rather than those of handwriting.

2 Take care with the following symbols: ə ɔ ɪ ʊ ɜ ɛ æ ɑ ɒ ʃ ʒ θ ð g. Make sure that you don't confuse these letter shapes:

> ɪ i   ɛ ʒ   ə a   æ ɑ a   ʊ u   z ʒ   ʒ ʒ   θ ə ɔ   ʊ u   m ʍ   s ʃ   ɒ ɑ

3 Here are a few hints on how to write some of the symbols:

ɒ is like **b** without an ascending stroke.
θ is written as **0** with a cross-stroke.
ð is like a reversed **6** with a cross-stroke.
f should not descend below the line.

4 Some transcription do's and don'ts

First the **do's**

❑ Do use *weak* and *contracted forms* wherever possible.

❑ Do show syllabic consonants with the syllabic mark: *bottle* /ˈbɒtl̩]/, *written* /ˈrɪtn̩/. The most frequent syllabic consonants in NRP are /l n/; syllabic /m/ and /ŋ/ are less commonly found. Syllabic /r/ is very common in General American and other rhotic accents (see Section B2 for more information).

❑ Do transcribe numbers or abbreviations in their full *spoken* form. Note that in abbreviations the stress always falls on the last item, e.g. *CD* /siː ˈdiː/, *CNN* /siː en ˈen/.

Now the **don'ts**

❑ Don't use any capital letters or show any punctuation.

❑ Don't include **c o q x y**, which don't occur in our English phonemic transcription system. (Note that these symbols are used for sounds in other languages.)

❑ Don't use *phonetic* symbols, e.g. [ʔ ɹ ɫ], in a *phonemic* transcription.

5 Other miscellaneous points to note

1 In our transcription system for English NRP, /ə/ occurs only in unstressed syllables. In stressed syllables you will generally find /ʌ/ or /ɜː/, e.g. *butter* /ˈbʌtə/, *burglar* /ˈbɜːglə/.

2 In NRP, and similar accents, /r/ only occurs before a vowel, e.g. *fairy* /ˈfɛːri/, but *far* /fɑː/, *farm* /fɑːm/. (See Section B2.) To indicate the possibility of linking r (see B4), many dictionaries use superscript r, e.g. /fɑːʳ/. You should never write the superscript r, but instead where there is linking r transcribe it *between* words with a full-size letter, e.g. *far off* /fɑː r ˈɒf/.

3 The '*happy* words' (see Section B3), ending in -**y**, -**ie** or- **ee**, have a vowel between KIT /ɪ/ and FLEECE /iː/, as do inflectional -**ies** and -**ied**. This neutralised phoneme (see Section B1) is indicated by the symbol **i**, e.g. *silly* /ˈsɪli/, *caddie* /ˈkædi/, *coffee* /ˈkɒfi/, *fairies* /ˈfɛːriz/, *married* /ˈmærid/. Similarly, words like *graduate, influence* have a vowel between /ʊ/ and /uː/, shown by the symbol **u**, e.g. *influence* /ˈɪnfluəns/.

4 The pronunciation of written **s** in plurals and verb endings, and '**s** found in possessives and the weak forms of *has* and *is*, is governed by the preceding sound.

❑ Following /s z ʃ ʒ tʃ dʒ/, s → /ɪz/, e.g. *buses* /ˈbʌsɪz/, *wishes* /ˈwɪʃɪz/, *George's* /ˈdʒɔːdʒɪz/.

❑ Following the fortis consonants /p t k f θ/, s → /s/, e.g. *Jack's boots* /ˈdʒæks ˈbuːts/.

❑ In all other cases, s → /z/, e.g. *roads* /rəʊdz/, *dreams* /driːmz/, *Sue's* /suːz/.

5 The ending -**ed** has the following patterning:

❑ Following /t/ and /d/, -**ed** → /ɪd/, e.g. *folded* /ˈfəʊldɪd/, *waited* /ˈweɪtɪd/.

❑ Following fortis consonants (except /t d/), -**ed** → /t/, e.g. *looked* /lʊkt/, *laughed* /lɑːft/.

❑ Following all other consonants or vowels, -**ed** → /d/, e.g. *seemed* /siːmd/, *pleased* /pliːzd/, *saved* /seɪvd/, *barred* /bɑːd/.

For several adjectives, -**ed** → /ɪd/, e.g. *crooked* /ˈkrʊkɪd/, *naked* /ˈneɪkɪd/. Other examples are: *ragged, aged, jagged, -legged* (as in *four-legged, bow-legged*), *rugged, wicked, learned, cursed, blessed, beloved.*

6 A number of verbs ending in **n** or **l** have two pronunciations and sometimes two spelling forms for the past tense, one in **-ed** and one in **-t**, e.g. *spelled/spelt*; *burned/burnt*. In British English, the pronunciation with /t/ is more common; American English favours /d/.

7 If transcribing from an audio recording, you must show all assimilations and elisions you can hear. When transcribing from a written text, it adds interest to show assimilations and elisions where these are possible (see Section B4).

Passages for transcription

Passages (slightly adapted from *Alice in Wonderland*, Ch. 1), graded in length, have been provided for you to use for transcription practice in the course of reading this book. Three are given below to start you off, and from then on there is an activity of this sort at the end of every unit in sections A and B. Mark sentence stress and intonation group boundaries. Show contracted forms wherever possible, even if not indicated as such in the text (i.e. transcribe *could not* as /kʊdn̩t/). A key, based on NRP, is to be found on the website.

Activity

10

Transcribe phonemically, showing intonation groups and sentence stress, and using weak and contracted forms wherever possible.

Transcription passage 1
And here Alice began to get rather sleepy, and went on saying to herself, in a dreamy sort of way, 'Do cats eat bats?' and sometimes, 'Do bats eat cats?'. For, you see, as she couldn't answer either question, it didn't much matter which way she put it.

Transcription passage 2
She felt that she was dozing off, and had just begun to dream that she was walking hand in hand with Dinah, her cat. She was saying to her very earnestly, 'Now, Dinah, tell me the truth. Did you ever eat a bat?', when suddenly – thump! Down she came on a heap of sticks and dry leaves, and the fall was over.

Transcription passage 3
Alice was not a bit hurt, and she jumped up on to her feet in a moment. She looked up, but it was all dark overhead. In front of her was another long passage, and the White Rabbit was still in sight, hurrying down it. There was not a moment to be lost. Away went Alice like the wind. She was just in time to hear it say, as it turned a corner, 'Oh my ears and whiskers, how late it's getting!'

HOW WE PRODUCE SPEECH

Introduction

In this unit, we're going to have a look at what are usually known as the **organs of speech** or the **speech mechanism**. But one curious thing about the organs of speech is that none of them started out that way. They are all 'designed' for purposes other than speech. For example, the lungs are primarily intended for breathing; the teeth and the tongue for chewing up food and passing it down to the stomach. This has sometimes led scientists to call speech an 'overlaid function'. Nevertheless, the human being is uniquely a *speaking* animal, and in the course of evolution, all the organs of speech have developed in very specialised ways often quite remote from their original purpose. Perhaps the best example of this is the larynx (see below). This was originally merely a device for keeping chewed-up food from entering the lungs, but it has evolved into one of the most intricate parts of the vocal apparatus, playing a crucial role in speech.

The overwhelming majority of the sounds found in human speech are produced by an **egressive pulmonic airstream**, i.e. an outgoing stream of air produced by the lungs contracting (partially collapsing *inwards*) and thus pushing the air contained within them *outwards*. This airstream then passes through the larynx (known familiarly as the 'Adam's apple') and along a tube of complex shape formed by the mouth and nose (termed the **vocal tract**). A variety of muscles interact to produce changes in the configuration of the vocal tract so as to allow parts of the speech organs to come into contact (or near contact) with other parts, i.e. to **articulate**. Phoneticians term these anatomical bits and pieces the **articulators** – hence the term for the branch of science known as **articulatory phonetics**, which actually forms the main basis of this book.

The organs of speech fall into three groupings, arranged here from top to bottom:

Location	System
HEAD	Articulatory system
THROAT	Phonatory system
CHEST	Respiratory system

The respiratory system

The respiratory system consists of the lungs and the bronchial /ˈbrɒŋkɪəl/ tubes which lead to the throat. Normally, breathing in (**inhalation**) and breathing out (**exhalation**)

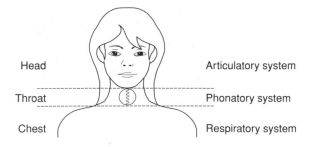

Head   Articulatory system

Throat   Phonatory system

Chest   Respiratory system

Figure A4.1 Divisions of the speech mechanism

both take a roughly equal space of time. But during speech, the lungs take in air rapidly and let it out slowly – in fact, about 1:8 in favour of exhalation. Speech consequently can be seen as a type of controlled breathing.

Activity

11

Breathe in and out. Then say /ɑː/ as in PALM. Hold it for as long as you can. Now try making the same noise on an ingressive airstream (i.e. breathing *in*). What difference can you notice?

When you did Activity 11 above, you will have noticed that it's very difficult to speak on an **ingressive** airstream for any length of time. Ingressive air may sometimes be used involuntarily for speech, for example when sobbing, or out of breath. Have you ever tried talking after having walked up several flights of stairs? A pulmonic ingressive airstream may also be employed when counting quickly (perhaps you remember playing 'hide and seek' as a child, and counting up to fifty as quickly as you could).

Activity

12

Try to recite a nursery rhyme, like *Mary Had a Little Lamb*, or some other familiar piece of verse breathing in. How many seconds can you go on for using just *one* breath?

In some languages certain words may be occasionally produced on an ingressive pulmonic airstream (for instance, French *oui* 'yes' is often said in this way). But no known language regularly uses an ingressive pulmonic airstream as part of its phonemic system.

All languages use the pulmonic egressive airstream as their main form of speech production. But a few sounds are made in a different way – for instance the click sounds we use occasionally to show disapproval (*tut-tut*) or enthusiasm. Although clicks aren't part of the English phonemic system, they are nevertheless meaningful in context. We call such phenomena that function alongside speech **paralinguistic** features – gestures, facial expressions and voice quality are other examples. Nevertheless, the sounds known as **clicks** – made with ingressive mouth air – are actually used as phonemes in several African languages. The best known of these are Zulu and Xhosa (actually two very similar languages) spoken in total by about twelve million people in South Africa.

The phonatory system

The bronchial tubes end in the windpipe – known technically as the **trachea** (/trəˈkɪə/ or /ˈtreɪkɪə/). At the very top of the trachea, we find the **larynx** /ˈlærɪŋks/, which can be regarded as the engine of the phonatory system. The larynx is clearly visible in grown males as a lump bobbing up and down in the neck; females have much smaller larynxes. Try feeling your larynx – easy for men but a bit more difficult for women.

The **vocal folds** (also called the vocal cords) vibrate very rapidly when an airstream is allowed to pass between them, producing what is termed **voice** – that is, a sort of 'buzz' which one can hear and feel in vowels and in some consonant sounds. The function of the larynx as a vibration source is termed **phonation** /fə'neɪʃn̩/.

The larynx is a box-like structure composed of cartilage, and inside it are the two vocal folds. These can be positioned by the two cartilages known as the **arytenoids** /ærə'tiːnɔɪdz/ (from Greek *arutaina*, 'serving spoon, ladle', so called because the cartilages were thought to be spoon-like in shape). The vocal folds temporarily close off the entrance to the trachea so protecting the lungs from inhaling small food particles. If this mechanism fails, as it sometimes does, we end up choking and spluttering, complaining that the food has 'gone the wrong way'. Food normally goes down the **oesophagus** /iː'sɒfəgəs/, the pipe leading to the stomach.

We can view the workings of the larynx in the old-fashioned way without too much difficulty by means of a **laryngoscope** /lə'rɪŋgəskəʊp/, which is a smart word for an angled rod with a mirror on the end (like the mirror a dentist uses to look at your teeth). Or, with more up-to-date technology, we can employ a fibre-optic cable by means of which clear still and moving images of the larynx can be obtained. We have not included a photographic image here because a wealth of material is to be found on the Internet: two excellent websites are http://www.voicedoctor.net/media/anatomy/anatview.html and http://www.phon.ox.ac.uk/~jcoleman/phonation.htm.

The gap between the vocal folds and/or the arytenoids is termed the **glottis** (adjective: **glottal**). With an organ as complex as the larynx, it is difficult to discuss the various settings using photographs or moving images. We shall, for our purposes, use a simplified model as illustrated in Figure A4.2 (note, incidentally, that our diagrams have the front of the larynx at the top – some of the images available on the Internet show the larynx the other way round).

For **voiceless** sounds, the vocal folds and the arytenoid cartilages are held wide apart as in relaxed breathing. This allows the pulmonic airstream to escape freely.

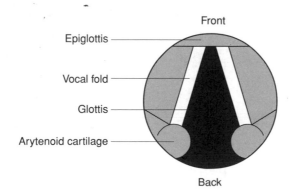

Figure A4.2 Simplified model of the larynx

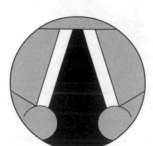

Vocal folds wide apart

Arytenoids wide apart

Figure A4.3 Glottal setting: voiceless

For **voice**, the vocal folds vibrate at high speed in the airstream produced by the lungs. The arytenoids are firmly closed. Vocal fold vibrations are far too fast to see with the naked eye, being comparable to the buzzing of an insect's wing. The vibration is constantly changing but occurs on average 130 times a second for male voices, and 230 times per second for females. Longer and larger vocal folds produce slower vibrations. The larger dimensions of the male vocal folds mean that men's voices are deeper in pitch than those of women.

The speed of vibration is termed **frequency**. Although the relationship is complex, we can say broadly that the higher the frequency of vocal fold vibration, the higher the pitch perceived by listeners (note that frequency is a *physical measurement* whilst pitch refers to the *perception* of the listener). Pitch change is crucial in language, being the basis of intonation and tone (see Section B6).

Activity

13

Say a vowel [ɑː] as in PALM. Prolong it. Press your hand on your larynx, and feel the buzz – the voicing. Now say a long [m] and feel the same thing. Now say a long [s]. Go on to say a [z]. Prolong it. Can you feel and hear the voicing for the [z] sound? Say [s z s z s z] and feel the contrast of voiceless and voiced in these sounds.

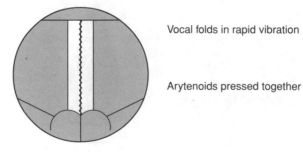

Vocal folds in rapid vibration

Arytenoids pressed together

Figure A4.4 Glottal setting: voice

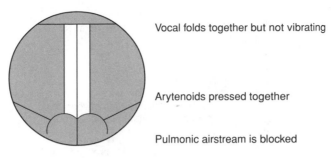

Vocal folds together but not vibrating

Arytenoids pressed together

Pulmonic airstream is blocked

Figure A4.5 Glottal setting: glottal stop

⭐ **Activity**

14

Say some voiced sounds: [ɑː], [m], [z]. Sing or hum them, changing the pitch up and down. This is easy to do with the voiced sounds but impossible with a voiceless sound like [f].

We shall soon see how important voicing is in language. In English, it is one of the phonetic variables which play a part in the fortis/lenis contrast (see A5).

Glottal stop [ʔ] is at the other extreme from voiceless (where the vocal folds are wide apart). The vocal folds and the arytenoids are close together so that the airstream coming from the lungs is momentarily stopped. On the release of the glottal closure, the blocked air rushes out with an effect rather like a weak cough, or the noise one makes when lifting a heavy weight.

Glottal stop functions as a phoneme in many languages, e.g. Arabic, Hawaiian and Farsi (also called Persian, which is the chief language of Iran). In English, [ʔ] is not a phoneme but plays a very important role as a reinforcement (or replacement) of fortis stop consonants (see Section B2).

⭐ **Activity**

15 ⊙ **Track 5**

Try saying this sentence using [ʔ] for /t/ as it might be in Cockney.

I've got to put a lot of butter on that little bit of bread
[aɪv ˈgɒʔə ˈpʊʔə ˈlɒʔə ˈbʌʔə r ɒn ðæʔ ˈlɪʔl̩ ˈbɪʔ ə ˈbred].

Note that because [ʔ] isn't a phoneme, we have to enclose this transcription in square brackets.

Creak is like a succession of glottal stops, one after another, sounding rather like an old door creaking open. The arytenoids are firmly pressed together whilst the

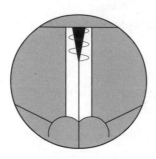

Front portion of vocal folds in slow vibration

Rear portion of vocal folds together but not vibrating

Arytenoids pressed together

Figure A4.6   Glottal setting: creak

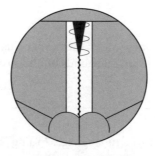

Front portion of vocal folds in slow vibration

Rear portion of vocal folds in rapid vibration

Arytenoids pressed together

Figure A4.7   Glottal setting: creaky voice

front portions of the vocal folds slowly vibrate. These vibrations (about 40 times per second) are slow enough almost to be heard individually.

Creaky voice is creak combined with voice. Though apparently more complicated, creaky voice is nevertheless easier to imitate and much commoner in language. Creaky voice is common in NRP English and also in much American speech, especially high-status varieties. In fact, if you listen to the samples of native-speaker English on the audio CD, you'll hear creaky voice in many of them.

Activity

> ### 16
>
> Can you produce creaky voice and creak? Say a long vowel [ɑː], going down the scale till it's as low a note as you can comfortably achieve – and then go lower again! You'll end up with creaky voice. Now take away the actual vowel sound leaving just the 'rattle' of creak.

In Danish many words are distinguished by whether or not they are said with creaky voice. This effect, known in Danish as *stød*, is indicated in transcription by [ʾ], e.g. *hun* /hun/ 'she' (pron.) – *hund* /hunʾ/ 'dog'. This means that in Danish creaky voice has a kind of phonemic function.

17 ☺ **Track 6**

Listen to these three pairs of words in Danish. In each case, the first word is said with normal voice whilst the second has added creaky voice, or *stød* (indicated in transcription by an apostrophe). Try imitating the words to see if you can mimic the effect of *stød*.

hun [hun] 'she'   *hund* [hun'] 'dog'
man [mɛn] 'one' (pronoun)   *mand* [mɛn'] 'man'
mor [moɒ] 'mother'   *mord* [moːˈɒ] 'murder'

For **whisper** the vocal folds are brought together but do not vibrate. The arytenoids are held apart leaving a gap at the rear of the larynx through which air passes at fairly high velocity.

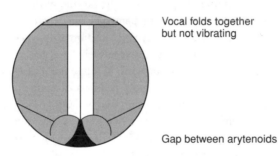

Vocal folds together but not vibrating

Gap between arytenoids

Figure A4.8 Glottal setting: whisper

A combination of voice and whisper is known as **breathy voice**. It is sometimes associated with 'sexy' voices, and breathy voice is skilfully used by popular singers – particularly women – as a special effect (to quote just one example from a former era, Marilyn Monroe). A significant aspect of such singing – as opposed to the classical tradition – is the deliberate introduction of a wide variety of different larynx settings and voice qualities.

18

Listen to a number of singers (on CD, cassette or minidisc so that you can hear the same piece over again) and try to discover what special voice quality effects are being employed. Do you notice any differences in the voices of male and female singers in this respect?

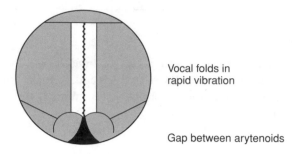

Vocal folds in
rapid vibration

Gap between arytenoids

Figure A4.9   Glottal setting: breathy voice

In many Indian languages (e.g. Hindi, Bengali) breathy voice is employed phonemically, some consonants being said with breathy voice and some with normal voice. In English, /h/ between vowels is often said with breathy voice, indicated by [ɦ], e.g. *behind* [bɪˈɦaɪnd]. In Afrikaans (spoken in South Africa), and also in much South African English, /h/ is breathy voiced in all contexts.

The various states of the glottis can be seen as forming a kind of chain relationship. Voiceless is at one extreme of openness of the larynx; glottal stop is at the other extreme of closed larynx state. Voice can be placed at the centre as the most frequent state of the larynx in most languages. Creaky voice and breathy voice are combinations of creak and voice, and whisper and voice, respectively.

All these possibilities are known to be used in language. For example, most languages employ voiced and voiceless in some way in consonant oppositions. English has glottal stop as a marker of certain fortis consonants. Other languages, e.g. Arabic, use glottal stop itself as a phoneme. Creaky voice and creak occur regularly in English as a part of the intonation process. Whisper and breathy voice are heard in /h/ and may also sometimes be used for special effects.

Activity

> ## 19 ☉ Track 7
>
> Listen to your CD and then try to imitate different glottal settings for this sentence in English:
>
> *Jack and Jill went up the hill to fetch a pail of water.*
>
> 1. Voice. 2. Whisper. 3. Breathy voice. 4. Creaky voice.

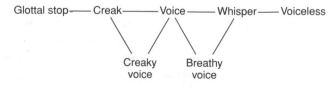

Figure A4.10   Chain relationship of glottal settings

The articulatory system

Without special equipment, it's impossible to view the anatomy of the respiratory system and difficult to examine that of the phonatory system. But most of the **articulatory system**, the third part of the speech mechanism, is quite easy to see – all you need is an ordinary mirror and decent illumination.

The articulatory system is contained in the head and throat above the larynx – termed the **supra-glottal vocal tract** (from Latin *supra* = 'above', hence 'above the glottis'), usually abbreviated simply to 'vocal tract'. We can distinguish three resonating cavities:

- ❑ Throat (or pharynx)   pharyngeal cavity
- ❑ Mouth   oral cavity
- ❑ Nose   nasal cavity

As the airstream passes through these cavities the nature of the vocal buzz is altered, increasing (or amplifying) some parts of it and diminishing (or damping) others. This is in many ways comparable to the difference made to the sound produced by a vibrating reed by the tube and bell of a saxophone (or other similar wind instruments). Alterations in the shape of the pharyngeal and oral cavities change the shape of the resonating chambers (i.e. the cavities) and modify the quality of the sounds produced, particularly the vowels. Furthermore, the air passing from the lungs can be blocked off by the articulators and released to make little pop-like explosions, or made to pass through narrowings to produce hiss-type noise.

It is convenient to illustrate the shape of the vocal tract by means of **cross-sections**. Rather than having detailed, realistic cross-sections (if you want to see one of these, go to http://www.phon.ox.ac.uk/~jcoleman/phonation.htm), it is better for our purposes to use a simplified model, as in Figure A4.11.

Pharyngeal, nasal and oral cavities

The pharynx is located directly above the larynx. At the upper end, the passageway splits in two – one portion leading to the **nasal cavity** (the space inside the nose) and the other to the **oral cavity** (the space inside the mouth). The position of the soft palate determines whether the airstream is directed into one or the other.

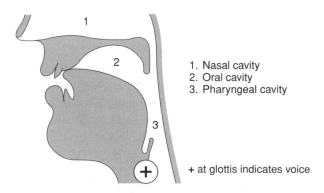

1. Nasal cavity
2. Oral cavity
3. Pharyngeal cavity

+ at glottis indicates voice

Figure A4.11 Simplified cross-section of vocal tract showing nasal, oral and pharyngeal cavities, as for articulation of /n/

20

Say a prolonged [m]. Now pinch your nostrils sharply. What happens? Do the same with [n] and [ŋ]. These consonants, where the airstream is allowed to resonate in the nasal cavity, are called nasals. When you block the point of the release at the nostrils, the airstream can no longer escape and the sound suddenly ceases.

The function of the soft palate can be likened to that of a railway points mechanism. It switches the airstream to flow either (1) out through the mouth (soft palate raised) and without passing through the nose, or (2) through the nose. In the case of (1) there is no nasal resonance and the resulting sound is termed **oral** or non-nasal. In the case of (2) (soft palate lowered) nasal resonance is added and the sound is termed **nasal**. See Figures A4.12 and A4.13 (p. 37) illustrating velic closure.

Most speech sounds are oral, i.e. made with a velic closure (soft palate raised). But nearly all languages have **nasal consonants**, e.g. [m n ŋ], and some also have **nasal vowels**, e.g. the vowels in the French phrase *un bon vin blanc* 'a good white wine'; see also Section C6. For nasal sounds, there is no velic closure.

Activity

21

Look in a mirror and say an oral vowel [ɑː] followed by a nasal sound [ɑ̃ː]. If you look at the back of your mouth, you may be able to see the velum moving up and down and looking very like a veil blowing in the wind.

In speech much of the action takes place in the oral cavity. We'll start at the lips to begin our description and then work backwards.

Lips (Latin labia; adj. bilabial = 'two lips')
The two lips can close to block the airstream, as for **bilabial** /p b m/ in English. Or the lips can allow air through, being so close together that audible friction is produced, as for the Spanish bilabial sound [β] spelt **b** or **v**, e.g. *Ibiza* or *aviso* 'warning'.

The lower lip can also be held close to the upper teeth, as for /f v/ (e.g. *fan*, *van*). Such lip–teeth articulations are termed **labio-dental**.

For vowels, the lips may be rounded (as in the English THOUGHT vowel), neutral (as in English PALM) or spread (as in English FLEECE). Consonants may also be lip-rounded; English /w/ has strongly rounded lips, and for most speakers, /r/ is also rounded. The lips can also be protruded – often even made 'trumpet-shaped', as for English /ʃ ʒ tʃ dʒ/, e.g. *ship*, *measure*, *aitch*, *bridge*.

✪ Activity

22 ☺ Track 8

Practise lip-rounding and spreading with vowel sounds, using a mirror. Say /iː/, as in FLEECE. Now say it whilst rounding your lips. You should now get a sound resembling the vowel [y], as in French *nu* or German *Bücher*, which we referred to in Section A2. Similar sounds exist in many other European languages, e.g. Dutch, Danish, Swedish, Norwegian, Finnish and Turkish.

Teeth (Latin dentes; adj. dental)

The term **dental** normally implies a sound made by the tongue-tip against or close to the front teeth, e.g. English /θ ð/. These articulations usually pose problems for non-native learners of English. In the languages of the world, dental fricatives similar to English /θ/ and /ð/ are not as unusual as is sometimes supposed. One or both are found, for example, in Greek, European Spanish, Icelandic, Welsh and in many varieties of Arabic.

But in fact, the teeth are important in one way or another for making a whole range of sounds, e.g. [θ ð f v s z ʃ ʒ]. It's really quite difficult to talk without them. If you don't believe us, ask anyone with false teeth!

✪ Activity

23

If you are a non-native speaker of English, try saying the dental sounds [θ] and [ð]. Use your mirror to check the position of your tongue and teeth. See if you can say the dental sounds by placing the tongue just behind the back of the upper front teeth. You should find it quite easy to produce [θ] and [ð] in this way.

Alveolar ridge (from Latin alveolus 'small hollow', referring to the tooth sockets)

Now let's deal with the roof of the mouth. The term **alveolar** /ælviˈəʊlə/ implies that the tongue-tip or blade is in contact or near-contact with the upper alveolar ridge, i.e. the ridge immediately behind the front teeth. A large number of the English consonants are alveolar articulations, e.g. /t d s z n/.

✪ Activity

24

Put your tongue on your teeth. Move it back to the gums and the sensitive ridged area just behind the gums. You can now feel your alveolar ridge, which is where the teeth fit into their sockets – or *alveoli*, to give them their Latin name.

Hard palate (adj. palatal)

The term 'palatal' means that the central portion of the tongue articulates with the hard palate, e.g. [j].

> **25**
>
> Move the tip of your tongue back from the alveolar ridge. As you do so, you'll notice that the roof of the mouth changes from ridged to smooth. This portion is called the hard palate – it feels hard because there's a bone inside it.

Note that when applied to the description of sounds 'palatal' is only used for those involving the *hard* palate. You'll recall that sounds formed by the back of the tongue against the soft palate are termed 'velar'. For /ʃ/, as in *ship*, a large portion of the tongue rises to articulate with the alveolar ridge and the front of the hard palate. Such articulations are termed **palato-alveolar**. Similar palato-alveolar articulations are heard in /ʒ/ in *measure*, /tʃ/ in *choke*, /dʒ/ in *joke*. (Note that some linguists nowadays use the term **post-alveolar** instead of palato-alveolar. See the International Phonetic Alphabet symbol chart, p. 258.)

Soft palate or velum (from Latin velum /'viːləm/ 'veil'; adj. velar)

> **26**
>
> If you feel brave, run your finger further back to determine where the hard palate joins the soft palate. You'll be aware of a sensation, called the 'gag reflex', which makes you want to vomit. Its purpose is to deter you from swallowing large objects.

One of the important functions of the soft palate was explained above, namely that of directing the airstream either into the nasal cavity (if lowered, i.e. absence of velic closure) or into the oral cavity (soft palate raised, velic closure). But the soft palate can also be used as a place of articulation – just like the other parts of the roof of the mouth described in this section. Sounds made with the back of the tongue against the soft palate are called **velar**. Note that /k g ŋ/ are all velar consonants, but only /k g/ have a velic closure.

Uvula (from Latin uvula 'little grape'; adj. uvular)

The velum ends in a lump of flesh called the **uvula**. It is quite possible to see this organ (which does indeed look something like a little pink grape!) and to make it vibrate, so producing a **uvular trill** [ʀ]. It's much the same kind of action as gargling. Several European languages, including French, German, Dutch, Danish, have uvular

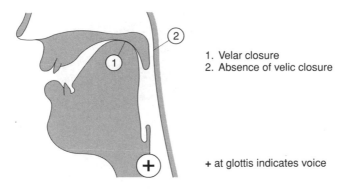

1. Velar closure
2. Absence of velic closure

+ at glottis indicates voice

Figure A4.12   Articulation of /ŋ/ showing velar closure but absence of velic closure

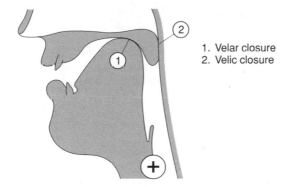

1. Velar closure
2. Velic closure

Figure A4.13   Articulation of /g/ showing both velar closure and velic closure

articulations for /r/, all with the airstream channelled between the uvula and the back of the tongue. Uvular /r/ is unusual in English but not unknown. Geordies (from the north-east of England) sometimes produce /r/ in this way.

 Activity

27

Try to produce a uvular trill [ʀ]. If you have difficulty, try going through the motions of gargling.

Tongue (Latin lingua; adj. lingual)

We'll now examine one of the most complex of the organs of speech – the tongue. The body of the tongue, consisting almost entirely of muscle, is very flexible and capable of assuming a wide variety of different shapes. Although it has no natural anatomical divisions, it is necessary for phonetic analysis to distinguish its various portions: tip, blade, front, back and root. See Figure A4.14.

The tip of the tongue is a very sensitive organ of touch – much more sensitive, in fact, than the finger tips – but this diminishes as we move towards the back of the tongue.

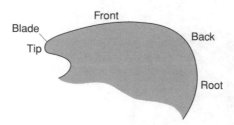

Figure A4.14 Divisions of the tongue

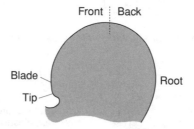

Figure A4.15 Tongue body raised, with tip and blade lowered, as for vowel articulations

Activity

> **28**
>
> While looking in a mirror, run the tip of your tongue back from the teeth along the hard palate. How far back can you get the tongue-tip to go? Can you feel the soft palate? Try saying [t]-type sounds with your tongue at various points along the roof of the mouth. Can you make a trilled [r] with the tip of your tongue?

The term 'front' is used for what at first looks as if it should be called the middle of the tongue. But look at Figure A4.15, which shows the **tongue arch** found in the articulation of vowels. You'll see that the front/back divisions are then quite appropriate.

Two other important facts about the tongue are that:

1. The sides of the tongue can be lowered for **lateral** sounds, e.g. [l].

Activity

> **29**
>
> Say [l] and then breathe in sharply. Where do you feel the cold air coming in? Along the mid-line of the tongue, or along one or both sides?

2. The tongue can be depressed making a groove down the mid-line. This is very important for the sounds [s] and [z].

You now have most of the necessary information about the anatomy and physiology of the organs of speech. To test yourself out on the basic facts, do Activity 31.

Activity

30

Say [s] and then breathe in sharply. Feel how the cold air rushes in via the channel formed along the groove down the mid-line of your tongue.

⭐ Activity

31

Fill in the blanks by consulting the text. Answers on the website.

1
2
3
4
5
6
7
8
9
10
11
12
13
14
15
16
17
18

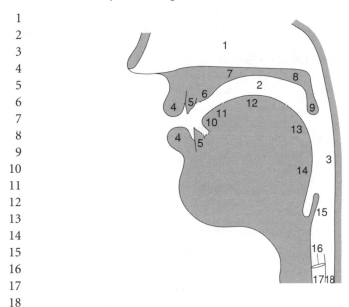

Figure A4.16 Exercise on speech mechanism

⭐ Activity

32

Transcribe phonemically, showing intonation groups and sentence stress, and using weak and contracted forms wherever possible.

Transcription passage 4
She was close behind it when she turned the corner, but the Rabbit was no longer to be seen and she found herself in a long, low hall, which was lit up by a row of lamps hanging from the roof. There were doors all round the hall, but they were all locked. Alice went all the way down one side and up the other, trying every door. Then she walked sadly down the middle, wondering how she was ever to get in.

A5   **CONSONANT POSSIBILITIES**

Consonant labels

Consonants are usually referred to by brief descriptive labels stating *energy*, *place of articulation* and *manner of articulation*, always in that order (Table A5.1).

Place of articulation

Place of articulation tells us *where* the sound is produced. The English places of articulation are shown in Figure A5.1 (they correspond to the column 'Place' in Table A5.1).

Other languages and varieties of English may have additional places of articulation. For instance, French /r/ is **uvular**, made with the back of the tongue against the uvula; it is symbolised phonetically as [ʀ] and can also be heard in traditional Geordie (Tyneside) accents; see Section C2. Indian languages (and most Indian English) have

Table A5.1   Consonant labels for English

Consonant	Energy	Place	Manner
p t k	fortis	bilabial alveolar velar	plosive
b d g	lenis	bilabial alveolar velar	plosive
tʃ dʒ	fortis lenis	palato-alveolar	affricate
f θ s ʃ h	fortis	labio-dental dental alveolar palato-alveolar glottal	fricative
v ð z ʒ	lenis	labio-dental dental alveolar palato-alveolar	fricative
w r j		labial-velar post-alveolar palatal	(central) approximant
l		alveolar	lateral (approximant)
m n ŋ		bilabial alveolar velar	nasal

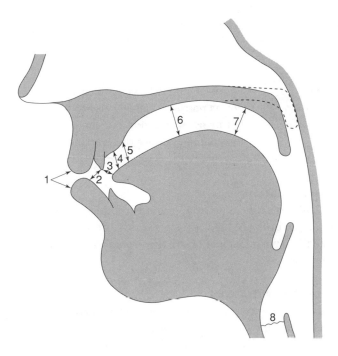

1. Bilabial (lower lip ↔ upper lip)
2. Labio-dental (lower lip ↔ upper front teeth)
3. Dental (tip of tongue ↔ rear of upper front teeth)
4. Alveolar (tip/blade of tongue ↔ alveolar ridge)
5. Palato-alveolar (blade/front of tongue ↔ rear of alveolar ridge/front of hard palate)
6. Palatal (front of tongue ↔ hard palate)
7. Velar (back of tongue ↔ velum)
8. Glottal (glottis)

Figure A5.1 English consonants: places of articulation

retroflex sounds made with the tip of the tongue curled back against the rear of the alveolar ridge (see Section C4). Some speakers of West Country English also make /r/ in that way (see Section C2).

Some consonants have two places of articulation resulting in what is termed a **double articulation**. An example is English /w/ which is articulated at the lips (bilabial) and at the velum (velar) and hence is termed labial-velar.

 Activity

33

Say these words and relate the consonants in bold to their places of articulation: *pub* (bilabial), *five* (labio-dental), ***this bath*** (dental), *side* (alveolar), *rarer* (post-alveolar), *change* (palato-alveolar), *you* (palatal), *king* (velar), *how* (glottal).

Table A5.2 Manner of articulation – stricture types

Nature of stricture	Effect of stricture
Complete closure	Forms obstruction which blocks airstream
Close approximation	Forms narrowing giving rise to friction
Open approximation	Forms no obstruction but changes shape of vocal tract, thus altering nature of resonance

Manner of articulation

Manner of articulation tells us *how* the sound is produced. All articulations involve a **stricture**, i.e. a narrowing of the vocal tract which affects the airstream. Table A5.2 summarises the three possible types of stricture: *complete closure, close approximation* and *open approximation*.

Active and passive articulators

The **active articulator** is the organ that *moves*; the **passive articulator** is the *target* of the articulation – i.e. the point towards which the active articulator is directed. Sometimes there's actual contact, as in [t] and [k]. In other cases, the active articulator is positioned close to the passive articulator, as in [s] or [θ]. With other articulations again, like English /r/, we find only a slight gesture by the active articulator towards the passive articulator.

The distinction of passive/active articulator isn't always possible. For instance, [h] is formed at the glottis. The descriptive label for place of articulation is in most cases derived from the *passive* articulator. Figure A5.1 shows the chief places of articulation for English.

Activity

> **34**
>
> Say /t/ as in *tight* [taɪt]. Now say /s/ as in *sauce* [sɔːs]. Can you feel that for /t/ the active articulator (tongue-tip/blade) and the passive articulator (alveolar ridge) block the airstream with a stricture of *complete closure*? But for /s/ the same articulators form a narrowing through which the airstream is channelled, i.e. a stricture of *close approximation*. Now say and compare the following sounds:
>
> ❑ English /k/ in *coat* (complete closure)
> ❑ Spanish /x/, the sound spelt **j** in *jefe* (close approximation)
> ❑ English /j/ in *yes* (open approximation).

Complete closure

Stops

Stop consonants have a stricture of complete closure in the vocal tract which blocks (i.e. *stops*) the airstream, hence the term **stop**. The soft palate is raised so that there's no escape of air through the nose. The compressed air can then be released in one of two ways:

❏ The articulators part quickly, releasing the air with explosive force (termed **plosion**). Sounds made in this way are termed **plosives**, e.g. English /p t k b d g/.

❏ The articulators part relatively slowly, producing **homorganic** friction, i.e. friction at the same point of articulation. Sounds made in this way are termed **affricates**, e.g. English /tʃ dʒ/.

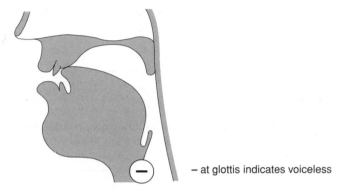

– at glottis indicates voiceless

Figure A5.2   Plosive [t] showing complete closure

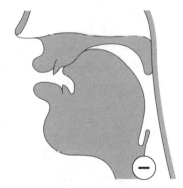

Figure A5.3   Affricates [tʃ] and [dʒ] showing palato-alveolar closure

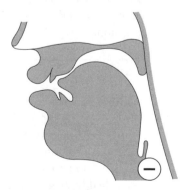

Figure A5.4   Affricates [tʃ] and [dʒ] showing release with homorganic friction

Figures A5.3 and A5.4 illustrate the stages in /tʃ/ as in *church*. In English, /tʃ/ and /dʒ/, as in *judge*, are affricates which function as phonemes (but see also Section B2).

Nasals

Like stops, **nasals** have a stricture of complete closure in the oral cavity, but the soft palate is lowered allowing the airstream to escape through the nose, e.g. English /m n ŋ/. In English, as in most languages, nasal consonants are normally voiced. However, a few languages, e.g. Burmese, Welsh and Icelandic, have voiceless nasals acting as phonemes, i.e. /m̥ n̥ ŋ̊/. Note that we employ here the diacritic for voiceless [̥] added below the symbol (above in the case of [ŋ]).

Activity

35 ☺ Track 9

Try imitating these examples, based loosely on Burmese words: [m̥a] 'notice'; [n̥a] 'nose'; [ŋ̊a] 'borrow'. (See Ladefoged and Maddieson 1996: 111.)

Trills and taps

For a **trill**, the active articulator strikes the passive articulator with a rapid percussive (i.e. beating) action. The two types of trill that most frequently occur in language are alveolar (the tongue-tip striking the alveolar ridge) and uvular (uvula striking the back of the tongue): see Figures A5.5 and A5.6. But other kinds are possible – for instance, a bilabial trill (see Activity 36).

Activity

36

You should find it easy to make a bilabial trill – it's just the *brrr* noise we sometimes use to mean: 'Isn't it cold!' But in a few African languages (e.g. Ngwe spoken in Cameroon) this sound is a phoneme and has its own phonetic symbol [ʙ]. Look in a mirror and then you'll be able to see, as well as feel, the rapid percussive lip action.

An alveolar trill is found in Spanish, e.g. *carro* 'cart'. The uvular trill [ʀ] is occasionally heard in French – but usually only in singing. Edith Piaf, a well-known French voice from the past, was renowned for her vibrant uvular trill.

A *single* rapid percussive movement (i.e. one beat of a trill) is termed a **tap**. Spanish is unusual in having a contrast of a tap /ɾ/ and a trill /r/, e.g. *caro* 'dear' /ˈkaɾo/ and *carro* /ˈkaro/. In many languages with trilled [r] (e.g. Welsh, Italian and Arabic) many speakers regularly pronounce taps, reserving the trill for careful speech.

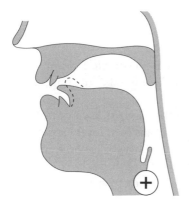

Figure A5.5 Alveolar trill [r]

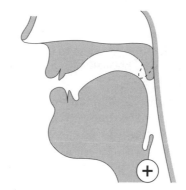

Figure A5.6 Uvular trill [ʀ]

37 ☺ **Track 10**

Try saying, between vowels, (1) an alveolar tap [aɾa] and (2) an alveolar trill [ara]. Then practise the uvular trill [ʀ] in the same context [aʀa].

One important point concerning transcription: note that in *phonetic* transcription the symbol for an alveolar trill, placed, of course, in square brackets, is [r]. The *phonetic* transcription symbol for the commonest type of English /r/ (a post-alveolar approximant, see p. 47) is an upside-down [ɹ]. Nevertheless, for *phonemic* transcription the rule is to employ the simplest letter shape possible, and consequently an ordinary /r/ (in slant brackets) is used for the English phoneme.

NRP, like virtually all other types of native-speaker English, has no regular trill articulation. Scots can usually produce a trill if called upon to do so but use a tap for /r/ in everyday speech. But many British regional accents, not only Scottish, but also Liverpool, and most Welsh varieties, regularly have an alveolar tap [ɾ] for /r/. A tap was also to be heard from old-fashioned traditional RP speakers (one famous example was the legendary Noël Coward). It was used for medial /r/, e.g. *carry*, *very*. Indeed, a tapped [ɾ] is still sometimes taught by elocutionists as 'correct' speech, especially for would-be actors.

38

Some people find it hard to make an alveolar trilled [r]. Don't despair! One way to begin is by saying a 'flappy' [d] using the very tip of your tongue, and as quickly as possible. Try it in words like *cross*, *brave*, *proof* [kdɒs bdeɪv pduːf]. Practise rapid 'flappy' [d] many times until you can change it into a true tap and then extend that into a trill.

Close approximation

Fricatives

The articulators are close to each other but don't make a complete closure. The airstream passes through a narrowing, producing audible hiss-like friction, e.g. English /f v θ ð s z ʃ ʒ h/.

Compared with most varieties of English, Scottish accents have two extra fricatives [x ʍ]. The voiceless velar fricative [x] is found mostly in local usages, e.g. *och!* 'oh', *loch* 'lake' ([x] also occurs in many European languages; see Section A2). The voiceless labial-velar fricative [ʍ] occurs in words spelt **wh**, such as *which, what, whether, wheel*. It is used not only by Scots but also by many Irish and some American speakers.

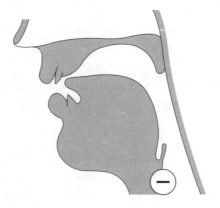

Figure A5.7   Fricative [s] showing narrowing at alveolar ridge

A useful term to cover both stops and fricatives is **obstruents**. All other consonant sounds, and also vowels, are classed as **sonorants**.

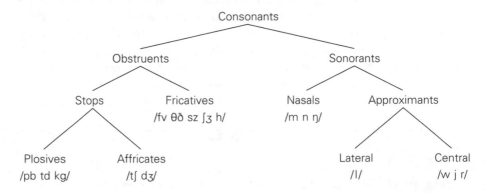

Open approximation

(Central) approximants

Approximants have a stricture of open approximation. The space between the articulators is wide enough to allow the airstream through with no audible friction, as in

English /w j r/. English /j/ and /w/ are like very short vowels – similar to brief versions of /iː/ and /uː/ (an old term for these sounds was in fact 'semi-vowels').

39

Say English /iː/ followed directly by /es/ in this way: /iː es/. If you say /iː/ quickly, you will end up with *yes*. Now try the same with /uː/. If you say a rapid /uː/ followed by /et/, you should end up with a sound close to /w/, and a word sounding like English *wet*. For non-native learners of English who don't have /j/ or /w/ in their languages this is a good way to learn the sounds.

In NRP, and most English regional accents, /r/ is a post-alveolar approximant – made with the tip of the tongue approaching the rear of the alveolar ridge. The phonetic symbol is [ɹ]. Remember that in phonemic transcription, because one tries to use simple symbol shapes wherever possible, it is shown with the ordinary letter /r/.

All the sounds so far described may if necessary be termed **central approximants** to distinguish them from the lateral approximants described below.

Lateral (approximant)

Lateral consonants are made with the centre of the tongue forming a closure with the roof of the mouth but the sides lowered. Typically, the airstream escapes without friction so producing a **lateral approximant**. This is true for most allophones of English /l/. However, if there's a narrowing between the lowered sides of the tongue and the roof of the mouth, and the air escapes with friction, the result is a **lateral fricative**.

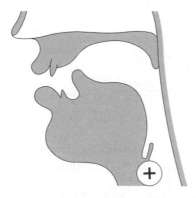

Figure A5.8 Approximant [ɹ] showing post-alveolar open approximation

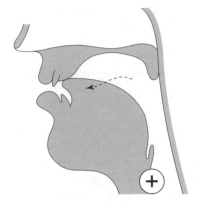

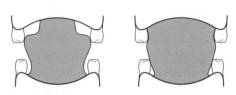

Figure A5.9 Lateral approximant [l]. Arrow indicates passage of airstream without friction over lowered sides of tongue

Figure A5.10 Transverse cross-sections of mouth viewed from front. Left: tongue sides lowered for lateral [l]; right: tongue sides raised as for non-lateral articulations, e.g. [t d]

 Activity

> ### 40 ☺ Track 11
>
> Say an [l] a number of times. Now try saying the sound, raising the tongue sides a little closer to the roof of the mouth, and forcing a stronger airstream through. This gives you a voiced lateral fricative, [ɮ]. Now try 'switching off' the voice. This results in a voiceless lateral fricative [ɬ], which is Welsh **ll**. A similar sound also occurs in English (usually represented as [l̥]) as an allophone of /l/, following fortis plosives, as in *close, place*.

Lateral fricatives are unusual in the languages of the world but by no means unknown. The most familiar to you may be the notorious Welsh **ll**. The voiceless lateral fricative (spelt double **ll**, and symbolised [ɬ]) is a frequent phoneme in Welsh. You can hear it in the place-name *Llanelli*. It's sometimes said to be 'impossible' for non-Welsh people to produce – a claim which is patently untrue, since not only do such sounds occur in many other languages but English itself has a similar articulation as an allophone of /l/: see below.

 Activity

> ### 41 ☺ Track 12
>
> Try saying these Welsh words which contain the voiceless lateral fricative: *llaeth* /ɬaiθ/ 'milk', *llaw* /ɬau/ 'hand', *llong* /ɬɔŋ/ 'ship', *allan* /'aɬan/ 'out', *ambell* /'ambɛɬ/ 'sometimes'.

42 ☉ **Track 13**

Just for fun, try saying the longest Welsh place-name. It's full of voiceless [ɬ] sounds:

Llanfairpwllgwyngyllgogerychwyrndrobwllllantysiliogogogoch

[ˈɬanvairpuɬˈgwɪŋɪɬgoˈgerəxwərnˈdrɔbuɬˈɬantɪˈsɪljoˈgogoˈgoːx]

Incidentally, the name in its present form was invented in the nineteenth century – apparently as a joke, or perhaps to bewilder the English! The village is known to the locals as *Llanfair P.G.* – much easier to pronounce! Even for the Welsh!

Welsh, Icelandic, Burmese, the South African languages Zulu and Xhosa, and many native American languages all have [ɬ]. The voiced lateral fricative [ɮ] is much more uncommon but does occur, for example, in Zulu and Xhosa.

43

Find a CD of Miriam Makeba (or another South African performer) singing folksongs in Zulu or Xhosa. Listen to it carefully and try to pick out the lateral fricatives (voiced and voiceless).

We have already mentioned in Activity 40 that English /l/ has a very common fricative allophone which is to be heard in words beginning /pl/ and /kl/. If a normally voiced phoneme is for whatever reason realised without voice, the effect is termed **devoicing**. As we have seen, this is shown by a diacritic in the form of a little circle, e.g. [l̥].

44 ☉ **Track 14**

Say these words with devoiced [l̥]: *clean, play, click, clock, please, plaster, plenty, cluster.* Some people (not all) produce a devoiced [l̥] following [t] as in *atlas, rattling, cutlet.* Do you?

Energy of articulation (fortis/lenis contrast)

The third possible distinction is **energy of articulation** (already mentioned briefly above). The English consonants /k/ and /g/ are both velar (place of articulation) and plosives (manner of articulation), yet they're obviously very different sounds. The same goes for /s/ and /z/, which are both alveolar fricatives, but are clearly not identical. So what's the difference?

Activity

45 ☉ Track 15

Say these words a number of times: *pack – back*. Compare the initial sound in each word /p – b/. Which sound do you hear as the stronger, more energetic articulation? Did you also notice that there is a slight 'puff of air' after the release of /p/ but not after the release of /b/?

Activity

46

Say /p/ and /b/ between /ɑː/ vowels: /ɑːpɑː/, /ɑːbɑː/. Put your fingers in your ears and listen for voice. Voice ceases during /p/, but continues all the way through /b/. Now do the same for /t/ and /d/, and /s/ and /z/: /ɑːtɑː/ and /ɑːdɑː/, /ɑːsɑː/ and /ɑːzɑː/. Voice ceases for the consonants /t/ and /s/, but continues throughout for /d/ and /z/.

English has two classes of consonant sound: one of the /t k s/ type with *stronger* and *voiceless* articulation and another of the /b d z/ type whose articulation is *weaker* and potentially *voiced*. The first class is termed **fortis** (Latin: 'strong'), and the second **lenis** (pronounced /ˈliːnɪs/ Latin: 'soft'). Consonants in English divide as follows (note that /h/ has no lenis counterpart).

Fortis   **Lenis**
p t k tʃ f θ s ʃ h   b d g dʒ v ð z ʒ

The fortis/lenis distinction applies in English only to the obstruents (i.e. stops and fricatives). The sonorants (nasals and approximants) do not have this contrast (hence the blank spaces in the 'Energy' column in Table A5.1).

The fortis/lenis contrast in English

Most languages have a contrast of a kind similar to the fortis/lenis contrast found in English. But the exact form of the contrast varies a lot from one language to another, and there are more phonetic signals for the fortis/lenis contrast in English than in most other languages.

There may also be very important differences in distribution. Many languages have no word-final fortis/lenis contrasts (even where the spelling would seem to indicate this). This goes for German, Dutch and Russian. In German, *Wirt – wird* 'host – became' are said exactly the same and *kalt – bald* 'cold – soon' form a good rhyme. Similarly, in Dutch, *hout – houd* 'wood – hold' are pronounced identically, and *maat* 'size' rhymes

Table A5.3 Fortis/lenis contrast in English

Fortis	Lenis
1 Articulation is stronger and more energetic. It has more muscular effort and greater breath force.	1 Articulation is weaker. It has less muscular effort and less breath force.
2 Articulation is voiceless.	2 Articulation may have voice.
3 Plosives /p, t, k/ when initial in a stressed syllable have strong aspiration (a brief puff of air), e.g. *pip* [pʰɪp].	3 Plosives are unaspirated, e.g. *bib* [bɪb].
4 Vowels are shortened before a final fortis consonant, e.g. *beat* [bit].	4 Vowels have full length before a final lenis consonant, e.g. *bead* [biːd].
5 Syllable-final stops often have a reinforcing glottal stop, e.g. *set down* [seʔt ˈdaʊn].	5 Syllable-final stops never have a reinforcing glottal stop, e.g. *said* [sed].

with *kwaad* 'angry'. Speakers of languages such as these usually have great difficulty with the frequent word-final fortis/lenis contrasts in English in pairs like *life – live*, *rate – raid*, *nip – nib*.

Table A5.3 summarises the main ways in which the fortis/lenis contrast is indicated in English.

The factors described in Table A5.3 are crucial in the fortis/lenis contrast in English. Energy of articulation has been mentioned already. Aspiration and glottalisation apply only to the fortis plosives /p t k/ and will be discussed in Section B2. Let's now examine the two remaining features, voicing and vowel length.

Voicing

In English, fortis consonants are voiceless, i.e. the vocal folds do not vibrate. Lenis consonants are *potentially* voiced. The word 'potentially' is important here. In many languages the essential difference between sounds like [s] and [z], or [p] and [b], is one of voicing; /p t k f s/ etc. are voiceless while their counterparts /b d g v z/ etc. are truly voiced. This is largely true, for example, of French, Spanish, Italian and many more. In such languages, the terms used for these phonologically opposed classes are voiceless and voiced.

But in English the difference is not as clear-cut. Although lenis consonants are potentially voiced, some voicing is lost in initial position, and final consonants are typically almost totally devoiced. Medially (i.e. between vowels, or other voiced sounds) lenis consonants have full voicing.

Activity

---

47 ⊙ **Track 16**

Say the following English words and note the degree of voicing in the different contexts:

	Initial	Medial	Final
/b/	ban	rabbit	cab
/d/	die	cider	side
/dʒ/	jar	margin	barge
/z/	zinc	daisy	daze
/v/	vet	favour	save

The difference in initial and final devoicing only affects lenis obstruents. The nasals /m n ŋ/, lateral /l/ and approximants /w j r/ do not undergo devoicing in the manner described following or preceding pause. Consequently, in words like *ram, long, wall, moon, yell*, the initial and final sounds are both fully voiced.

Activity

48

Jim bought books, bags and magazines at Gateshead Station
['dʒɪm 'bo̞ːt 'bo̞ks 'bæɡz ən mæɡə'ziːnz ət ̬ɡeɪtshed 'steɪʃn̩]

In this example, the vowels and fully voiced consonants are underlined, and those with devoicing shown by the 'devoiced' diacritic: [̥]. Transcribe the following utterances and mark the consonants in the same way.

A big bag full of gold.
David rode off on Grandad's old bike.

Vowel length

In all varieties of English (except Scottish: see Section C3), vowels are shortened before fortis consonants but have full length in all other contexts (i.e. word-finally, before lenis consonants, and before nasals and /l/). This pre-fortis shortening is most obvious in stressed **monosyllables** (i.e. single-syllable words) and is termed **pre-fortis clipping**.

⭐ **Activity**

49 ⏺ **Track 17**

Say these sets of English words. The vowels have full length in final position and before lenis consonants. If you are not a native English speaker, you can also do this exercise with a native speaker or ask your tutor to provide a model.

wheat	*we*	*weed*	*peace*	*pea*	*peas*
note	*no*	*node*	*bought*	*bore*	*bored*
sauce	*saw*	*sawed*	*juice*	*Jew*	*Jews*
state	*stay*	*stayed*	*weight*	*way*	*weighed*
white	*why*	*wide*	*hurt*	*her*	*heard*

Secondary articulation

It often happens that the production of a speech sound involves certain types of modification. Besides the main articulation, there may also be an additional **secondary articulation**. The chief kinds of modification are listed below (see also Figure A5.11). Notice that all the terms include '-ised' or '-isation'.

Labialisation adds lip-rounding and is shown phonetically with the diacritic [ʷ] *after* the symbol.

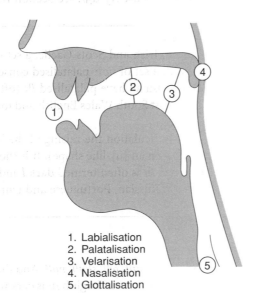

1. Labialisation
2. Palatalisation
3. Velarisation
4. Nasalisation
5. Glottalisation

Figure A5.11 Secondary articulation locations

50

Look in a mirror and say *me*. What shape are your lips? Now say *more*. Where does the lip-rounding begin? Now say the words *door, saw, core, bore*. You'll find that lip-rounding typically starts in the consonant preceding the rounded vowel. We can show these labialised consonants as [dʷ sʷ kʷ bʷ].

51

Say the word *sheep*. Do you have lip-rounding for /ʃ/? English native speakers usually do.

Palatalisation adds to the main articulation the raising of the front of the tongue towards the hard palate (tongue takes on an [i]-like shape with a possible [j] off-glide). It is shown by [ʲ] placed *after* the symbol.

52

Say the English words *tune, dune, new, mew, assume, beautiful, putrid*. These all involve palatalised consonants [tʲ dʲ nʲ mʲ sʲ bʲ pʲ]. (But note that for *tune, dune* most NRP speakers nowadays use /tʃ dʒ/: see Section B2.)

In some languages, e.g. Russian, Irish and Scots Gaelic, a set of palatalised consonants contrasts phonemically with a set of non-palatalised consonants.

French, Italian, German and Welsh all have palatalised /l/ (often termed **clear *l***) in all contexts. The same is true of most South Wales English and much southern Irish English.

Velarisation adds to the main articulation the raising of the back of the tongue towards the velum (the tongue takes on an [u]-like shape). It is shown by [~] written *through* the symbol, e.g. [ɫ]. Velarised /l/ is often termed **dark *l*** and is found not only in English, but also (for example) in Russian, Portuguese and Dutch.

53 ☺ **Track 18**

Say the following words in English: *still, tell, shall, bull*. And these in French: *style, tel, halle, boule*. Note that in this context English /l/ is dark whereas French /l/ is clear.

Table A5.4 Secondary articulation

Modification	Description	Symbol	Example
Palatalisation	Addition of front tongue raising to hard palate	ʲ after symbol	*tune* [tʲuːn]
Velarisation	Addition of back tongue raising to velum	~ through symbol	*still* [stɪɫ]
Labialisation	Addition of lip-rounding	ʷ after symbol	*talk* [tʷɔːk]
Glottalisation	Addition of glottal stop	ˀ before symbol	*stopwatch* [ˈstɒˀpwɒˀtʃ]
Nasalisation	Addition of nasality	~ above symbol	*morning* [ˈmɔ̃ːnĩŋ]

Activity

54

Certain varieties of English, e.g. much American and Scottish, some Australian, have a velarised dark *l* in all contexts. Is your word-initial /l/ clear, or dark, in words like *leaf, lame, less, look, long*? What about medial position, e.g. *willow, follow, teller, sullen*?

Glottalisation adds reinforcing glottal stop [ʔ]. The English fortis stops /p t k tʃ/ are regularly glottalised when syllable-final (see Section B2). Glottalisation is symbolised as [ˀ], e.g. *lipstick* [lɪˀpstɪˀk].

Nasalisation adds nasal resonance through lowering the soft palate. It is shown by the diacritic [~] placed above the symbol. In English, and many other languages, vowels preceding nasals are regularly nasalised, e.g. *strong man* [strɒ̃ŋ mæ̃n].

Note that most writers take only the oral strictures of open approximation into account (e.g. labialisation, palatalisation, velarisation). We have extended the concept to cover two other articulatory modifications, i.e. glottalisation and nasalisation.

Articulatory setting

In addition to differences between individual consonants, one can also consider other characteristics of consonant articulations which have to do with the articulatory **setting** of a particular language. This term refers to shapings of the speech organs which are continuous *throughout* the speech process. Setting varies from one language to another and, within the same language, from one accent to another.

To give just a few examples:

❑ Spanish is characterised by a dental setting (tongue between teeth) which means that sounds such as /t d n s l/ are dental rather than alveolar. (This, together with syllable-timed rhythm (see Section B5), is perhaps why English speakers have been known to refer to Spanish as sounding rather like a 'machine gun with a lisp'!)

- Portuguese has semi-continuous nasalisation – something also found in much American English (see Section C1). European Portuguese also has notable velarisation (not obvious in the Brazilian variety).
- In Hindi and other Indian languages there is a retroflex setting so that many articulations are made with the tip of the tongue curled back against the alveolar ridge (see pp. 40–1). This retroflex setting is also a well-known feature of almost all varieties of Indian English.
- Many types of Arabic have tongue-root retraction producing a pharyngealised setting.

NRP English typically has loose lips, and relaxed tongue and facial muscles – very much opposed to French with its pouting lip-rounding, and tense tongue and facial muscles (something imitated to great effect by Peter Ustinov in his portrayal of Hercule Poirot). A characteristic of most English is to use a tapered tongue setting for alveolar consonants with a small area of contact. Compare the blunter tongue setting for alveolars found in some other languages, e.g. Dutch, where a larger portion of the tongue is used for these sounds. The looser lip setting and the relaxed tapered tongue shape of English alveolars seem to be one reason why fortis stops in English are frequently realised with aspiration.

Setting can also vary noticeably from one language variety to another. Just within British English we can find several examples: West Country English (e.g. Bristol) often has a type of retroflex setting; South Wales English has a tendency towards palatalisation; whilst Liverpool English is velarised (Scouse is popularly termed 'adenoidal', presumably in reference to the voice quality induced by the velar setting). Pharyngealisation is characteristic of English as spoken in much of North Wales.

Activity

55

Transcribe phonemically, showing intonation groups and sentence stress, and using weak and contracted forms wherever possible.

Transcription passage 5
Suddenly she came upon a little three-legged table, all made of solid glass. There was nothing on it but a tiny golden key, and Alice's first idea was that this might belong to one of the doors of the hall. But, alas! Either the locks were too large, or the key was too small. At any rate, it would not open any of them. However, the second time round, she came upon a low curtain she had noticed before, and behind it was a little door about fifteen inches high. She tried the little golden key in the lock, and to her great delight it fitted.

VOWEL POSSIBILITIES

Introduction

Vowels can't be described in the same way as consonants. For vowels there's always considerable space between the articulators so that in terms of manner of articulation all vowels are approximants. Nor can we effectively use place of articulation – all we can do is distinguish broadly whether the front, centre or back of the tongue is raised towards the roof of the mouth. Finally, our third variable (voicing or energy of articulation) is of little help. Vowels are typically voiced, so that there are no voiced/voiceless or fortis/lenis contrasts.

It is possible to use another means of description, namely acoustic data, and acoustic phoneticians have now made enormous advances in this area. But obtaining such information and interpreting it still involves considerable time and effort. In language teaching, dialect research, and many other branches of practical phonetics, a speedy but reasonably accurate way of describing vowels is what is actually required.

The most generally used description of vowel sounds is based on a combination of articulatory and auditory criteria, and takes into account the following physical variables:

1   Tongue shape
2   Lip shape
3   Whether tongue and/or lip shape are held constant or undergo change (i.e. is the vowel a *steady-state vowel* or is it a *diphthong*?)
4   Position of the soft palate (nasal or non-nasal).

Finally, we have a non-physical variable which operates in a large number of languages:

5   Duration.

Tongue shape

Change in the shape of the tongue is perhaps the most important of all these factors. Let's first examine the variable of **tongue height**, namely how close the tongue is to the roof of the mouth. For some vowels, it is very easy to see and feel what is going on, as you can test for yourself in the following two activities.

  Activity

56

Say the English vowel /ɑː/, as in PALM. Put your finger in your mouth. Now say the vowel /iː/ (as in FLEECE). Feel inside your mouth again. Look in a mirror and see how the front of the tongue lowers from being close to the roof of the mouth for /iː/ to being far away for /ɑː/. Now you know why doctors ask you to say 'ah' when they want to see inside your mouth; the tongue is at its lowest when you say /ɑː/.

Activity ⭐

57

Now say these English vowels: /iː/, as in FLEECE, /ɛː/, as in SQUARE, /æ/, as in TRAP. Can you feel the tongue moving down? Then say them in reverse order: /æ/, /ɛː/, /iː/. Can you feel the tongue moving up?

As the tongue lowers, the oral cavity opens and increases in size. Consequently, the oral cavity is bigger for /ɑː/ than it is for /iː/, and as a result it produces a lower-pitched resonance.

Activity ⭐

58

Now take another set of English vowels and say them a number of times: /ɑː/, as in PALM, /ɔː/, as in THOUGHT, /uː/, as in GOOSE.

For the vowel /ɑː/ in PALM, the tongue is fairly flat in the mouth. For /ɔː/ in THOUGHT, the back of the tongue rises, and for /uː/ in GOOSE is closer again. We cannot see or feel the back of the tongue as easily as the front, and the lip-rounding for /ɔː/ and /uː/ obscures our view. But X-ray photography (and similar imaging techniques) confirm the raising of the back of the tongue for vowels like /ɔː/ and /uː/.

This provides us with an important aspect of vowel description. If the upper tongue surface is *close* to the roof of the mouth (like /iː/ in FLEECE and /uː/ in GOOSE) the sounds are called **close** vowels. Vowels made with an *open* mouth cavity, with the tongue far away from the roof of the mouth (like /æ/ in TRAP and /ɑː/ in PALM), are termed **open** vowels.

We also need to know which *part* of the tongue is highest in the vowel articulation. If the *front* of the tongue is highest (as in the first type /iː/ and /ɛː/), we term the sounds **front** vowels. If the *back* of the tongue is the highest part, we have what are called **back** vowels (the second type, like /ɔː/ and /uː/).

Although we can look into the mouth cavity, it is impossible to view directly what is happening in the pharynx – but this can be observed with X-ray imaging and similar techniques. As a consequence, we know that the open vowels like /ɑː/ have the tongue root pushed back so that the pharynx cavity is small. For the other open vowels, and to an extent for all back vowels, the pharynx cavity is reduced in size.

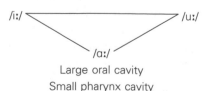

Small oral cavity   /iː/   /uː/   Fairly large oral cavity
Large pharynx cavity   Fairly large pharynx cavity

                                    /ɑː/
                              Large oral cavity
                              Small pharynx cavity

The cardinal vowels

It was not until early in the twentieth century that a reasonably accurate system of describing and classifying vowels was devised. In 1917, the British phonetician Daniel Jones (1881–1967) produced his system of **cardinal vowels** (often abbreviated to **CVs**), a model which is still widely employed to this day.

For any vowel, the tongue must be arched into a hump (termed the **tongue arch**), as illustrated in Figures A6.1–A6.4. We can always distinguish the highest point of the tongue arch for any vowel articulation. There is an **upper vowel limit** beyond which the surface of the tongue cannot rise in relation to the roof of the mouth – otherwise friction will be produced. The vowels at the upper vowel limit are the front vowel [i] and the back vowel [u].

> ★ **Activity**
>
> **59**
>
> Say a close front vowel, e.g. /iː/ in FLEECE. Now try to put your tongue even closer to the roof of your mouth. You will hear friction. Do the same for /uː/ in GOOSE. Once again a kind of fricative will be the result.

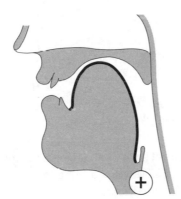

Figure A6.1 Tongue arch for [i]

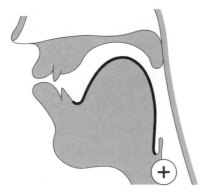

Figure A6.2 Tongue arch for [u]

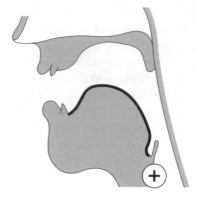

Figure A6.3 Tongue arch for [a]

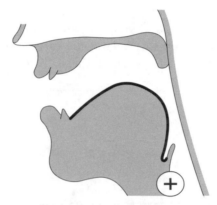

Figure A6.4 Tongue arch for [ɑ]

There is also a **lower vowel limit** beyond which the tongue cannot be depressed. This gives us two other extreme vowels – a front vowel [a] and a back vowel [ɑ].

We have now established the closest and most front vowel [i]; the closest and most back vowel [u]; the most open front vowel [a]; the most open and most back vowel [ɑ].

If we join up the highest points of the tongue arches for these four vowels, we arrive at the oval shape shown in Figure A6.5; this space is termed the **vowel area**.

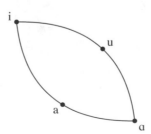

Figure A6.5 Vowel area

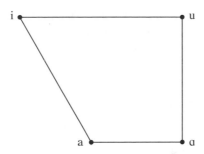

Figure A6.6 Vowel quadrilateral

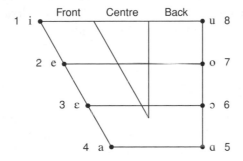

Figure A6.7 Primary cardinal vowels shown on a vowel diagram

For the sake of simplicity, the lines were straightened to form a four-sided figure (often termed the vowel quadrilateral), as in Figure A6.6. Other vowels were estimated auditorily (i.e. by ear) at roughly equal steps related to assumed tongue height. This gave four intermediate vowels – two front [e ɛ] and two back [o ɔ]. The full series of eight sounds was termed the **primary cardinal vowels** (named after the cardinal points of the compass: North, South, East, West). The quadrilateral was then for convenience divided up by lines as in Figure A6.7. The resulting figure is termed the **vowel diagram**.

What the cardinal vowel model provides is a mapping system which presents what is essentially auditory and acoustic information in a convenient visual form. The approach can be faulted in some ways, mainly in that no account is taken of the pharyngeal cavity. Nevertheless, linguists have found it a very useful way of dealing with vowel quality for many practical purposes. The cardinal vowel model has been adopted by phoneticians all over the world and, in 1989, a vowel diagram closely based on it was introduced on to the International Phonetic Alphabet symbol chart. The full revised 1996 version is illustrated on p. 258.

Note the labelling system for the cardinal vowels:

[i]:	front close	[u]:	back close
[e]:	front close-mid	[o]:	back close-mid
[ɛ]:	front open-mid	[ɔ]:	back open-mid
[a]:	front open	[ɑ]:	back open

Below, we give some rough indications of what the primary cardinal vowels sound like (what is technically termed **vowel quality**). To do so, we use, for comparison, average vowel qualities in familiar European languages:

[i]:	French *vie*	[u]:	German *Schuh*
[e]:	German *See*	[o]:	German *so*
[ɛ]:	French *crème*	[ɔ]:	English *awe*
[a]:	French *patte*	[ɑ]:	unrounded English *box*

It must be emphasised that the above are intended only as rough guides. The quality of the vowels in natural languages has considerable variation from one accent to another. To overcome this problem and in order to define the cardinal vowel qualities, Jones made a series of audio recordings, and these have served as a standard for other phoneticians using the system. A recording of the CVs by Daniel Jones himself can be heard if you visit this website: http://www-uilots.let.uu.nl/~audiufon/data/e_cardinal_vowels.html.

Activity

---

60 ☻ **Track 19**

Listen to the recording of the primary cardinal vowels on your audio CD; get to know them so that you can recognise them and reproduce them with ease. At the same time, learn to associate the vowel with its number and symbol and its place on the diagram. Listen to the vowels again, and repeat them, this time using your mirror and noting carefully the shape of the lips.

Lip shape

Change of lip shape is also a significant factor in producing different vowel qualities. The main effects of lip-rounding are: (1) to enlarge the space within the mouth; (2) to diminish the size of the opening of the mouth. Both of these factors deepen the pitch and increase the resonance of the front oral cavity. The lip shapes of the primary CVs follow the pattern typically found in languages world-wide. Front and open vowels have spread to neutral lip position, whilst back vowels have rounded lips. (The UPSID survey of world languages, carried out by the University of California, has shown that over 90 per cent of front and back vowels are unrounded and rounded respectively; Maddieson 1984.)

The shape of the lips can be shown on vowel diagrams by means of the following **lip-shape indicators**:

Unrounded, ☐ e.g. /eɪ/ in FACE
Rounded, ◯ e.g. /oʊ/ in GOAT in many American varieties.

Although front unrounded vowels are the norm, nevertheless a number of languages (including many spoken in Europe) also have rounded front vowels; this goes for French, German, Dutch, Finnish, Hungarian, Turkish and the major Scandinavian languages. For example, French has the rounded front vowels /y ø œ/, as in *tu* 'you', *peu* 'little' and *neuf* 'nine'; German rounded front vowels include /yː øː œ/, as in *Stühle*

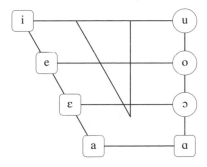

Figure A6.8 Lip shape of primary cardinal vowels

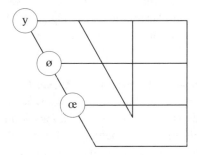

Figure A6.9 Front rounded cardinal vowels

'chairs', *Goethe* (name), *Götter* 'gods'. Unrounded back vowels are much less common but are, for instance, to be heard in some languages of the Far East, like Japanese and Vietnamese. To cover these cases, a set of **secondary cardinal vowels** was devised, with reverse lip positions (i.e. front rounded, back unrounded) and these can be found on the official IPA chart (p. 258). For many purposes, it is only necessary to be familiar with three front rounded vowels as shown in Figure A6.9.

Activity

61 ☉ **Track 20**

Listen to the recording of the three secondary cardinal vowels /y ø œ/; get to know them so that you can recognise them and reproduce them with ease. Look in a mirror when you pronounce them to check that your lips are rounded.

You can find more information on the cardinal vowels in the *Handbook of the International Phonetic Association* (1999: 10–13).

Additional vowels

Other vowels are now included in the latest version of the vowel diagram incorporated into the International Phonetic Alphabet. The most important of these is the central vowel [ə] (termed **schwa** after the name of the vowel in Hebrew and similar

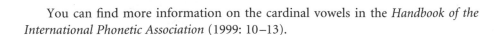

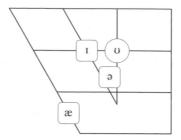

Figure A6.10   Additional vowels

to the *bon*ʊs vowel of English). In addition, the following vowels are significant because of their frequent occurrence in languages: centralised CV 2 [ɪ] (similar to KIT) and centralised CV 7 [ʊ] (similar to FOOT). See Figure A6.10. Another vowel shown is a front vowel between CVs 3 and 4, namely [æ] – termed 'ash' (from the name for the letter in Old English). This sound is similar to General American TRAP.

Steady-state vowels and diphthongs (Vowel Glides)

If the positions of the tongue and lips are held steady in the production of a vowel sound, we term it a **steady-state** vowel. In other books you may encounter the terms 'pure vowel' or 'monophthong' /ˈmɒnəfθɒŋ/ (Greek for 'single sound'; note the spelling with **phth**). If there is an obvious change in the tongue or lip shape, we term the vowel a **diphthong** (meaning 'double sound' in Greek, pronounced /ˈdɪfθɒŋ/; note again the spelling with **phth**). For a sound to be considered a diphthong, the change – termed a **glide** – must be accomplished in one movement within a single syllable without the possibility of a break. Apart from steady-state vowels, most languages also have a number of diphthongs; this goes for English and for other European languages, e.g. Dutch, Danish, German, Spanish and Italian. French is the best-known example of a language which is usually analysed as having only steady-state vowels.

   The starting-point of a diphthong is shown in the usual way and the direction of the tongue movement is indicated by an arrow. Figure A6.11 illustrates by means of a cross-section the change in tongue position for the English diphthong /aɪ/ as in PRICE. This corresponds to an arrow on a vowel diagram.

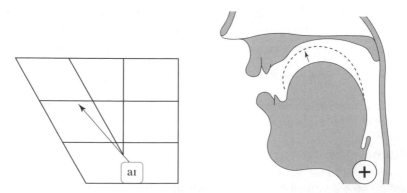

Figure A6.11   Vowel diagram representing English /aɪ/ as in PRICE. The cross-section shows the raising of the front of the tongue

To allow for possible change in lip shape in diphthongs, two additional lip-shape indicators are employed:

⬭ From spread to rounded, e.g. /əʊ/ in GOAT
⬬ From rounded to spread, e.g. /ɔɪ/ in CHOICE

Note that the indication goes from left to right as in handwriting. (These lip-shape indicators were devised by J. Windsor Lewis 1969.)

Position of the soft palate

Nasal vowels, produced with the soft palate lowered (see Section A4), are found in many languages all over the world. European languages with nasal vowel phonemes include French (see Activity 62), Portuguese and Polish. These sounds are common in African languages (for example, Yoruba, spoken in Nigeria) and are also to be heard in a European language now spoken in South Africa – Afrikaans (see Activity 63).

⭐ **Activity**

62 ⊙ Track 21

Listen to your audio material and practise making the nasal vowels in the French words given here: *brun* 'brown' /brœ̃/, *train* 'train' /trɛ̃/, *banc* 'bench' /bɑ̃/, *bon* 'good' /bɔ̃/. (Most present-day speakers of standard French have no contrast /œ̃ – ɛ̃/, using /ɛ̃/ for both.) Compare the oral vowels: *boeuf* 'ox' /bœf/, *très* 'very' /trɛ/, *bas* 'low' /ba/, *beau* 'beautiful' /bo/.

⭐ **Activity**

63 ⊙ Track 22

Listen to these Afrikaans sounds on your CD: *kans* 'chance' /kɑ̃s/, *mens* 'human being' /mɛ̃s/, *ons* 'us' /ɔ̃s/.

Duration

Duration is merely the time taken for any sound. But measuring sounds in isolation only gives us *absolute* values. Duration is only of linguistic significance if one considers the *relative* length of sounds, i.e. the duration of each sound has to be considered in relation to that of other sounds in the language.

Many languages have a phonemic contrast of longer versus shorter duration in vowel sounds, although very often this is combined with differences of vowel quality. This is true of English where the checked vowels like /ɪ/ are shorter than the free vowels like /iː/ (see Sections A2 and B3). Similar phonemic pairs are found in many other languages, e.g. German, Dutch and the Scandinavian languages.

Practical applications of the vowel diagram

In this book we shall use the following system for vowel description. The areas of the vowel diagram will be designated in the way shown in Figure A6.12.

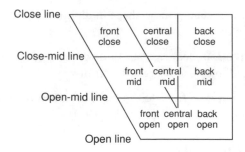

Figure A6.12 Areas of the vowel diagram

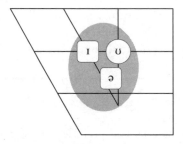

Figure A6.13 Central versus peripheral vowels

We shall also distinguish between central vowels (i.e. those in or near the central-mid position of the diagram) and peripheral vowels (i.e. those around the edges, or periphery, of the vowel diagram) (Figure A6.13).

64

Transcribe phonemically, showing intonation groups and sentence stress, and using weak and contracted forms wherever possible.

Transcription passage 6

Alice opened the door and found that it led into a small passage. She knelt down and looked along the passage into the loveliest garden you ever saw. How she longed to get out of that dark hall, and wander about among those beds of bright flowers and cool fountains. But she was not able even to get her head through the doorway. 'And then, if my head *would* go through,' thought poor Alice, 'it would be of very little use without my shoulders. Oh, how I wish I could shut up like a telescope! I think I could, if I only knew how to begin.' For, you see, so many out-of-the-way things had happened lately, that Alice had begun to think that nothing was really impossible.

Section B
DEVELOPMENT

PHONEME AND SYLLABLE REVISITED

The phoneme revisited

In Section A2 we introduced the phoneme. We shall now return to examine the concept a little more closely, and consider its place in linguistic organisation. You'll recall that the phoneme is an abstract unit which may be realised as any one of a number of allophones. Allophones are the concrete entities of speech. The allophones of a particular phoneme typically have **phonetic similarity**, that is to say, they have both articulatory and acoustic features in common (stated loosely, this implies that they are produced in much the same way by the speaker and sound much the same to the listener).

Taken to the finest level of analysis, no two realisations of a phoneme are ever totally identical. Even if we ask the same person to produce the same sound under carefully controlled conditions, there will still be very slight differences between one utterance and the next. However, this perfectionist approach is not very useful in linguistic analysis. In reality, most allophones can be placed in fairly well-defined categories, and it is usually possible to provide descriptive rules to predict their occurrence in a particular phonetic context.

Complementary distribution and free variation

Let's take the case of the English phoneme /l/. This has three clearly defined recurring allophones (see Figure B1.1). It is possible to state, in broad terms, the chief phonetic contexts where the particular allophones of the phoneme /l/ are likely to occur:

❑   clear [l] occurs before vowels;
❑   dark (velarised) [ɫ] before a consonant or a pause;
❑   voiceless (fricative) [l̥] occurs initially in a stressed syllable following /p/ or /k/.

We can demonstrate the distribution of the allophones of the /l/ phoneme with the example in Figure B1.2.

The occurrence of allophones in this instance is therefore predictable. They can be considered as *complements* to each other; where one occurs the other cannot. Such an allophonic patterning, which is very frequent in language, is termed **complementary distribution**.

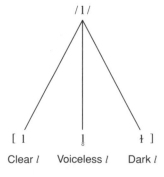

Figure B1.1   Chief allophones of English /l/

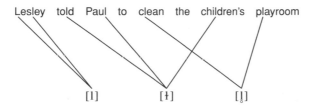

Figure B1.2 Distribution of allophones of /l/

Nevertheless, not all the allophones of all phonemes can be accounted for in this way. For example, in NRP English the pronunciation of /t/ in words like *Britain* varies. Some people realise the sound as alveolar [t] and others produce a glottal stop [ʔ]: ['brɪtn̩] vs. ['brɪʔn̩]. Many speakers alternate between these possibilities. To take an example from another language, for /r/ some speakers of Dutch employ an alveolar [r] while others use a uvular fricative or approximant (which we can symbolise as [ʀ]). But some Dutch people vary between [r] and [ʀ] in the same position in the word, using the alveolar type on one occasion and the uvular type on another. Such variation cannot be accounted for in terms of complementary distribution, since we cannot predict from the context which allophone will be selected. In such cases, the allophones are said to be in **free variation**, implying that the realisation of one allophone rather than another appears to be a matter of chance.

Nevertheless, there may often be additional, possibly non-linguistic, factors involved, so free variation is not always as 'free' as it might appear at first sight! It's frequently the case that social influences are at work, and that speakers' use of particular allophones on any given occasion may be determined by matters such as the formality of the circumstances, or perhaps the socio-economic background of the people they are with at the time. For example, Australian schoolchildren may pronounce the vowel in *start* in different ways. In the playground, speaking to other schoolmates, they might use a 'broad Australian' front vowel quality [staːt]. But back in the classroom, talking to a teacher, the same pupils might employ a more back vowel [stɑːt], which has greater social prestige. Similarly, a London hotel receptionist might use glottal stop [ʔ] for /t/ in words like *butter* and *bottle* ['bʌʔə 'bɒʔɫ] when talking to other members of staff, but on turning round to address a customer might instead realise this phoneme as an alveolar plosive ['bʌtə 'bɒtɫ] to take account of the more formal context.

Furthermore, although the concept of complementary distribution is a useful one, it can sometimes pose problems. Take the case of /j/ and /ŋ/. In English syllables, /j/ only occurs before a vowel (**pre-vocalically**), while /ŋ/ only occurs following a vowel (**post-vocalically**); they are therefore in complementary distribution. However, they cannot be analysed as belonging to the same phoneme, for two reasons. One is that they lack any sort of phonetic similarity; /j/ is a palatal approximant, while /ŋ/ is a velar nasal. Secondly, and even more crucially, they could not possibly be considered as members of the same phoneme by mother-tongue speakers of the language concerned. No English speaker could ever accept that *young* could be transcribed as */ŋʌn/ or */jʌj/. Native speakers have an awareness of phonemes and hear them as significant linguistic units; differences between allophones of the same phoneme, on the other hand, either pass unnoticed or are shrugged off as insignificant. In the final analysis, native-speaker intuition has to be regarded as the most decisive factor in the allocation of allophones to phonemic categories.

Neutralisation

Sometimes two phonemes may show overlap in phonetic realisation. Take the case of /m/ and /n/ in English, where these occur before labio-dental /f/ (or /v/), as in *emphatic, infatuated*, etc. In both cases, the realisation of /m/ and /n/ may be a labio-dental nasal, which is represented by the symbol [ɱ], giving [ɪɱˈfætɪk] and [ɪɱˈfætʃueɪtɪd]. In this case, there is no way (apart from spelling) of knowing whether [ɱ] should be assigned to /m/ or to /n/. Both are nasal and voiced; /m/ is bilabial while /n/ is alveolar. Since /m/ and /n/ are never in opposition in this context, we can assign [ɱ] to either of the phonemes /m/ or /n/. The opposition between /m/ and /n/ has undergone **phoneme neutralisation**.

Another example of neutralisation are the vowels in French pairs like *patte – pâte* ('paw' – 'paste'), *là – las* ('there' – 'weary'). Traditionally, French speakers selected /a/ for the first word in each pair and /ɑ/ for the second; but in connected speech many used a vowel somewhere between the two. Thus for these speakers there was potential neutralisation of the phonemes /a/ and /ɑ/. In present-day French this neutralisation has become established in the language and today probably only a minority still make a consistent contrast.

Yet another case of phoneme neutralisation is the realisation of stops in syllable-initial clusters after /s/ in English: *spar* /spɑː/, *star* /stɑː/, *scar* /skɑː/. After /s/, the fortis stops have none of the energy and aspiration which characterises the other allophones of /p t k/. In fact, phonetically, these realisations are in most ways close to the allophones of /b d g/. Since there is no possibility in English of a contrast of the type /spɑː – *sbɑː/, it would be perfectly reasonable to regard these allophones in this context as varieties of /b d g/, and symbolise thus: */sbɑː, sdɑː, sgɑː/. But this is never actually done even though perhaps the influence of spelling tradition is probably the main factor for their allocation to the /p t k/ fortis category. It is interesting to note that in Welsh phonetically similar sequences are actually spelt **sb** and **sg**, e.g. *sbectol* 'spectacles', *sgyrt* 'skirt' (although Welsh words with initial /st/ are spelt **st**, e.g. *sticill* 'stile').

Neutralisation is also found in the final sound in words like *happy, toffee, Johnnie* (generally called the '*happ*ʏ words'). This vowel was formerly regarded as /ɪ/ in descriptions of traditional RP (e.g. Jones 1962: 68). Present-day speakers of NRP realise the vowel short (like KIT /ɪ/) but with a fairly close vowel quality (similar to FLEECE /iː/) and, if asked, many native speakers express doubt about whether this vowel belongs to the KIT or FLEECE phoneme. It is to take account of the neutralisation of these two vowels that modern transcription systems use the special symbol **i** (see also the transcription guide in Section A3).

Different systems in different accents

In providing a complete phonemic analysis of a language, account must be taken of its different varieties. The phonemic system may vary considerably from one accent to another, some possessing an extra phoneme contrast or, alternatively, lacking a phoneme contrast present in other varieties. Sections C2–C4 provide considerable detail

Table B1.1 Different phoneme systems in different varieties of English

Most varieties of English	/ʊ/	/ʌ/
Northern English	/ʊ/	

Most varieties of English	/uː/	
Welsh English	/ɪu/	/uː/

on this question with reference to English varieties, but we can nevertheless consider one or two examples at this point.

In most types of English, there is a STRUT – FOOT contrast /ʌ – ʊ/, giving minimal pairs like *tuck* vs. *took*. However, in the north of England, broadly from just above Birmingham up to the Scottish border, this opposition is lost in basilectal accents; all words of this type have /ʊ/, and there is no /ʌ/ in the phoneme system. On the other hand, most varieties of Welsh English have an extra vowel /ɪu/ giving a contrast in pairs like *through – threw* /θruː/ – /θrɪu/. This means that Welsh English has an additional phoneme contrast GOOSE – JUICE /uː – ɪu/ as compared with most other varieties of English.

Compared to NRP speakers, most Scots, many Irish, and some Americans have an additional phoneme /ʍ/ that is a voiceless labial-velar fricative. This extra phoneme provides a contrast with /w/ in pairs like *where – wear, which – witch*.

Most types of English have no voiceless velar fricative phoneme [x]. Nevertheless, certain speakers use this sound in foreign names and loanwords from, for example, German, Yiddish, Scots Gaelic or Spanish (e.g. *Bach, chutzpah, Sassenach, rioja*). Another example, at least for some speakers, is voiceless [ɬ] used in Welsh place-names like *Llangollen*. Such sounds which are not part of the basic phoneme system are termed **marginal phonemes**.

As will be seen, a valid phonemic analysis can only be made for one particular accent of a language at any one time. It is sometimes found that the differences between phonemic systems (see Section C1), especially vowels, are very great indeed. For instance, accents in Scotland, Northern Ireland and the north-east of England have vowel systems which are very different from most varieties of English.

The syllable revisited

The structure of a syllable can be represented in this way:

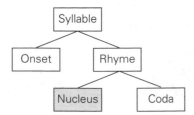

For example, in the word *strands*, /str/ is the **onset** and /ændz/ is the **rhyme**, which consists of the **nucleus** /æ/ and the **coda** /ndz/. The only obligatory element here is the nucleus, normally a vowel. If there is no vowel, then certain consonants can function in its place (see below). The onset is an optional element, as is the coda. Note that the syllable nucleus plus the coda provide the potential for words to rhyme in poetry; hence the term 'rhyme'.

We have now seen that the syllable consists of an obligatory vowel potentially surrounded by consonants. We can therefore define a vowel as a speech sound which functions as the syllable nucleus. A consonant is a speech sound which typically occurs at the **margins** of the syllable. (We need hardly say that we are dealing with speech sounds here and *not* the letters of spelling. A word like *thought* /θɔːt/ has just three sounds – two consonants and a single vowel.)

A selection of possible vowel and consonant structures for English syllables is shown below.

awe	/ɔː/	V
saw	/sɔː/	C V
ought	/ɔːt/	V C
sawn	/sɔːn/	C V C
lawns	/lɔːnz/	C V CC
draw	/drɔː/	CC V
drawn	/drɔːn/	CC V C
straw	/strɔː/	CCC V
strands	/strændz/	CCC V CCC
glimpsed	/glɪmpst/	CC V CCCC

From this it can be seen that the English syllable can consist of up to three consonants in initial position (as in *straw*) and as many as four in final position (as in *glimpsed*). Note that a syllable which ends in one or more consonants (like *sawn*) is called a **closed** syllable; whilst one ending in a vowel (like *saw*) is termed an **open** syllable. A sequence of consonants at the margin of a syllable is called a **consonant cluster**.

In any language, there are constraints on the possible combinations of sounds which occur in consonant clusters. For instance, English doesn't permit syllable onsets such as /pn ps vw/ but these do occur in French (examples: *pneu* 'tyre', *psychologie* 'psychology', *voilà* 'there', 'there you are'). English has no /tl/ onsets, but these do exist in Welsh (*tlws* /tluːs/ 'pretty'). In the onset, Spanish permits no clusters with initial /s/ of the type /sp st skw str/ etc., although these are commonly found in English.

All languages have CV-type open syllables. Most European languages allow both open and closed syllables – although in some (e.g. Spanish) there may be constraints on the types of consonant found in coda position. Samoan allows no consonant clusters and has only open syllables, whilst Yoruba (a major Nigerian language) permits only open syllables or codas of /m/ or /n/. If such languages borrow words from European languages like English, these loanwords are usually altered in terms of syllable structure. So, in Yoruba, *Christmas* is *Kérésìmesì*, and *stone* (measure of weight) is *sítónù*.

65

Look at the following Samoan words and see if you can guess the English originals. Take account also of (1) the more economical vowel system of Samoan as compared with English; (2) that there are no /b/ or /g/ phonemes; (3) that /r/ is a marginal phoneme found only in loanwords and sometimes replaced by /l/. Answers on the website.

naifi, sipuni, sasa, kirisimasi, sikaleti, kapiteni, kirikiti, kalapu, silipa, parakarafa.

Some languages have more complex onset and coda structures than English. For instance, Georgian is reported as having up to six consonants in onset position (Catford 1988: 208).

Languages do not use all the combinations possible in their phoneme inventories. In English we can state a number of constraints which are operative on syllable structure, for example:

1   /ŋ/ never occurs in onsets.
2   /h j w/ never occur in codas.
3   /r/ never occurs in codas in non-rhotic (see p. 89) varieties of English (e.g. NRP).
4   The lenis fricatives /v ð z ʒ/ never occur in onset clusters.
5   In three-element onset clusters the initial consonant is invariably /s/.
6   /t d θ/ never combine with /l/ in onset clusters.
7   Nasals never combine with stops in onsets.
8   Nasals combining with stops in coda clusters are invariably homorganic, e.g. /mp ŋk/ but not */mk np/.

66

Which of these are permissible syllables in English? Explain why. (Answers on the website.)

spraːθs   vwaːks   gwaːmz   kraːh   ŋaːs   knaːj
draːw   ʃraːlts   skwaːksθs traːvz   dlaːmg   ʒraːnk

So far we have discussed syllables in monosyllabic words but, of course, many words are polysyllabic. In such cases we have to divide the word up before we can attempt a syllable analysis. This is not always easy to do in a language like English which has a complex syllable structure. To take a much-quoted example, the word *extra* /ˈekstrə/ certainly contains two syllables. But what form would these take?

1 'e + kstrə
2 'ek + strə
3 'eks + trə
4 'ekst + rə
5 'ekstr + ə/

We can eliminate the first and the last suggestions since they clearly conflict with the formulations for syllable onsets and codas stated above. The remaining three (nos. 2, 3 and 4) are more problematical. Many native speakers would go for no. 2, taking into account the likely realisation of the consonants in the /str/ sequence, but the decision is by no means clear-cut.

Activity

67

Take one of the 'Alice' transcription passages in this book and underline all the polysyllabic words. Bearing in mind the constraints mentioned so far in terms of English syllable structures, try to split the polysyllabic words into component syllables. Compare your results with other members of your class. You may find that they differ, since placing syllable boundaries is often a matter for debate.

Activity

68

Consonant clusters are often simplified in connected speech. Say these words slowly. Then say the sentences containing the words at normal conversational speed. What will be the likely differences in your pronunciation of the coda clusters? See Section B4 for more about this phenomenon.

asked   risked   texts   sixths

1 We've asked Jack to leave.
2 I risked my money on the favourite.
3 Dan sent Jo three texts last week.
4 It takes up over five sixths of the computer's memory.

Consonant/vowel distinction

What is it about certain sounds that makes them candidates for syllable nucleus status? It is significant that the sounds which can occur as a syllable nucleus are those which have the most **sonority** – i.e. those which, other things being equal, have the greatest 'carrying power'. The sonority of a sound is closely related to its acoustic make-up; sounds composed largely of musical tones, like vowels, are more **sonorous** than those which have more significant acoustic noise elements (plosion and hiss), like stops and fricatives.

One example of an attempt to construct a sonority scale is shown in Figure B1.3.

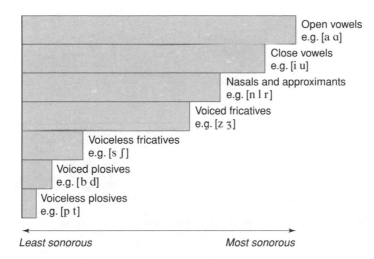

Figure B1.3 Relative sonority scale

Table B1.2 Consonants classed according to sonority

Vowels		Most sonorous
Nasals Lateral (approximant) (Central) approximants	SONORANTS	↓ ↓ ↓
Voiced fricatives Voiceless fricatives Voiced plosives Voiceless plosives	OBSTRUENTS	↓ ↓ ↓ Least sonorous

Table B1.2 shows how it is possible to classify sounds in terms of sonority. On this basis we can consider three types of sound:

❑ vowels, which typically form the syllable nucleus;
❑ obstruents, which are found invariably at the margins of syllables (onset or coda);
❑ those in the intermediate category – the sonorant consonants (i.e. nasals and approximants) – typically occur at syllable margins but, if there is no vowel in a syllable, certain of these sounds can function as a nucleus. We then term them syllabic consonants (see Section A2). Such consonants are likely to be realised with greater energy and extra length, giving them more prominence. Look at the examples in English in Figure B1.4.

B

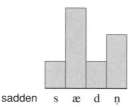

grunts   g   r   ʌ   n   t   s

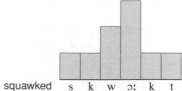

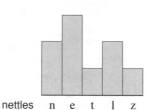

squawked   s   k   w   ɔː   k   t

sadden   s   æ   d   ṇ

nettles   n   e   t   ḷ   z

Figure B1.4 Prominence in vowels and consonants

You will note from the above that sonorants are also more likely to feature towards the centre of syllables. This is significant for the ordering of consonant clusters, so that, for example, /kl/ as in *clay* is a possible onset, whereas /lk/ is not. On the other hand, /kl/ is not found in coda position, whereas /lk/ as in *bulk* is to be found in this context.

Compare this categorisation with how we earlier divided up sounds as vowels and consonants in terms of manner of articulation (see Section A5). There is considerable, even if not complete, overlap.

A consonant was then defined as an articulation which involves any of the following strictures:

❑   blocking the airstream completely (i.e. stops, trills and taps)
❑   hindering the airstream sufficiently to give rise to audible friction (i.e. fricatives)
❑   blocking the airstream, but allowing nasal escape (i.e. nasals)
❑   blocking the airstream centrally, but allowing lateral escape (i.e. laterals)

All other sounds, i.e. the central approximants and the vowels themselves, which involve only strictures of open approximation, are classed as articulatory vowels.

Relationship of phonetics and phonology

In this unit we have concerned ourselves with two of the main traditional preoccupations of phonologists – namely the phoneme and the syllable. Although we have not dealt with these topics in any kind of detail, the discussion will provide an indication of how theoretical phonology approaches such matters, and what relationship phonology has to phonetics. Phonetics provides the data for describing speech; phonology generalises from these so as to produce deeper insights into the structures and patterns of language sound systems. A rough-and-ready analogy is that phonetics provides the ingredients and phonology gives you the recipe for baking the cake.

As the word 'practical' in the title of this book would suggest, most of the phonological aspects of the book are indeed severely practical in nature. We have confined ourselves to noting the most significant surface aspects of the patterning of sounds in English (concentrating on NRP, but also comparing this accent with other varieties). But we have not attempted to dig below the surface and discuss what lies behind such matters (a tremendous amount can be said about the placement of syllable boundaries, for example). If you wish to provide yourself with the resources for a more thorough theoretical approach to phonology, you could as a first step try reading introductory surveys such as Carr (1999) and McMahon (2001) (see the Further Reading section). These will provide you with a basis to enable you to deal with more complex works on the English sound system, and perhaps those of other languages, later on in your linguistic career. You can find a more advanced treatment, which brings together a number of different modern approaches to phonology, in Ewen and van der Hulst (2001).

Activity

69

Transcribe phonemically, showing intonation groups and sentence stress, and using weak and contracted forms wherever possible.

Transcription passage 7
There seemed to be no use in waiting by the door, so she went back to the table, half hoping she might find another key on it, or at any rate a book of rules for shutting people up like telescopes. This time she found a tiny bottle on it – 'which certainly was not here before,' said Alice. Tied round the neck of the bottle was a paper label, with the words 'Drink me', beautifully printed on it in large letters. It was all very well to say that, but wise little Alice was not going to do things in a hurry.

ENGLISH CONSONANTS

B2

Overview of the English consonant system

We've already discussed the various possibilities for producing consonant sounds. Now we're going to examine in greater detail how these sounds function in present-day English. It is usual to provide an overview in the form of a consonant grid with the following conventions: *place* on the horizontal axis, *manner* on the vertical axis; fortis precedes lenis in each pair.

Table B2.1 English consonant grid

	Bilabial	Labio-dental	Dental	Alveolar	Palato-alveolar	Palatal	Velar	Glottal
Plosive	p b			t d			k g	[ʔ]³
Affricate					tʃ dʒ			
Nasal	m			n			ŋ	
Fricative		f v	θ ð	s z	ʃ ʒ			h
(Central) Approximant	w²			r¹		j	w²	
Lateral (Approximant)				l				

Notes

1 /r/ is post-alveolar.

2 /w/ is labial-velar with two strictures (see Section A5).

3 In NRP [ʔ] is an allophone. Hence the square brackets.

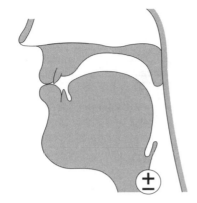

± at glottis indicates that fortis
is voiceless and lenis is voiced

Figure B2.1   English /p/ and /b/ (hold stage)

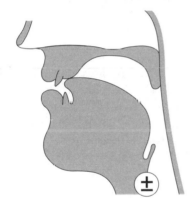

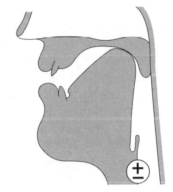

Figure B2.2   English /t/ and /d/
(hold stage)

Figure B2.3   English /k/ and /g/
(hold stage)

Stop consonants

The English stop phonemes (1) plosives /p t k b d g/ and (2) affricates /tʃ dʒ/ occur in initial, medial and final contexts.

Stops (i.e. plosives and affricates) have three stages:

❑   in the **approach** stage, the articulators come together and form the closure;
❑   in the **hold** stage, air is compressed behind the closure;
❑   in the **release** stage, the articulators part and the compressed air is released, either (1) rapidly with plosion in the case of plosives, or (2) slowly with friction in the case of affricates.

See Figure B2.4 below.

Plosives /p t k b d g/

In all cases a closure is made at some place in the vocal tract:

❑   at the lips for bilabial /p b/;
❑   tongue-tip against alveolar ridge for alveolar /t d/;
❑   back of tongue against velum for velar /k g/.

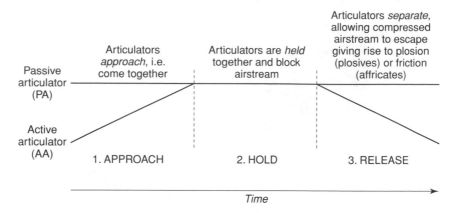

Figure B2.4 Articulation timing diagram showing the stages of a stop

Affricates /tʃ dʒ/

English has two **phoneme affricates**, namely /tʃ/ and /dʒ/; see Section A5 for cross-section diagrams of /tʃ dʒ/. A closure is formed between a large area of the tip, blade and the front of the tongue with the rear of the alveolar ridge and the front of the hard palate. The palato-alveolar closure is released relatively slowly, thus producing friction at the same place of articulation (i.e. homorganic). Like the palato-alveolar fricatives /ʃ ʒ/, these affricates are strongly labialised, with trumpet-shaped lip-rounding. Fortis /tʃ/ is energetically articulated (though without aspiration); lenis /dʒ/ is weaker and has potential voice.

Phonetic affricates

In addition there are the following phonetic affricates resulting from a sequence of two homorganic consonants:

/tr/	*try*	[tɹ̥]	fortis post-alveolar affricate
/dr/	*dry*	[dɹ]	lenis post-alveolar affricate
/ts/	*cats*	[ts]	fortis alveolar affricate (/t/ often has glottal reinforcement or replacement)
/dz/	*lads*	[dz]	lenis alveolar affricate

Affrication is also heard from many speakers who produce bilabial affricates [pɸ bβ] as realisations of the sequences /pf bv/, e.g. *helpful, obvious.*

Fortis/lenis opposition in stops

The fortis stops /p t k tʃ/ have energetic articulation and are voiceless; lenis stops /b d g dʒ/ have weaker articulation and have potential voice (see Section A5). In addition, aspiration (for plosives) and pre-glottalisation are important distinguishing features.

Aspiration

Aspiration (symbolised phonetically by [ʰ]) occurs when fortis plosives /p t k/ are initial in a stressed syllable, and takes the form of a delay in the onset of voicing, an effect often compared to a little puff of air. The link with stress is significant; in *com'petitor* [kəm'pʰetɪtə] aspiration is heard on the /p/, and not on the unstressed /k/ or the two [t]s; compare '*competent* ['kʰɒmpətənt]. In initial clusters with /s/, e.g. *stool*, *spool*, *school*, aspiration is absent. See below for devoicing of /l r j w/ following fortis plosives.

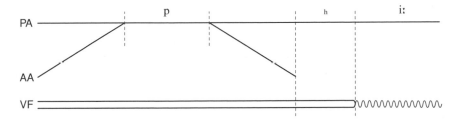

Figure B2.5   Delayed voice onset time (aspiration) in English /p/, as in *peak* (VF = vocal folds)

 Activity

70

A test for aspiration is to put a feather or a piece of paper in front of your mouth and then pronounce the consonants [p t k]. If you're a native speaker of English, the paper should move noticeably.

Try the same test with the lenis non-aspirated [b d g]. The paper should move less or not at all. Now try the clusters [sp st sk] as in *spy*, *sty*, *sky*. Does the paper move now?

Aspiration is a feature of most English accents (a few varieties, e.g. some Lanca-shire, and most Scottish and South African English, have very weakly aspirated stops). Languages split between those with aspiration (e.g. standard German, the Scandinavian languages and Welsh) and those without, e.g. southern varieties of German, Dutch and the Romance languages (French, Spanish, Italian, Portuguese, Romanian). Some languages (e.g. Korean) distinguish voiceless vs. aspirated voiceless vs. voiced stops; many Indian languages have a four-term distinction (voiceless vs. aspirated voiceless vs. voiced vs. aspirated voiced). Non-aspiration languages tend to have firmer closures for voiceless plosives; the articulators form a tight, efficient valve, with a brisk release of the compressed air. Aspirated articulations have looser closures which act like an inefficient 'leaky' valve from which the air is released somewhat more slowly.

Pre-glottalisation in stops
English syllable-final fortis stops are accompanied by a reinforcing glottal stop at or before the hold stage. Termed (**pre-**)**glottalisation**, or **glottal reinforcement**, this is one of the most significant phonetic markers of final fortis stops in many English accents. In NRP the pattern of glottal reinforcement is as follows.

❑ Syllable-final fortis stops are regularly glottalised before another consonant, e.g. *I don't like that fat guy* [aɪ ˈdəʊnˀt laɪˀk ˈðæˀt ˈfæˀt ˈgaɪ], *sleepwalker* [ˈsliːˀpwɔːkə], *locksmith* [ˈlɒˀksmɪθ], *watchdog* [ˈwɒˀtʃdɒg]. Note that /tʃ/ also has optional glottalisation in medial position, e.g. *kitchen* [ˈkɪˀtʃɪn].

❑ In the following contexts both glottalised and non-glottalised forms are to be found:
(a) before pause: *short* [ˈʃɔːˀt] or [ˈʃɔːt];
(b) before /h/, *shorthand* [ˈʃɔːˀthænd] or [ˈʃɔːthænd];
(c) word-finally preceding a vowel: *short of money* [ˈʃɔːˀt əv ˈmʌni] or [ˈʃɔːt əv ˈmʌni].

❑ The most frequently glottalised consonant is /t/. In particular, pre-glottalisation (and glottal replacement, see below) very commonly affects a small group of high-frequency words, namely: *it, bit, get, let, at, that, got, lot, not* (and contracted forms: *don't, can't, aren't, isn't,* etc.), *what, put, but, might, right, quite, out, about.*

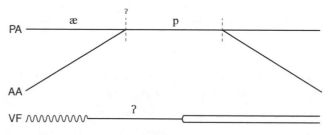

Figure B2.6 Pre-glottalisation in English /p/ as in *laptop*

Glottal replacement (an effect also known as 'glottalling') occurs when [ʔ] is substituted for /t/ so that, for example, *shortbread, shorten, sit down* are realised as [ˈʃɔːʔbred, ˈʃɔːʔn̩, sɪʔ ˈdaʊn]. This may also occur where /p k/ are followed by a homorganic stop or nasal, e.g. *stepbrother* [ˈsteʔ brʌðə], *took care* [ˈtʊʔ kɛː].

Activity ✪

71

Do you glottalise the underlined stop consonant in any of these words or phrases?

no̲t true; *pu̲t right*; *it's go̲t twisted*; *tra̲p door*; *a̲tlas*; *po̲t luck*.

Types of release

Nasal release

When a plosive is followed by a homorganic nasal, the closure is not released in the usual way. Instead, the soft palate lowers, which allows the airstream to pass out through the nasal cavity; this is termed **nasal release**, e.g. *submit, partner.* Nasal release of /t d/ is also heard in final /tn dn/ leading into a syllabic nasal, e.g. *shorten* [ˈʃɔːtn̩], *rodent* [ˈrəʊdn̩t]. With fortis plosives, there is typically accompanying glottalisation,

e.g. *witness* ['wɪˀtnəs], *help me* ['helˀp mi]. In present-day NRP, fortis plosives normally undergo glottal replacement in this context, e.g. ['wɪʔnəs 'helʔ mi]. German is
notable for the common occurrence of nasal release giving rise to syllabic nasals (often
with assimilation: see Section B4), e.g. *leben* 'to live' ['leːbm̩], *beten* 'to pray' ['beːtn̩],
sagen 'to say' ['zaːgŋ̍].

Lateral release

In English, /t/ and /d/ can have **lateral release**, i.e. the alveolar closure is released by
lowering the sides of the tongue, e.g. *settle, partly, muddle, paddling*. Following /t/, there
is initial devoicing of /l/: ['setl̥], ['pɑːtl̥li]. A similar type of articulation is found in
the sequences /kl ɡl pl bl/, as in *prickly, struggling, grappling, bubbly* where the tongue
takes up the alveolar position for /l/ during the hold stage of the stop.

Lateral release in English often leads into syllabic laterals. In many accents, such
as Cockney, lateral release is lacking and instead a vowel /ə/ or /ʊ/ is inserted, giving
e.g. *settle* ['seʔəl] or ['seʔʊl]. Of late, possibly as a result of the spread of London influence,
realisations without lateral release have become increasingly common among younger
NRP speakers. As opposed to what happens with syllabic /n/, glottalisation is not
usually found in NRP in this context.

Sequences such as, for example, /pt ɡb kd ɡtʃ dɡ/, as in *stopped, rugby, back door,
big cheese, bad guys*, where a plosive consonant is immediately followed by a stop,
are termed *overlapping stops*. In such cases, the plosive has inaudible release and the
second stop has inaudible approach.

> **⊛ Activity**
>
> **72**
>
> Take a paragraph from any of the extracts in Section D and underline all
> the examples of overlapping stops that you can find. Then transcribe them
> phonemically.

In English, in a sequence of three stops, the central consonant (always alveolar
/t/ or /d/) lacks both audible approach and release stages. In fact, /t d/ in this context
are elided in all but ultra-careful speech, e.g. *clubbed together* /'klʌb tə'ɡeðə/, *she looked
quite young* /ʃi 'lʊk kwaɪt 'jʌŋ/ (see Section B4 on elision).

Sequences of homorganic stops result in a single articulation with a prolonged hold
stage, e.g. /ɡɡ/ (phonetically [ɡː]) as in *big game*. Where the first of such a homorganic
sequence is fortis, the stop typically has glottal reinforcement and, frequently, glottal
replacement.

Other types of allophonic variation

Alveolar /t d/ have a wide range of variation in NRP. Intervocalic /t/ is frequently
realised as a very brief voiced stop which can be shown as [[t̬], e.g. *British, pretty,
but I, pathetic, that I*. This realisation is particularly common in high-frequency words

and expressions. The brevity of the tap and the shortening of the preceding vowel serve to maintain the contrast with /d/. Unlike American English, there is no tendency to reduce the contrast /t – d/ in pairs such as *clouted – clouded, writing – riding, waiter – wader*. (See Section C1.)

73

Are you a 't-voicer'? Say the following words and phrases and ask others in your class to judge.

*be*t*ter*; *phonetics*; *bottle*; *pre*t*ty*; *pretty apathetic*; *not a lot of*; *what a pity*; *quite a lot*

If you do voice /t/, do you think the resulting sound is the same as /d/ or different? Check by saying pairs like *whiter – wider, waiter – wader*. Do you also extend t-voicing to contexts before syllabic /n/, e.g. *cotton, Britain*? Or do you replace /t/ here by glottal stop?

Nasals

The bilabial and alveolar nasals /m n/ occur in all contexts, but velar /ŋ/ occurs only syllable-finally following checked vowels. For all three nasals, the place and manner of articulation is similar to that of the corresponding stops /b d g/ (see above). However, the soft palate is lowered (i.e. there is no velic closure; see Section A4), thus adding the resonance of the nasal cavity. See Figures B2.7 (below) for /m/, A4.11 (p. 33) for /n/, and A4.12 (p. 37) for /ŋ/.

The soft palate anticipates the action of other articulators, and consequently vowels are nasalised preceding nasals, e.g. *farm* [fɑ̃ːm], *lawn* [lɔ̃ːn], *gang* [gæ̃ŋ]. This tendency can be very noticeable in certain varieties, e.g. most American English.

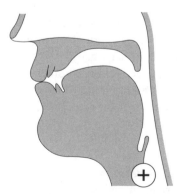

Figure B2.7 English /m/

Activity

74

Try saying the following text substituting non-nasal stops [b d g] for the nasals [m n ŋ].

> *Good morning, Mr Armstrong. I'm most sorry but I can't come in this morning owing to an appalling attack of influenza. I'm going to remain at home and with any luck I'll be in again on Monday morning. End of message.*

(A useful technique if you want a good excuse for staying away from work!)

Fricatives

All fricatives, except /h/, occur in fortis/lenis pairs. (Return to Sections A2 and A5 if you're unsure of the contrast between lenis and fortis consonants.)

Labio-dental fricatives /f v/

The lower lip makes near contact with the upper front teeth resulting in labio-dental friction. Lenis /v/ has potential voice.

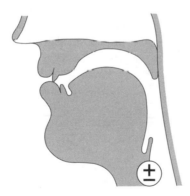

Figure B2.8 English /f/ and /v/

Dental fricatives /θ ð/

The tongue-tip makes near contact with the rear of the upper teeth resulting in dental friction. Lenis /ð/ has potential voice, and often has the tongue withdrawn, being realised as a type of weak dental approximant.

Initial /ð/ occurs only in the following function words: *the, this, that, these, those, then, than, thus, there, they, their, them, thence*; also in the archaic words *thou, thee, thy, thine, thither*.

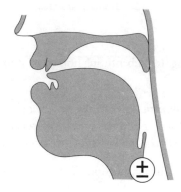

Figure B2.9 English /θ/ and /ð/

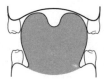

Figure B2.10 Transverse cross-section of mouth viewed from front showing grooved tongue shape for /s/ and /z/

Alveolar fricatives /s z/

The tip/blade of the tongue makes near contact with the alveolar ridge. Air is channelled along a deep groove in the tongue, producing alveolar friction characterised by **sharp** hiss (see Figure B2.11). These are sometimes termed **grooved** fricatives; see Figure B2.10. Lenis /z/ has potential voice.

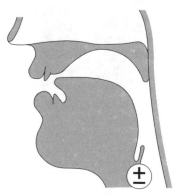

Figure B2.11 English /s/ and /z/

Palato-alveolar fricatives /ʃ ʒ/

A large portion of the tongue (tip/blade/front) makes near contact with the alveolar ridge and the front of the hard palate. The airstream is channelled through a shallower groove than for /s z/. In addition, /ʃ ʒ/ have strong trumpet-shaped lip-rounding similar to that of /tʃ dʒ/. The resulting hiss is **graver** (i.e. lower pitched) than that of /s z/.

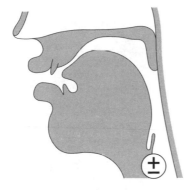

Figure B2.12 English /ʃ/ and /ʒ/. Note trumpet-shaped lip-rounding

/ʒ/ is notably restricted in its distribution occurring mainly in medial position, e.g. *usual, pleasure*, etc. In initial and final position it is found only in recent French loanwords, e.g. *genre, beige*. In most cases, there are alternative pronunciations with /dʒ/.

Glottal fricative /h/

Phonetically, /h/ is like a voiceless vowel. The articulators are in the position for the following vowel sound and a strong airstream produces friction not only at the glottis but also throughout the vocal tract. Consequently, there are as many articulations of /h/ as there are vowels in English (and for that reason no cross-section diagram is provided). In English, /h/ occurs only preceding vowels.

Approximants

Lateral (approximant)

The tip and blade of the tongue form a central closure with the alveolar ridge, while the sides of the tongue remain lowered. The airstream escapes over the lowered sides.

Clear *l* occurs before vowels, e.g. *leap*, and before /j/, as in *value*. The tongue shape is slightly palatalised with a convex upper surface giving a close front vowel [i]-type resonance (see Figure A5.9).

Dark *l* occurs before consonants and pause. The articulation is slightly velarised (see Section A5), with a concave upper surface, giving a back-central vowel [ʊ]-type resonance, e.g. *still* [stɪɫ], *help* [heɫp]. Dark *l* is often a syllable-bearer, when it will be of longer duration [ɫ̩], e.g. *hospital* /ˈhɒspɪtl̩/ [ˈhɒspɪtɫ̩]. Younger NRP speakers, especially those brought up in the area of London or the South East, nowadays regularly have a vocalic dark *l* sounding rather like [ʊ], especially following central and back vowels, e.g. *doll* [dɒʊ], *pearl* [pɜːʊ]. Traditional RP speakers tend to stigmatise this feature (see p. 142), which is nevertheless one of the striking changes going on in present-day English.

The allophonic distribution of clear and dark *l* quoted above is true of NRP and most varieties of English, but other English accents show different patterns. For example, most Welsh and Irish accents have only clear *l* in all contexts, while many Scottish and American varieties have only dark *l*. See Sections C1 and C2.

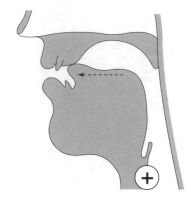

Figure B2.13　English dark *l* showing velarised tongue shape (cf. clear *l* as shown in Figure A5.9). Arrow shows lateral passage of the airstream

Activity

75

Try saying the following sentences (1) with dark *l* only, (2) with clear *l* only:

I'm told that this model will only be available for a little while longer.
Lesley feels awfully guilty putting you to all this trouble.
Delia's told me she'll call round at twelve.

Post-alveolar approximant /r/

The sides of the tongue are raised and the tongue-tip may move towards the rear of the alveolar ridge in a stricture of open approximation. See Figure A5.8 (p. 47). Although /r/ is classed as post-alveolar, this tongue raising is probably more important than the tongue-tip movement (which is in fact absent for many individuals). Most NRP speakers have accompanying lip-rounding and protrusion.

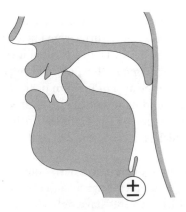

Figure B2.14　English post-alveolar affricates [tɹ̥ dɹ] as in **train, drain**: hold stage

The sporadic occurrence in times past of an alveolar tap [ɾ] in traditional RP in intervocalic contexts, e.g. *borrow, marry*, has been mentioned in Section A5. Nowadays, tap [ɾ] is rarely heard from NRP speakers although it is found in many regional accents. Curiously, it is still taught by elocutionists as 'correct speech'. Another recent development is that some young speakers (especially in the south-east of England) use a labio-dental approximant, symbolised as [ʋ].

Distribution – rhotic vs. non-rhotic accents

A very significant feature of English is the split of accents into two groups according to /r/ distribution. In **rhotic** varieties, /r/ is pronounced in all contexts. Rhotic speech comprises most American varieties – including General American and Canadian – Scottish, Irish, much Caribbean, and the regional accents of the West Country of England. In **non-rhotic** varieties, /r/ is pronounced only before a vowel. Non-rhotic speech includes most of England and Wales, much American English spoken in the southern and eastern states, some Caribbean, Australian, South African, and most New Zealand varieties of English. Note that English as spoken by most African Americans, from all areas of the USA, is typically non-rhotic.

In non-rhotic varieties, /r/ is typically pronounced across word boundaries, e.g.

car /kɑː/   *car alarm* /ˈkɑː r əˈlɑːm/
matter /ˈmætə/   *matter of fact* /ˈmætə r əv ˈfækt/

This is a type of **liaison** termed **linking r**. See Section B4 for further discussion of this and other types of r-liaison.

Activity

76

Go round your class and discover who has a rhotic form of English. Which part of the English-speaking world do they come from?

Palatal approximant /j/

The palatal approximant /j/ is a brief [i]-vowel-like glide. In NRP, the sequences /tj dj/ are typically replaced by palato-alveolar affricates /tʃ dʒ/ not only within the word (e.g. *module* /ˈmɒdʒuːl/) but also across word boundaries, particularly involving *you, your*, e.g. *can't you* /ˈkɑːntʃu/, *did you* /ˈdɪdʒu/, *mind your own business* /ˈmaɪndʒɔː r əʊn ˈbɪznəs/. It is also nowadays the most frequent pronunciation in stressed syllables, e.g. *Tuesday* /ˈtʃuːzdeɪ/, *dual* /ˈdʒuːəl/. Such forms, which were formerly not accepted in traditional RP, are still stigmatised by some members of the older generation as 'lazy speech'.

77

In your idiolect, are the beginnings of these words the same or different?

chews – Tuesday; *choose – tune*; *Jew – due*; *June – dune*; *jukebox – duke*; *jewel – dual*.

If they are different, is *tune* /tjuːn/, /tʃuːn/ or /tuːn/? And is *duke* /djuːk/, /dʒuːk/ or /duːk/? Ask round the class and compare results.

Labial-velar approximant /w/

For /w/ there are two strictures of open approximation: (1) labial and (2) velar. Like /j/, /w/ is like a brief vowel glide. The [u]-like glide has strong lip-rounding.

A few speakers still strive to produce an additional phoneme contrast, with a voiceless labial-velar fricative, symbolised as /ʍ/, used in all words beginning **wh**, e.g.

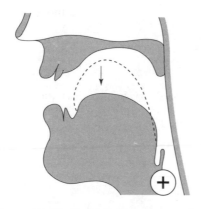

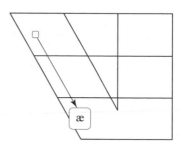

Figure B2.15 English /j/: sequence /jæ/ as in *yam*. Cross-section shows approximate change in shape of tongue

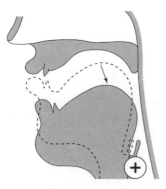

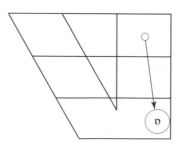

Figure B2.16 English /w/: sequence /wɒ/ as in *watt*. Cross-section shows approximate change in shape of tongue

where – wear /ʍɛː – wɛ:/. Those who produce this sound have often undergone speech training of some kind. Over-correct forms are not infrequently to be heard on radio; for example:

Isle of Wight */aɪl əv 'ʍaɪt/
the ways of the world */ðə 'ʍeɪz əv ðə 'ʍɜːld/

It is probable that the phoneme /ʍ/ was extinct in the everyday language of England by the eighteenth century. But it is somewhat more often heard in American English, and is still a living feature of all Scottish varieties and also much Irish English.

Activity

78

Do you have any friends or relatives who say /ʍ/ for **wh**? If so, is it natural to them or were they taught to say it in school, or by a speech trainer?

Other types of allophonic variation

Devoicing
All nasals are typically voiced throughout and there is none of the devoicing characteristic of the fricatives and stops. Only when following /s/ in initial clusters are /m n/ partially devoiced [m̥ n̥], e.g. *smoke* [sm̥əʊk], *snow* [sn̥əʊ].

Similarly, /l/ is also typically voiced, not showing initial and final devoicing. It is, however, voiceless and fricative [l̥] in initial clusters following the voiceless plosives /p k/ in stressed syllables, e.g. *plain*, *claim* [pl̥eɪn kl̥eɪm]. (The cluster /tl/ does not occur in initial position.) The same holds true for /w j/, e.g. *queen*, *cute* /kw̥iːn kj̊uːt/. This effect corresponds to the aspiration of the fortis plosives found in other contexts (see above).

· In stressed syllable-initial clusters, a completely voiceless post-alveolar fricative [ɹ̥] is realised following fortis plosives /p k/, e.g. *price*, *crease*. In the sequence /pr/, bilabial friction may be heard. The sequences /tr dr/, e.g. *troop*, *droop*, are realised as post-alveolar affricates, [tɹ̥ dɹ] (see p. 80).

Palatalisation
Preceding /j/, plosives are palatalised [pʲ bʲ tʲ dʲ kʲ gʲ], e.g. *pure*, *beauty*, *tune*, *dune*, *cure*, *angular*. As stated above, the sequences /tj dj/ are frequently reduced in NRP to /tʃ dʒ/, so giving no contrast between words like *juice* and *deuce*, *chewed* and the first syllable of *Tudor*. In these contexts, /j/ is devoiced and fricative [j̊], e.g. *pure*, *tuna*, *cue*; it may be realised as a voiceless palatal fricative [ç] (similar to the sound known in German as the *ich-Laut*, in words like *ich* 'I', *Bücher* 'books'). The sequence /hj/ in *huge*, *human* is also frequently realised in this way [ç], e.g. *humid* /hjuːmɪd/ [çuːmɪd].

Other fricatives preceding /j/ are also palatalised, e.g. *fuse, views, assume, presume*. Following /s/, NRP deletes traditional /j/, e.g. *suit, suicide* (at one time /sjuːt 'sjuːɪsaɪd/, nowadays typically /suːt 'suːɪsaɪd/). These well-established forms nevertheless occasionally suffer criticism from some older-generation speakers.

Before /j/ and /ɪə/, the nasals /m n/ are strongly palatalised, e.g. *mute, near* [mʲuːt nʲɪə].

Labialisation

Consonants preceding /w/ are strongly labialised, e.g. *switch* [sʷwɪtʃ], *language* ['læŋgʷwɪdʒ]. Following the fortis alveolar and velar plosives /t k/, as in *entwine, quick*, /w/ is in addition devoiced, [ɪn'tw̥aɪn], [kw̥ɪk]; the remaining voiceless plosive /p/ is not found in this context. Note that the friction for [w̥] in this case is bilabial and not velar.

Advanced/retracted

Consonants may be **advanced** or **retracted**. This depends on the consonants adjacent to them. Alveolar consonants are particularly prone to place variation. The plosives /t d/ are advanced to dental when adjacent to dental fricatives (shown by means of the diacritic [̪] below the symbol), i.e. articulated with the tongue-tip behind the teeth: [t̪ d̪] in *eighth, hid them*. The same goes for /n l/ [n̪ l̪], e.g. *anthem, both numbers, healthy, faithless*.

For /k g/, the velar closure is advanced before front vowels and /j/ – an effect shown in phonetic transcription by the diacritic [₊], e.g. *key, cue* [k₊iː k₊juː]. The closure is retracted before back vowels (shown by [-]), cf. *corn, cob* [k-ɔːn k-ɒb]. /ŋ/ is advanced [ŋ₊] after front vowels and retracted [ŋ-] after velars, e.g. *singsong*.

Before labio-dental /f v/, both /m/ and /n/ may be realised as labio-dental nasal [ɱ], e.g. *in front*; thus, despite the spelling, the consonant clusters in *emphasis* and *infant* are normally pronounced identically.

Activity

79

Transcribe phonemically, showing intonation groups and sentence stress, and using weak and contracted forms wherever possible.

Transcription passage 8
'No, I'll look first,' she said, 'and see whether it's marked "poison" or not', because she had read several nice little stories about children who had got burnt, and eaten up by wild beasts, and other unpleasant things, all because they *would* not remember the simple rules their friends had taught them. For instance, a red-hot poker will burn you if you hold it too long. If you cut your finger *very* deeply with a knife, it usually bleeds. Alice had never forgotten that if you drink much from a bottle marked 'poison', it is almost certain to disagree with you, sooner or later.

B

B3

ENGLISH VOWELS

Overview of the English vowel system

The terms 'checked' and 'free' were introduced in Section A2, but we can now say a little bit more about this distinction. In English, checked vowels cannot occur in word-final stressed open syllables. This implies that there are no words like */'tɪ 'te/, etc., whereas we do find free vowels in this environment, e.g. /'tiː 'taɪ/ (*tea*, *tie*), etc. Note that, in similar phonetic contexts, checked vowels are shorter than free vowels. Since /ə/ is never stressed, it must be regarded as standing outside the checked/free classification. As it is always short, we are discussing it here together with the checked vowels.

Let's now examine in overview (Figure B3.1) the complete vowel system of English NRP.

The terms 'fronting, backing and centring diphthong' are explained below. See Section A2, Table A2.2 for the vowel keywords and symbols.

Checked steady-state vowels and /ə/

The checked steady-state vowels of English are shown in Figure B3.2.

Front vowels /ɪ e æ/

/ɪ/   KIT   front-central, close-mid
/e/   DRESS front mid
/æ/   TRAP   front open

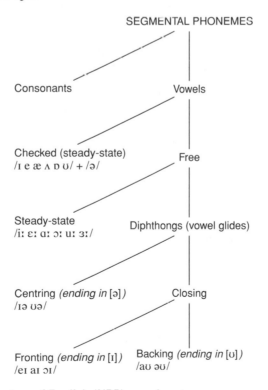

Figure B3.1 Overview of English (NRP) vowel system

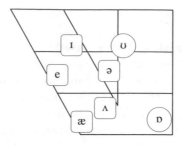

Figure B3.2 English (NRP) checked vowels and /ə/

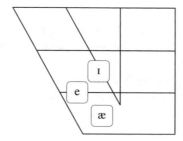

Figure B3.3 English (NRP) front vowels before dark *l* in *pill, bell, pal*

The English front checked vowels share the following characteristics:

❑   they are unrounded;
❑   they are centralised and/or lowered before dark *l*, e.g. *pill, bell, pal* (see Figure B3.3);
❑   they are raised before velars, e.g. *pick, peck, pack*.

Many NRP speakers have a lengthened TRAP vowel in certain common words, such as *bad, mad, bag, man*; this is also true of many southern regional varieties and traditional RP.

 Activity

> ## 80
>
> Do you have vowels of the same length in the words listed below? Or is the first vowel regularly longer?
>
> *mad – had*
> *man – plan*
> *bag – stag*
> *jam – tram*
>
> If you do have lengthening of this sort, can you think of any other words which regularly contain a lengthened TRAP vowel? Ask friends and relatives the same questions.

Traditional RP front vowels had closer qualities, an effect which is especially notice-able with TRAP (making it sound amusingly similar to SQUARE to young ears). This feature is still to be heard from some of the older generation – one often imitated example being the British Queen. See also Section C5 for discussion of language change affecting TRAP.

Central vowels /ʌ ə/

/ʌ/   STRUT   central open-mid
/ə/   *bonus*   central mid

STRUT varies considerably – some speakers use a much more front quality.

In word-final position, the *bonus* vowel is noticeably open, and overlapping to a degree with STRUT. Some English speakers, indeed many, may regard these two vowels as being in allophonic relationship. Since /ə/ is always (by definition) unstressed, then /ʌ/ could be regarded as the stressed allophone of /ə/. For many speakers, the two vowels in *butter* /ˈbʌtə/ are very similar, or identical.

Remember that in the accents of the north of England, roughly from just above Birmingham to the Scottish border, STRUT is absent and words containing /ʌ/ are instead pronounced with the FOOT vowel /ʊ/. See Sections B1 and C1.

Activity

81

Although native English speakers outside the north of England usually have a contrast STRUT – FOOT /ʌ – ʊ/, nevertheless not all may consider that they contrast the STRUT vowel /ʌ/ and the *bonus* vowel /ə/. How do you yourself pronounce the syllable *drum* in the following words: *drum – humdrum – conundrum*? Do you say them with a STRUT vowel, a FOOT vowel or a *bonus* vowel? Or do they vary?

Back vowels /ɒ ʊ/

/ɒ/   LOT   back open (rounded)
/ʊ/   FOOT   back-central close-mid (rounded)

The checked back vowels have potential lip-rounding, but in modern NRP, such round-ing is typically very weak. FOOT is often unrounded and central, especially in the high-frequency word *good*. See above for the use of the FOOT vowel in STRUT words in Northern England. In certain words LOT varies with STRUT, e.g. *accomplish, constable*. In some northern varieties this is extended to more words, e.g. *none, one*.

Worry words

Non-native learners of English often confuse STRUT and LOT words. This is because the STRUT vowel, as well as having a regular spelling with **u** (e.g. *bus, hurry*), can also be represented orthographically by **o**, as in *worry*. We shall therefore term these the '*worry* words'. Here's a list of the most frequent words of this type: *done, none, son,*

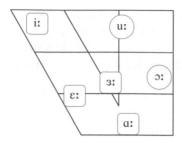

Figure B3.4   English (NRP) free steady-state vowels

ton, won, one, honey, money, front, month, London, Monday, wonder(ful), monk, monkey, onion, sponge, among, tongue, above, glove, love, lovely, shove, oven, dozen, govern, government, slovenly, colour, cover, come, some, Somerset, comfort, comfortable, compasses, company, accompany, other, brother, mother, smother, borough, thorough, nothing and (last but not least!) *worry*.

Another spelling for STRUT is **ou**, as in: *country, double, trouble, young, couple, touch, nourish, flourish, southern, cousin, courage, enough, tough, rough*.

This is an area of sound–spelling relationship which is especially significant for non-natives, since it is a problem which affects learners from virtually all language backgrounds.

Free steady-state vowels

The free steady-state vowels are long in open syllables, and also when preceding nasals, lateral approximants and lenis stops and fricatives. Before fortis stops and fricatives, under the influence of pre-fortis clipping (see Section A5), these vowels are much shorter.

Front steady-state vowels /iː ɛː/

| /iː/ | FLEECE | front close |
| /ɛː/ | SQUARE | front open-mid |

The FLEECE vowel /iː/ is generally realised as a slight diphthongal glide [ɪi], except where shortened by pre-fortis clipping. Compare *knee* (long, diphthongal) with *neat* (short, steady-state). Preceding dark *l*, there is usually a *centring* glide, so that for many speakers there is no contrast with /ɪəl/, e.g. *reel – real*. English native speakers often seem unsure of how to transcribe words like *feel*, i.e. either as /fiːl/ or as /fɪəl/. Thus for them, the effect of dark *l* would appear to be to neutralise the contrast.

The final vowel in words like *happy, coffee, movie*, etc. (usually referred to as the '**happ**Y words'; see Wells 1982: 165–6) is nowadays much closer than in traditional RP. Indeed, most speakers of English would regard it as falling into the FLEECE rather than the KIT category; this is especially true of younger NRP speakers. Traditional RP speakers, Northerners (in particular Yorkshire and Lancashire) and most Scots regard the 'happy' vowel as /ɪ/ and this is how it has until recently been classified. At one time, traditional RP had a very open vowel in this context, sounding almost like /e/: ['hæpe]. This is hardly ever heard today and strikes most NRP users as archaic. For most English speakers the *happy* vowel provides an example of phoneme neutralisation (see Section B1), with no clear choice possible between KIT and FLEECE in this context. This is why most modern pronunciation dictionaries show it with the compromise symbol **i**.

SQUARE /ɛː/ is typically a steady-state vowel in present-day NRP. For past generations, a centring glide of an [ɛə] type was usual, and this is still to be heard as a variant pronunciation. In most phonetics books, the symbol for this vowel is **eə** – but this certainly does not reflect the typical pronunciation of the twenty-first century. This is why the Oxford dictionaries show it with ɛ, and we have followed their example.

Central steady-state vowels /ɜː ɑː/

/ɜː/   NURSE   central open-mid
/ɑː/   PALM   central open

NURSE /ɜː/ was more open in traditional RP – a feature nowadays often regarded as 'affected'.

The BATH words

In what are termed the BATH words, e.g. *craft, pass, dance* (see below), most British varieties apart from NRP and those in the south-east of England choose TRAP. NRP, London and East Anglia have PALM in these items. Some speakers, for instance many Northerners and Midlanders whose speech is otherwise largely NRP, may retain TRAP in BATH words, thus keeping a characteristic of their local speech. (This is often cited as an example of 'accent loyalty'.) Worldwide, North American accents choose TRAP, South Africa chooses PALM, while Australia, New Zealand and the Caribbean are variable.

The set of BATH words consists chiefly of words where orthographic **a** occurs before (1) a nasal (+ consonant), e.g. *chance*, or (2) a fricative (+ consonant), e.g. *task*. The following list provides a selection of the commonest words.

Pre-nasal

an   *banana*. Note also: *aunt*
am   *drama, example, sample* (but *ample, exam* with /æ/)
ance   *chance, dance, France* (but *romance, finance, cancer* with /æ/)
and   *command, demand, reprimand* (/æ/ in single-syllable words, e.g. *bland*)
ans   *answer*
ant   *advantage, chant, grant, plant, can't, shan't*

Pre-fricative

af   *after, craft, draft, staff*. Note also: *laugh, draught*
alf/alv   *half, calf, halve, calve*
ask   *ask, task, basket*
asp   *gasp, grasp, clasp*
ass   *brass, glass, pass, class* (but *ass, classical, classify* with /æ/)
ast   *cast, castle, fast(en), ghastly, master, plaster* (but **-astic** is usually /æ/, e.g. *plastic, elastic, fantastic*)
ath   *bath, path, father, rather* (but *maths* with /æ/)

In NRP there are also a number of words which vary between /æ/ and /ɑː/ (e.g. *drastic, plastic*) and all words containing the prefix **trans-**, e.g. *transport*.

Activity

82

How do you yourself pronounce the following words – with the TRAP vowel or the PALM vowel?

Prance, bask, brass, rather, task, dancer, answer

If possible, ask people from other parts of the English-speaking world. Does everyone have the same distribution? If not, try to analyse the differences.

Activity

83

Even if you are from the south-east of England, or an NRP speaker, you'll find some BATH words are pronounced in two ways. Which vowel (TRAP or PALM) do you use in the following:

chaff, graph, photograph, askance, bastard, lather, plastic, Glasgow, Basque, trans- (e.g. *transport*)?

Back steady-state vowels /ɔː uː/

/ɔː/ THOUGHT back mid (rounded)
/uː/ GOOSE back-central close (rounded)

Like other back vowels in English, THOUGHT and GOOSE are rounded – although with many speakers the rounding in GOOSE may be minimal or absent.

The GOOSE vowel is generally realised with a glide of an [ʊu] type, except where shortened by pre-fortis clipping. For many younger NRP speakers a striking change has occurred in recent years whereby this vowel has become much more fronted and unrounded. Older-generation speakers sometimes interpret this new GOOSE vowel as FLEECE, and may even confuse pairs such as *two – tea, through – three*, etc. The fronting is perhaps most obvious following /j/, as in *news, confuse, huge*, etc.

The THOUGHT vowel is the most strongly lip-rounded of all vowels in present-day NRP English. For most speakers this vowel replaces traditional /ʊə/ in common words such as *sure, you're/your, poor*, and has increasingly extended to many other items. See below.

Free diphthongs

Free diphthongs – also termed vowel glides – fall into a number of categories based on direction of tongue movement. English has **closing** diphthongs (tongue rises, thus *closing* the space between the tongue and the roof of the mouth) and **centring** diphthongs (tongue lowers towards the *central* vowel [ə]). The closing diphthongs can be further subdivided into **fronting** (moving towards a close *front* vowel [ɪ]) and **backing** (moving towards a close *back* vowel [ʊ]). See Figures B3.5–B3.6.

Symbolisation and lip-shape indicators
All diphthongs are shown with two symbols as explained below:

- ❏ fronting diphthongs end with ɪ, e.g. /eɪ/ FACE
- ❏ backing diphthongs end with ʊ, e.g. /aʊ/ MOUTH
- ❏ centring diphthongs end with ə, e.g. /ɪə/ NEAR

The diphthongs /eɪ aɪ ɪə/ are lip-spread throughout their articulation and are therefore represented by ☐ on vowel diagrams. The diphthongs /ʊə ɔɪ/ involve a change from rounded to unrounded (represented by ⨆). The diphthongs /əʊ aʊ/ move from lip-spread to lip-rounded (represented by ◗). NRP English has no vowel glides which are completely lip-rounded throughout.

Fronting diphthongs /eɪ aɪ ɔɪ/
/eɪ/	FACE	front mid → ɪ
/aɪ/	PRICE	central open → ɪ
/ɔɪ/	CHOICE	back open-mid (rounded) → ɪ

Traditional RP had a closer starting-point for FACE, a more front starting-point for PRICE, and a more open starting-point for CHOICE. These may still be heard from some conservative speakers. In modern NRP, the glide in FACE is very slight where it is affected by pre-fortis clipping but more extensive elsewhere. Before dark *l*, in FACE, PRICE, CHOICE, the final element is frequently [ə], e.g. *ale* [eəł], *mile* [maəł], *oil* [ɔəł].

Backing diphthongs /aʊ əʊ/
/aʊ/	MOUTH	central open → ʊ
/əʊ/	GOAT	central close-mid → ʊ

Traditional RP had back starting-points for these diphthongs, and these are still to be heard from some older speakers. GOAT in particular still shows very considerable variation. Many NRP speakers now have a more front articulation which can sound similar to /eɪ/ to older-generation ears, leading to potential confusion with pairs such as *cone/cane*, *go/gay*, etc. For certain speakers, the [ʊ] element may be minimal or lost entirely before dark *l*, making pairs such as *pole/pearl*, *whole/hurl* near-homophones.

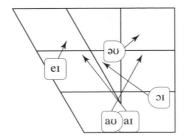

Figure B3.5 English (NRP) fronting and backing (closing) diphthongs

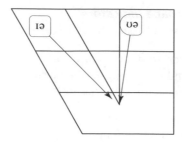

Figure B3.6 English (NRP) centring diphthongs

Many NRP speakers born in London, or influenced by London speech, employ [ɒ] rather than [əʊ] before dark *l*, giving an extra diphthong of an [ɒʊ] type. This can be heard in words like *gold, revolt*, etc.

Centring diphthongs /ɪə ʊə/

/ɪə/   NEAR   front close → ə
/ʊə/   CURE   back-central close → ə

Despite the symbolisation, most NRP speakers have a closer starting-point (similar to FLEECE) and may consider NEAR words as being a sequence /iː/ + /ə/. Very open terminations were found in some traditional RP, and are now considered by many to be 'affected'. Some, especially younger NRP speakers, have a prolonged [ɪː] vowel – losing the glide – in open syllables, e.g. *beer* [bɪː].

In the case of CURE, again many NRP speakers have a closer starting-point (similar to GOOSE) and may consider CURE words as a sequence of /uː/ + /ə/. Increasingly, in common words, e.g. *poor*, /ʊə/ is replaced by the THOUGHT vowel and, for some speakers, the /ʊə/ diphthong hardly exists. In words of the *cure, tour* type, it is replaced by /ɔː/, whereas in words like *brewer, jeweller* it is thought of as a sequence /uː/ + /ə/.

Note that traditional RP included SQUARE as a third centring diphthong of an [ɛə] type which can now be regarded as a steady-state vowel (see above).

Vowel sequences with /ə/ termination /aɪə aʊə/

In the common sequences /aɪə/ and /aʊə/, the [ɪ] or [ʊ] element is generally reduced, and may be altogether absent – an effect which has been termed **smoothing** (Wells 1982: 286). Nevertheless, words like *shire* and *shower* are normally distinct. The contrast of /aʊə/ and /ɑː/ (i.e. *shower* and *Shah*) was formerly absent in the relaxed speech of some traditional RP speakers – but this suffered a degree of stigmatisation, often being labelled 'affected'. In modern NRP (as indeed in other forms of English) a clear contrast of /aʊə – aɪə – ɑː/ seems to be well maintained. An exception to this is the word *our*, which is commonly pronounced /ɑː/ not only in unstressed contexts but also when stressed.

You can hear a degree of smoothing in other sequences, e.g. /eɪə/ as in *conveyor*, /əʊə/ as in *thrower*, /ɔɪə/ as in *royalist*. Extreme reductions such as the levelling of /eɪə/ and /ɛː/ (*layer – lair*) or /əʊə/ and /ɜː/ (*slower – slur*) are again characteristic of a type of traditional RP which was often branded 'affected'. These extreme smoothings are unusual in modern NRP.

Activity

84

Transcribe phonemically, showing intonation groups and sentence stress, and using weak and contracted forms wherever possible.

Transcription passage 9

However, this bottle was not marked 'poison', so Alice risked tasting it, and found it very nice. It had a sort of mixed flavour – cherry tart, custard, pineapple, roast turkey, toffee and hot buttered toast – so she very soon finished it off. 'What a curious feeling;' said Alice. 'I must be shutting up like a tele-scope!' And so she was indeed. She was now less than a foot high, and her face brightened up at the thought that she was now the right size for going through the tiny door into that lovely garden. First, however, she waited for a few minutes to see if she was going to shrink any further. She felt a little nervous about this. 'It might end, you know, with me going out altogether, like a candle. I wonder what I'd be like then.'

FEATURES OF CONNECTED SPEECH

B4

The surprises of connected speech

All languages modify complicated sequences in connected speech in order to simplify the articulation process – but the manner in which this is done varies from one language to another. Furthermore, most native speakers are totally unaware of such simplification processes and are often surprised (or even shocked!) when these are pointed out to them.

 Activity

85 ⊙ **Track 23**

Say these English words and phrases, firstly following the transcription in column 1 and then in column 2.

	1 Citation forms	2 Connected speech forms
headquarters	/hed ˈkwɔːtəz/	/heg ˈkwɔːtəz/
main course	/meɪn ˈkɔːs/	/meɪŋ ˈkɔːs/
matched pairs	/mætʃt ˈpɛːz/	/mætʃ ˈpɛːz/
perhaps	/pəˈhæps/	/præps/

The differences between the **citation forms** and the modified **connected speech forms** are not just a matter of chance: clear patterns are distinguishable.

Phonetic conditioning

Phonetic conditioning is a term used to cover the way in which speech segments are influenced by adjacent (or near-adjacent) segments, causing phonemes to vary in their realisation according to the phonetic context. We can distinguish three main types: (1) allophonic variation; (2) assimilation; (3) elision.

Throughout the sections on English segments, we have discussed deviations from the target forms of phonemes. This results from phonetic conditioning and is responsible for much of any range of allophones occurring in complementary distribution. We shall now proceed to deal with the two other types of phonetic conditioning.

Assimilation

Where, as a result of phonetic conditioning, one phoneme is replaced by a second under the influence of a third we term the effect **assimilation**.

Take the English word *broadcast*, which in careful pronunciation is /ˈbrɔːdkɑːst/, but in connected speech may well become /ˈbrɔːgkɑːst/. Here, one phoneme /d/ has been replaced by a second /g/ under the influence of a third /k/. This could be stated as a rule:

/d/   →   /g/   before /k/

We can distinguish here the two forms of the word *broad*: (1) /brɔːd/, (2) /brɔːg/, where form (1) can be considered the **ideal form**, corresponding to the target that native speakers have in their minds. This is what is produced in the slowest and most careful styles of speech; it often bears a close resemblance to the spelling representation. Form (2), more typical of connected speech, is termed the **assimilated form**.

Patterns of assimilation in English

Direction of influence

1   Features of an articulation may anticipate (i.e. *lead into*) those of a *following* segment, e.g. English *white pepper* /waɪt ˈpepə/ → /waɪp ˈpepə/. We term this **leading assimilation**.
2   Articulation features may be held over from a *preceding* segment, so that the articulators *lag* in their movements, e.g. English *on the house* /ɒn ðə ˈhaʊs/ → /ɒn nə ˈhaʊs/. This we term **lagging assimilation**.

In many cases there is a two-way exchange of articulation features, e.g. English *raise your glass* /ˈreɪz jɔː ˈglɑːs/ → /ˈreɪʒ ʒɔː ˈglɑːs/. This is termed **reciprocal assimilation**.

Types of influence

1   Assimilations involving a change in place of articulation are termed **place assimilation**. For instance, final alveolars in ideal forms are often replaced by bilabials (preceding /p b m/) or velars (preceding /k g/) or palatals (preceding /ʃ/), e.g. *woodpecker* /ˈwʊdpekə/ → /ˈwʊbpekə/, *wet blanket* /wet ˈblæŋkɪt/ → /wep

'blæŋkɪt/, *night-cap* /'naɪtkæp/ → /'naɪkkæp/, *statement* /'steɪtmənt/ → /'steɪpmənt/, *weed-killer* /'wiːd kɪlə/ → /'wiːg kɪlə/, *horseshoe* /hɔːsʃuː/ → /hɔːʃʃuː/. Place assimilation is very common in English.

2   Assimilations may involve a reduction of the fortis/lenis contrast, a type which is termed **energy assimilation**. In stressed syllables, energy assimilations are less frequent in English than in most other languages, but they do occur in a few common words and phrases, e.g. *I have to* (meaning 'must') /hæf tə/, *I used to* /juːst tə/, *newspaper* /'njuːzpeɪpə/ → /'njuːspeɪpə/. In unstressed syllables, they occur regularly, e.g. *it was spectacular* /ɪt wəz spek'tækjulə/ → /ɪt wəs spek'tækjulə/.

3   Assimilations may involve a change in the manner of articulation, e.g. an ideal form containing a fricative may be replaced by a nasal or a lateral. This is termed **manner assimilation**.

Nasal and lateral assimilations occur in English, mainly affecting initial /ð/ in unstressed words, e.g.

join the army /'dʒɔɪn ði 'aːmi/ → /'dʒɔɪn ni 'aːmi/
fail the test /feɪl ðə 'test/ → /feɪl lə 'test/
till they meet again /tɪl ðeɪ miːt ə'gen/ → /tɪl leɪ miːt ə'gen/

Nasal assimilations are especially common in French, e.g. *un demi* /œ dəmi/ → /œ nmi/, *on demande* /ɔ dəmɑd/ → /ɔ nmɑd/.

Co-occurrence of assimilations
Assimilations of different types may occur simultaneously, e.g. *behind you* /bə'haɪndjuː/ → /bə'haɪndʒuː/. Here both *place* and *manner* assimilation affects /d/ and /j/ of the ideal form:

/d/ (alveolar plosive)   /j/ (palatal approximant)

/dʒ/ (palato-alveolar affricate)

More than one phoneme may be affected by an assimilation, e.g. *point-blank range* /pɔɪnt blæŋk 'reɪndʒ/ → /pɔɪmp blæŋk 'reɪndʒ/.

Elision
A change from the ideal form in connected speech may involve the deletion of a phoneme, e.g. English *tasteless* /'teɪstləs/ → /'teɪsləs/. The phoneme is said to be **elided** and the process is termed **elision**.

Frequently, assimilation processes lead to elision, e.g. English *mind-boggling* /'maɪndbɒɡlɪŋ/ → /'maɪmbbɒɡlɪŋ/ → /'maɪmbɒɡlɪŋ/.

Historical assimilation and elision
We can distinguish between **contemporary assimilation and elision** vs. **historical assimilation and elision** processes. In contemporary assimilation/elision (using 'contemporary' in the sense of 'present-day'), there is an ideal form. The assimilation (or elision) takes place only in a certain phonetic context and, in most cases,

assimilation or elision is optional. Once the original ideal forms become extinct, and the assimilated/elided forms are fixed, we term such cases historical assimilation and elision, e.g. *cupboard* /'kʌbəd/, where the form */'kʌpbɔːd/ has died out. The 'silent letters' of English spelling provide frequent reminders of historical elision, e.g. *talk, comb, know, could, gnome, whistle, wrong, iron*. See Section C5 for a more general discussion on language change.

Activity

86

Go through two or three pages of one of the extracts in Section D and find more examples of 'silent letters' in English.

There is a tendency nowadays for some historical elisions and assimilations to revert back to the original forms as a result of the influence of spelling. For instance, in modern NRP English, /t/ is frequently pronounced in *often* (formerly only /'ɒfən/).

Activity

87

How do you pronounce the following words: *always, falcon, historical, hotel, often, perhaps, towards, Wednesday*? Do you know how your parents said these words? And what about your grandparents (or people of similar age)? See Section C5.

Liaison

The converse of elision is **liaison**, i.e. the insertion of an extra sound in order to facilitate the articulation of a sequence. We have seen (Section B2) that accents of English can be divided into two groups according to /r/ distribution, namely rhotic accents where /r/ is pronounced in all contexts, as opposed to non-rhotic accents (like NRP) where /r/ is pronounced only preceding a vowel. In these latter varieties orthographic **r** is regularly restored as a link across word boundaries, e.g.

sooner /'suːnə/	*sooner or later* /'suːnə r ɔː 'leɪtə/
sure /ʃɔː/	*sure enough* /'ʃɔː r ɪ'nʌf/

This is termed **linking r**. With most speakers of non-rhotic English, it is also possible to hear linking *r* when there is no **r** in the spelling. This is termed **intrusive r**.

the sofa in the catalogue /ðə 'səʊfə r ɪn ðə 'kætəlɒg/
my idea of heaven /maɪ aɪ'dɪə r əv 'hevən/
we saw a film /wi 'sɔː r ə 'fɪlm/
bourgeois immigrants /bʊəʒwɑː r 'ɪmɪgrənts/
via Australia /vaɪə r ɒ'streɪliə/

Intrusive *r* is heard after the vowels /ɑː ɔː ə/ and the diphthongs terminating in /ə/. Instances with other vowels hardly ever occur: /ɛː/ is invariably spelt with **r** (except possibly in the word *yeah* as a form of *yes*); final /ɜː/ almost always has **r** in the spelling. Many native speakers are aware of the existence of intrusive *r* and many seem to make a conscious effort to avoid it (especially after /ɑː/ and /ɔː/). It is often considered by English people (particularly the older generation) as 'lazy' or 'uneducated' speech. Nevertheless, it is a characteristic feature of NRP, and is also heard from the over-whelming majority of those who use any non-rhotic variety of English. Some native speakers will insert a glottal stop in examples like those given above, in a conscious effort to avoid producing an /r/ link. But, interestingly, many of those who condemn intrusive *r* vociferously are unaware of the fact that they regularly use it themselves.

French is notable for an elaborate system of liaison, e.g. *Elle est assez intelligent*, where 'est' and 'assez', pronounced /e/ and /ase/ in citation form, recover the final con-sonants when they occur pre-vocalically in connected speech: /ɛl ɛt asɛz ɛ̃tɛliʒɑ̃/.

Related to liaison is **epenthesis**, which is the insertion into a word of a segment which was previously absent. In all varieties of English, including NRP, speakers often insert a homorganic stop after a nasal in examples such as the following: *once* /wʌnts/, *length* /leŋkθ/, *something* /ˈsʌmpθɪŋ/. As a result, words like *sense* and *scents* may be pronounced in the same way.

✪ **Activity**

88

Some speakers distinguish the following pairs. Others, pronouncing an epenthetic consonant, say them identically: *mince – mints*; *prince – prints*; *patience – patients*; *chance – chants*; *tense – tents*; *Samson – Sampson*; *Thomson – Thompson*. What do you do? Check with friends. Can you think of any other examples of the same phenomenon?

Patterns of assimilation in English

General observations
Assimilation and elision tend to be more frequent in:

❑ unstressed rather than stressed syllables;
❑ rapid rather than slow tempo;
❑ informal rather than formal registers.

1 Leading assimilation of place of final alveolars

Alveolar → bilabial in context preceding bilabial
/t/ → /p/ ⎫
/d/ → /b/ ⎬ preceding /p b m/ and less commonly /w/.
/n/ → /m/ ⎭

footpath /ˈfʊppɑːθ/, *madman* /ˈmæbmən/, *pen pal* /pem ˈpæl/, *in March* /ɪm ˈmɑːtʃ/, *runway* /ˈrʌmweɪ/

Alveolar → velar in context preceding velar

/t/ → /k/ ⎫
/d/ → /g/ ⎬ preceding /k g/
/n/ → /ŋ/ ⎭

gatecrash /ˈgeɪkkræʃ/, *kid-gloves* /kɪg ˈglʌvz/, *painkiller* /ˈpeɪŋkɪlə/

Note that in NRP the allophone of /p k/ representing orthographic **t** is almost invariably strongly pre-glottalised and never has audible release: [ˀp ˀk], e.g. *footpath* [ˈfʊˀppɑːθ], *gatecrash* [ˈgeɪˀkkræʃ]. Often there will be complete glottal replacement [ˈfʊʔpɑːθ], [ˈgeɪʔkræʃ]. Similarly, /b g/ representing orthographic **d** indicate a single articulation with a prolonged hold stage [bː gː], e.g. *redbrick* [ˈrebːrɪk], *Red Cross* [regː ˈkrɒs].

Alveolar → palato-alveolar in context preceding palato-alveolar

/s/ → /ʃ/ ⎫ preceding /ʃ/
/z/ → /ʒ/ ⎭

spaceship /ˈspeɪʃʃɪp/, *news sheet* /ˈnjuːʒ ʃiːt/

Reciprocal assimilation with /j/

The plosives /t d/ merge regularly with *you* and *your* in a process of reciprocal assimilation of place and manner. The fricatives /s z/ have similar reciprocal assimilation with any word-initial /j/:

/t/ + /j/ → /tʃ/
/d/ + /j/ → /dʒ/
/s/ + /j/ → /ʃʒ/
/z/ + /j/ → /ʒʒ/

suit yourself /ˈsuːtʃɔːˈself/, *find your umbrella* /ˈfaɪndʒɔː r ʌmˈbrelə/
nice yellow shirt /ˈnaɪʃ ˈʒeləʊ ˈʃɜːt/, *where's your cup?* /ˈwɛːʒ ˈʒɔː ˈkʌp/

Assimilations of this sort are especially common in tag-questions with *you*:

You didn't do the washing, did you? /ˈdɪdʒu/
You should contact the police, shouldn't you? /ˈʃʊdn̩tʃu/

Assimilation is also frequent in the phrase *Do you*. This is often written *d'you* in informal representations of dialogue: *D'you come here often?* /dʒu ˈkʌm hɪə r ˈɒfn̩/.

2 Lagging assimilation involving /ð/

Initial /ð/ in unstressed words may be assimilated following /n l s z/:

on the shelves /ɒn nə ˈʃelvz/, *all the time* /ɔːl lə ˈtaɪm/, *what's the matter?* /ˈwɒts sə ˈmætə/, *how's the patient?* /haʊz zə ˈpeɪʃn̩t/.

Lagging assimilations are most frequent preceding *the*. Nevertheless, a difference is still to be heard (except at very rapid tempo) between *the* and *a* as a result of the lengthening of the preceding segment and possible differences in rhythm. With words other than *the*, assimilation of this type is less frequent – though by no means uncommon – particularly in unstressed contexts.

> *in this context* /ɪn nɪs ˈkɒntekst/, *when they arrive* /wen neɪ əˈraɪv/, *will they remember?* /ˈwɪl leɪ rəˈmembə/, *was there any reason for it?* /wəz zɛː r ˈeni ˈriːzn̩ fɔː r ɪt/.

3 Energy assimilation

In English, energy assimilation is rare in stressed syllables. Two obligatory assimilations are *used to* and *have to* (where equivalent to 'must'), e.g.

> *I used to play cricket* /aɪ ˈjuːstə ˈpleɪ ˈkrɪkɪt/, *I used two* (main verb) /aɪ ˈjuːzd ˈtuː/
> *I have to write him a letter* /aɪ ˈhæftə ˈraɪt ɪm ə ˈletə/, *I have two* (main verb 'possess') /aɪ ˈhæv ˈtuː/

There are also some word-internal energy assimilations, generally with free variation between two possible forms:

> *newspaper* /ˈnjuːspeɪpə/ or /ˈnjuːzpeɪpə/; *absurd* /əpˈsɜːd/, /əbˈsɜːd/ or /əbˈzɜːd/; *absolute* /ˈæpsəluːt/ or /ˈæbsəluːt/; *absorb* /əbˈzɔːb/ or /əbˈsɔːb/; *obsession* /əpˈseʃn̩/ or /əbˈseʃn̩/.

Although energy assimilations across word boundaries are rare in stressed syllables, they do occur in *unstressed* contexts, but only in the form lenis to fortis. This is particularly true of final inflexional /z/ (derived from the **s** of plurals, possessives and verb forms), and also with function words such as *as* and *of* and auxiliary verbs:

> *of course* /əf ˈkɔːs/, *it was stated* /ɪt wəs ˈsteɪtɪd/, *as soon as possible* /əs ˈsuːn əs ˈpɒsəbl̩/, *if she chooses to wait* /ɪf ʃi ˈtʃuːzɪs tə ˈweɪt/, *my sister's teacher* /maɪ ˈsɪstəs ˈtiːtʃə/.

Note that fortis to lenis assimilations, e.g. *back door* */bæɡ ˈdɔː/, *not bad* */nɒd ˈbæd/) are not found in English. Such assimilations are common in many languages such as French and Dutch.

Patterns of elision in English

Elision of /t d/ in consonant sequences

Elision of /t/ or /d/ is common if they are central in a sequence of three consonants:

> *past tense* /pɑːs ˈtens/, *ruined the market* /ˈruːɪn ðə ˈmɑːkɪt/, *left luggage* /lef ˈlʌɡɪdʒ/, *failed test* /feɪl ˈtest/.

Elisions such as these may remove the /t d/ marker of past tense in verbs but the tense is usually (not always) clear through context. Elision of /t d/ is not heard before /h/: *smoked herring* /ˈsməʊkt ˈherɪŋ/. If /nt/ or /lt/ are followed by a consonant, there is normally no elision of /t/ (except at very rapid tempo), though /t/ will be glottally reinforced [ˀt] or replaced by [ʔ]. Note that the vowel before /nt/ and /lt/ is shortened: *spent time* /'spent 'taɪm/ ['spenˀt 'taɪm] or ['spenʔ 'taɪm]; *Walt Disney* /wɔːlt 'dɪzni/ [wɔˀlˀt 'dɪzni] or [wɔˀlʔ 'dɪzni]. Sequences of consonant + /t + j/ and consonant + /d + j/ generally retain /t/ and /d/, but often have reciprocal assimilation to /tʃ/ and /dʒ/:

I've booked your flight /aɪv 'bʊktʃɔː 'flaɪt/, *I told your husband* /aɪ 'təʊldʒɔː 'hʌzbənd/

The verb forms *wouldn't you, didn't you*, etc. are regularly heard with this assimilated form: /'wʊdn̩tʃu, 'dɪdn̩tʃu/ (see above).

The sequence /skt/ has elision of /k/ instead of, or if preceding consonants, in addition to /t/:

masked gunman /mɑːst 'gʌnmən/ or /'mɑːs 'gʌnmən/, *they asked us* /ðeɪ 'ɑːst əs/

Other notable elisions

The following are examples of connected speech forms not covered by what has been stated already:

1 /h/ is regularly elided from the weak forms of function words (see also Section A3), e.g. *I think he will have told her* /aɪ 'θɪŋk i wɪl əv 'təʊld ə/. This is to be heard even in formal speech registers in all varieties of English. Because of the linguistic insecurity attached to **h**-dropping in England and Wales (see Section C2), it is not uncommon for children to be quite wrongly corrected by teachers or speech trainers for eliding /h/ in this context.

2 Another notable elision connected with weak forms is the deletion, in informal registers, of the dental fricative /ð/ in *'em*. Although often condemned as slipshod speech, this form in fact has a long history going back hundreds of years and is to be heard in NRP and all other accents of English.

3 Two common words have frequent alternative forms with elision of dental fricatives /θ ð/: *months* /mʌns/, *clothes* /kləʊz/.

4 Forms of numerals, e.g. *fifth, twelfth*, do not elide /θ/ but may instead elide the preceding consonant: /fɪθ, twelθ/.

5 Elision of /v/ in *of* is especially common before /ð/, e.g. *three of the websites* /'θriː ə ðə 'websaɪts/, *one of the lads* /'wʌn ə ðə 'lædz/. It is also heard at more rapid tempo before other consonants: *a piece of paper* /ə 'piːs ə 'peɪpə/, *as a matter of fact* /əz ə 'mætrə 'fækt/.

   In more rapid speech, /v/ is sometimes elided before /m/ in the verbs *give, have, leave*: *give me a chance* /'gɪ mi ə 'tʃɑːns/, *do you have my number* /duː ju 'hæ maɪ 'nʌmbə/, *leave me alone* /'liː mi ə'ləʊn/.

6 The sequence /tt/ is normally reduced to /t/ in three common verbal forms, i.e. *ought to, want to, got to*: *we ought to visit him* /'wi ɔːtə 'vɪzɪt ɪm/, *I want to leave* /aɪ 'wɒntə 'liːv/ (some speakers will further reduce this to /aɪ 'wɒnə 'liːv/ in more rapid speech), *they've got to go now* /ðeɪv 'gɒtə 'gəʊ naʊ/.

7 When *going to* is used as a tense-former, it is typically pronounced /gənə/, e.g. *What's going to happen* /'wɒts gənə 'hæpən/. This form (sometimes shown as 'gonna' in dialogue) is often criticised by prescriptivists, but is in fact the norm in colloquial NRP and all other varieties of native-speaker English.

⭐ **Activity**

89

Transcribe phonemically, showing intonation groups and sentence stress, and using weak and contracted forms wherever possible.

Transcription passage 10

She tried to fancy what the flame of a candle looks like after the candle is blown out, since she could not remember ever having seen such a thing. After a while, finding that nothing more happened, she decided to go into the garden at once. But poor Alice! When she got to the door, she discovered that she had forgotten the little golden key, but when she went back to the table for it, she found she could not possibly reach it. Alice could see it quite plainly through the glass, and she tried her best to climb up one of the legs of the table, but it was too slippery. When she had tired herself out with trying, the poor little thing sat down and cried.

STRESS AND RHYTHM

B5

Introduction

We're moving on now from dealing with the segments – i.e. the vowel and consonant sounds – to tackling **supra-segmental** features, namely stress, rhythm (which we shall deal with in this section) and intonation (which we'll come to in Section B6). Unlike vowels and consonants, which are single speech sounds, supra-segmental features normally stretch over more than a single segment – possibly a syllable, a complete word or phrase, whole sentences, or even more.

We introduced the concept of stress in Section A3 and from then on we've been employing it for our transcriptions – so you should be quite used to the general idea. But now let's examine stress more closely so as to discover:

❑ what is implied in phonetic terms
❑ what role stress has to play in the sound system of English.

Below we shall employ the distinction first made in Section A3 between **word stress** (stress in the isolated word) and **sentence stress** (stress in connected speech).

What Is stress?

In English, four phonetic variables appear most significant as indicators of stress: **intensity**, **pitch variation**, **vowel quality** and **vowel duration**.

1   **Intensity** in physiological terms is the greater breath effort and muscular energy associated with stressed syllables. It's closely related to what is perceived by the listener as **loudness**.

2   **Pitch variation** appears to be, as far as English is concerned, the most important single factor in determining stress. In English, higher pitch tends to be associated with stronger stress. We shall come back to discuss pitch and intonation in more detail in Section B6.

3   **Vowel quality**, i.e. whether a vowel is central or peripheral (see Figure A6.13, Section A6), also determines stress. Take the English vowels in the noun *present* /ˈprezənt/ as opposed to the verb *(to) present* /prəˈzent/. The stressed syllables contain the peripheral vowel DRESS /e/, whereas the unstressed syllables have a central vowel /ə/. (Note that in the first word, it is possible for the vowel in the unstressed syllable to be further reduced to a syllabic consonant /n̩/; in the second word some speakers may use another non-peripheral vowel, KIT.)

Some degree of vowel centralisation in unstressed contexts is a feature of many languages; as a result, unstressed vowels sound somewhat 'fuzzy' as compared with those in stressed syllables, which retain distinct peripheral vowels on the edges of the vowel diagram. As you can see from our example above, what is unusual about English is that this process generally goes one stage further. The peripheral vowel in the unstressed syllable is actually replaced by another phoneme – most commonly by /ə/, sometimes by /ɪ/ or /ʊ/, or even a syllabic consonant, e.g. *attention* /əˈtenʃn̩/, *excitable* /ɪkˈsaɪtəbl̩/. The effect is termed **vowel reduction** and is one of the most characteristic features of the English sound system. Neglect of vowel reduction is one of the commonest errors of non-native learners of English, and results in unstressed syllables having undue prominence.

90

Make phonemic transcriptions of the following pairs, noting the occurrence of non-central vowels in stressed syllables against central vowels/syllabic consonants in unstressed syllables:

compound (noun)	*(to) compound*
progress (noun)	*(to) progress*
permit (noun)	*(to) permit*
frequent (adj.)	*(to) frequent*

---

4   **Duration of vowels** is an important factor in indicating stress. In English, other things being equal, vowels are shorter in unstressed than in stressed syllables, cf. English *sarcasm* [ˈsɑːkæzm̩], *sarcastic* [sɑˈkæːstɪk], *TV* [ti̯ˈviː].

Word stress

We shall distinguish two degrees of stress and 'unstressed', as in:

                              2   1
categorical /kætəgɒrɪkl̩/

The strongest stress is **primary** stress (indicated by 1 in the example); the next level, **secondary** stress (indicated by 2) – anything else is treated as **unstressed**. Primary stress is normally shown by a vertical mark ['] placed *above* the line (as we have been doing throughout this book). Where it's necessary to show a secondary stress, this is shown by a vertical mark *below* the line, thus: [,], e.g. ‚cate'gorical, ‚eccen'tricity, ‚expla'nation, 'cauli‚flower, 'goal‚keeper, etc. Note that unstressed syllables are left unmarked. For most purposes, it is sufficient to show only *primary* stress, and from now on we shall normally ignore secondary stresses and also leave them unmarked, e.g. cate'gorical, 'cauliflower, etc.

In certain languages, stress always falls on a syllable in a particular position in the word; we shall term this **language invariable stress**. For example, in Czech and Slovak, stress is on the first syllable; in Italian, Welsh and Polish, stress is on the penultimate (last but one); other languages, such as Farsi, have word-final stress. In certain languages, notably French and many Indian languages, such as Hindi and Gujarati, native speakers don't seem to consider stress to be of significance. In French, for example, although in isolated words stress is invariably on the final syllable, things are very different in the flow of speech (see Section C6).

In English and many other languages (e.g. German, Russian, Danish, Dutch), stress not only can occur at any point in the word but, crucially, is fixed for each individual word; this we may term **lexically designated stress**. In such languages, stress is furthermore of great importance for the phonetic structure of the word and cannot as a rule be shifted in connected speech.

Table B5.1 Characteristics of stressed and unstressed syllables

	Stressed	Unstressed
1 Intensity	Articulation with greater breath/muscular effort. Perceived as greater loudness	Less breath/muscular effort. Perceived as having less loudness
2 Pitch	Marked change in pitch	Syllables tend to follow the pitch trend set by previous stressed syllable
3 Vowel quality	May contain any vowel (except /ə/) Vowels have clear (peripheral) quality Glides have clearly defined second element	Generally have central vowels /ə ɪ ʊ/ or syllabic consonants Vowels may have centralised quality Glides tend to lose second element
4 Vowel duration	Vowels have full length	Vowels are considerably shorter

Despite the significance of stress, it's curious that few languages show stress in orthography (an exception is Spanish where any word which does not conform to regular Spanish stress patterns has the stressed syllable indicated by an acute accent, e.g. *teléfono* 'telephone'; see Section C6). In English, although it's often very difficult for a non-native to predict the primary stress from the written form of the word, there's no such help. Nevertheless, native speakers are generally able to guess the stress of unfamiliar words, and this implies that there is an underlying rule system in operation, even though the rules for stress are complex and have numerous exceptions. In fact, linguists have moved from the view once held, which claimed that there were few rules for predicting English stress, to a standpoint where some would say that stress is completely predictable. Furthermore, any prescriptive rule system which aimed at being even reasonably comprehensive would have to be tremendously complex.

Some word stress guidelines

From the point of view of non-native learners, it's probably best to consider English stress as being in part rule-governed, and only to concern themselves with learning the most useful and frequent patterns. Together with the guidelines which follow, the traditional advice to the non-native English learner of noting and memorising the stress pattern of words when you first meet them must still apply. Nevertheless, it is possible to note a few useful stress guidelines.

Words consisting of two or three syllables

Rough guide: primary stress on first syllable, e.g. 'culture, 'hesitant, 'motivate.

Longer words (four or more syllables)

Rough guide: there is a tendency for the **antepenultimate** syllable to have primary stress, i.e. the last but two, e.g. *credi'bility, com'municate, methodo'logical*, etc.

Prefix words

Rough guide: in shorter words beginning with a prefix, the primary stress typically falls on the syllable **following** the prefix: *inter'ference, in'tend, ex'pose, con'nect, un'veil*. **Exception**: a large number of nouns, e.g. 'output, 'interlude, 'congress, 'absence.

Numerous verbs with prefixes are distinguished from nouns by stress. We can term this **switch stress**. The noun generally has stress on the prefix, while the verb has stress on the syllable following the prefix:

Verb	Noun
(to) in'sert	(the) 'insert
(to) ex'cerpt	(the) 'excerpt
(to) con'duct	(the) 'conduct
(to) up'date	(the) 'update

Word endings

Certain word endings may act as stress attractors, falling into two groups.

Stress on ending itself

ade (nouns), **-ain** (verbs), **-ee** (nouns), **-eer**, **-esque** (adjs/nouns), **-esce** (verbs), **-ess** (verbs), **-ette** (nouns), **-ique** (nouns/adjs), **-oon**, **-self/-selves**, e.g. *pa'rade, ab'stain, interview'ee, engi'neer, gro'tesque, conva'lesce, as'sess, statu'ette, cri'tique, lam'poon, her'self, your'selves*.

Stress on syllable preceding ending

-ative, -itive, -cient, -ciency, -eous, -ety, -ian, -ial, -ic, -ical, -ident, -inal, -ion, -ital, -itous, -itude, -ity, -ive, -ual, -ular, -uous, -wards /wədz/, e.g. *al'ternative*, *'positive*, *'ancient*, *de'ficiency*, *ou'trageous*, *pro'priety*, *pe'destrian*, *super'ficial*, *melan'cholic*, *'radical*, *'accident*, *'criminal*, *o'ccasion*, *con'genital*, *infe'licitous*, *'multitude*, *incre'dulity*, *a'ttentive*, *per'petual*, *'secular*, *con'spicuous*, *'outwards*. Note that many of these lead to antepenultimate stressing.

Stress in English compounds

Incorrect stressing of compounds doesn't normally hinder intelligibility, yet this area is a very significant source of error – even for advanced non-native learners. To provide a complete guide is impossible since there are indeed many irregularities. But knowing a few simple guidelines can make compound stress very much easier for non-natives to learn. Even if you still have to use some guesswork, it allows you to get things right, perhaps, nine times out of ten.

Compounds in English are of two types: those which have their main stress on the *initial* element of the compound and those which have the main stress on the *final* element.

❏   **Initial Element Stress (IES)** with main stress on the first part of the compound, e.g. *'apple pip*, *'office boy*, *'Russian class*.
❏   **Final Element Stress (FES)** with main stress on the last element of the compound, e.g. *apple 'pie*, *office 'desk*, *Russian 'salad*. Note that many books term this 'double stress' or 'equal stress'.

Stress guidelines for compounds

(1) Word shape

Compounds written as *one word* nearly always have IES, but those written as *two words*, or with a *hyphen*, can be of either stress type.

(2) The Manufactures Rule (FES)

The most useful guides in terms of allocating stress in compounds are the 'Manufactures Rule' and the 'Location Rule'.

The **Manufactures Rule** implies that if the compound includes a material used in its manufacture (e.g. an *apple pie* is a pie made of apples), then FES applies, e.g. *apple 'pie*, *plum 'brandy*, *paper 'bag*, *cotton 'socks*, *diamond 'bracelet*. Compare non-manufactured items, which instead take IES, e.g. *'apple-tree*, *'paper clip*, *'plum stone*, *'cotton-reel*, *'diamond cutter*.

(3) Location Rule (FES)

The **Location Rule** describes the strong tendency for a compound to take FES if location is in some way involved.

(a) FES applies if the first element is the name of a country, region or town: e.g. *Turkish de'light*, *Russian rou'lette*, *Burmese 'cat*, *Scotch 'mist*, *Lancashire 'hotpot*, *Bermuda 'shorts*, *Brighton 'rock*, *London 'pride*.

(b) The vast majority of place-names, geographical features etc. have FES. This category includes:

- ❑ regions, towns, suburbs, districts, natural features, e.g. *East 'Anglia, New 'York, Castle 'Bromwich, Notting 'Hill, Silicon 'Valley, Land's 'End, Botany 'Bay*.
- ❑ bridges, tunnels, parks, public buildings and sports clubs, e.g. *Hyde 'Park, (the) Severn 'Bridge, Paddington 'Station, Carnegie 'Hall, Manchester U'nited*.
- ❑ all street names, except *street* itself, e.g. *Church 'Road, Trafalgar 'Square, Thorner 'Place, Churchill 'Way, Fifth 'Avenue*. Cf. *'Church Street, Tra'falgar Street*, etc.

(c) **Parts of a building** tend to have FES, e.g. *back 'door, bedroom 'window, garden 'seat, office 'chair*. **Exceptions**: compounds with *-room* are IES, e.g. *'living room, 'drawing room* (but *front 'room*).

(d) FES applies where **positioning** of any sort is involved, e.g. *left 'wing, Middle 'Ages, upper 'class, bottom 'line*. Time location also tends to FES, e.g. *morning 'star, afternoon 'tea, January 'sales, April 'showers, summer 'holiday*.

Activity

> **91**
>
> Think of more examples of the Location Rule. Can you think of any counter-examples not already mentioned?

Further useful guides related to the above

(1) The vast majority of **food items** have FES, e.g. *poached 'egg*. Note that these are often covered by either the 'Manufactures Rule' or the 'Location Rule', e.g. *Worcester 'sauce, Welsh 'rabbit, Christmas 'pudding, fish 'soup*. **Exceptions**: some items take IES because they can also be regarded as part of the living plant or animal, e.g. *'chicken liver, 'orange juice, 'vine leaves*. Other significant exceptions are: *-bread, -cake, -paste*, e.g. *'shortbread, 'Christmas cake, 'fish paste*.

(2) Names of **magazines**, **newspapers**, etc. have FES (many involve place or time and are covered by the 'Location Rule'), e.g. (the) *Daily 'Post, (the) Western 'Mail, (the) Straits 'Times, Vanity 'Fair, (the) New 'Statesman*.

Other stress patterns

(3) IES applies to compounds including the names of **academic subjects**, **skills**, etc, e.g. *'technical college, 'French teacher* (i.e. a person who teaches French).

(4) Nouns formed from **verb + particle** take IES, e.g. *'make-up, 'come-back, 'look-out, 'backdrop*. **Exceptions** are few, but note: *lie-'down, look-'round, set-'to*. These patterns have changed in the recent history of the language. See Section C5.

(5) Nouns ending in *-er* or *-ing + particle* take FES, e.g. *hanger-'on, passer-'by, washing-'up*.

(6) Compounds formed from **-ing + noun** are of two types:

❑   IES applies where *an activity is aided by the object* (i.e. a '*sewing machine* helps you to sew), e.g. '*sewing machine*, '*running shoes*, '*scrubbing brush*, '*washing machine*.
❑   FES applies where *a compound suggests a characteristic of the object, with no idea of aiding an activity*, e.g. *leading* '*article*, *running* '*water*, *casting* '*vote*, *sliding* '*scale*.

Sentence stress

When discussing transcription (Section A3) we noted that many of the potential stresses of word stress are lost in connected speech (i.e. sentence stress). The general pattern is that words which are likely to lose stress completely are those which convey relatively little information. These are the words important for the structure of the sentence, i.e. the **function words** (articles, auxiliary verbs, verb *be*, prepositions, pronouns, conjunctions). The **content words** (nouns, main verbs, adjectives, most adverbs), which carry a high information load, are normally stressed.

I've 'heard that 'Jack and 'Jane 'spent their 'holidays in Ja'maica.
FF   C   F   C   F   C   C   F   C   F   C

(C = content word, F = function word).

There are certain exceptions to the general pattern stated above:

1   Two sets of function words frequently receive stress:
    (a) *wh*-words where these form questions, e.g. *where, why, how*;
    (b) demonstratives, e.g. *this, that, these, those*.
    These particular function words often add significant information; the demonstratives also provide contrast (see below).
2   Function words normally receive stress when they indicate a contrast:

    I said give 'her a kiss, not 'him.

3   Prepositions are frequently stressed where a contrast is stated or implied:

    Would you call yourself a jazz lover?
    Actually, I know very little a'**bout** jazz. I prefer classical music.

    It is noteworthy that *repeated* lexical items are not generally stressed: 'There have been 'traffic jams in 'Dagenham and 'areas 'close to Dagenham.' A similar effect can be heard in items which are direct equivalents:

    Are you 'fond of 'chocolate then?
    'Given the 'chance, I'll 'eat 'tons of the stuff.

4   At more rapid tempo, the number of unstressed syllables will increase, and more lexical words will be unstressed, e.g. 'I've heard that 'Jack and 'Jane spent their 'holidays in Ja'maica'.

Stress and rhythm

Sentence stress is the basis of rhythm in English. Stressed syllables tend to occur at roughly equal intervals of time. This is because the unstressed syllables in between give the impression of being compressed if there are many and expanded if there are few.

Activity

92 ☉ **Track 24**

Say the following sentences (stressed syllables are indicated by __ ; unstressed by **.** .) Tap out the stresses with a ruler.

'Jimmy's 'bought a 'house near 'Glasgow.

— **.** — **.** — **.** — **.**

'Sally's been 'trying to 'send you an 'e-mail.

— **.** **.** — **.** **.** — **.** **.** — **.**

'Alastair 'claimed he was 'selling the 'company.

—**.** **.** — **.** **.** —**.** **.** — **.** **.**

Notice how the stressed syllables give the impression of coming at regular intervals; if you pronounce the words in a regular 'singsong' manner, it's possible to tap out the rhythm with a pencil. Try doing so. We term this effect **stress-timing**, and it's characteristic of languages such as English, Dutch, German, Danish, Russian, and many others.

Related to this feature is the variable length of vowels in polysyllabic words. Look at the following example, and notice how the syllables compress as more are added. (The lines underneath give an approximate indication of vowel length.)

The ban's back in place　　*The banner's back in place*　　*The banister's back in place*
/bænz/　　　　　　　　/'bænəz/　　　　　　　　/'bænɪstəz/

——　　　　　　　　　—**.**　　　　　　　　　— **.** **.**

Activity

93

Say these words, noting how the vowel tends to shorten somewhat as unstressed syllables are added.

——　　　　——　　　　—
mean　　*meaning*　　*meaningful*
see　　　*seedy*　　　*seedily*
red　　　*ready*　　　*readily*
myrrh　　*murmur*　　*murmuring*

Other languages work on a different principle, **syllable-timing**, giving the impression of roughly equal length for each syllable regardless of stressing. Take this example from French:

Je voudrais descendre au prochain arrêt s'il vous plaît ☉ Track 25
/ʒvudre dɛ'sãdr | o prɔʃɛ̃ a're | si vu 'ple |/

Here each syllable appears to have approximately equal time value, except for the final one of each group, which is extended. Other languages with a tendency to equal syllable length are: Spanish, Greek, Turkish, Polish, Hindi, Gujarati.

Stress-timing appears to operate for all types of English spoken by native speakers, possibly with the exception of those strongly influenced by Creoles, such as the English of the West Indies. Some types of English employed as a second language (e.g. the English used by many Indians and Africans) absorb the syllable-timing of the mother tongue of the speakers, but such varieties can be very difficult for others to understand. As has been shown, stress-timing is achieved mainly by lengthening certain vowels at the expense of others: vowels tend to be lengthened in stressed syllables and shortened in unstressed syllables.

Activity

94

Transcribe phonemically, showing intonation groups and sentence stress, and using weak and contracted forms wherever possible.

Transcription passage 11

'Come on, there's no use crying like that!' said Alice to herself, rather sharply. 'I advise you to leave off this minute!' She generally gave herself very good advice (though she very seldom followed it), and sometimes she scolded herself so severely as to bring tears into her eyes; and once she remembered trying to box her own ears for having cheated herself in a game of croquet she was playing against herself, for this curious child was very fond of pretending to be two people. 'But it's no use now,' thought poor Alice, 'to pretend to be two people! Why, there's hardly enough of me left to make *one* respectable person!'

SPEECH MELODY

B6

Pitch movement

Variation in speech melody is an essential component of normal human speech. Indeed, if it's absent for any reason listeners reject the speech and claim it to be literally inhuman ('robot-like'). This is a major problem which has to be faced by a person who has had the larynx removed owing to cancer or some other disease. Equipment is available which can produce a voicing buzz but this as yet still cannot mimic realistically the pitch variation of natural speech.

Pitch refers to human perception, i.e. whether one perceives sounds as 'high' or 'low'. The most important physical factor in determining pitch is the **frequency** (i.e. speed of vibration) of the vocal folds; in general terms, the higher the frequency, the higher the perceived pitch and vice versa.

Many students find it difficult to judge whether pitch is rising or falling; the following simple analogy may help. The engine of a motor car when 'revving up' to start produces a series of *rising* pitches. When the car is cruising on the open road, the engine pitch is more or less *level*. On coming to a halt, the engine stops with a rapid *fall* in pitch.

Activity

---

95 ⊙ Track 26

Imitate the **pitches** just described, using a prolonged [aː] vowel.

(1) Rises ('revving up to start')

(2) Level pitch ('open road')

(3) Fall ('coming to a halt')

Tone languages

Pitch variation has an important role to play in communication, adding meaning additional to that conveyed by the segmental phonemes. We can distinguish two significant ways in which pitch functions, namely (1) **(lexical) tone** and (2) **intonation**.

In many languages, it is possible to use pitch differences to distinguish the *dictionary meaning* of words. This function of pitch is known as **tone** and such languages are termed **tone languages**. Tone languages may make use of different numbers of pitch levels. Two levels (high and low) or three (high, mid and low) are common.

Activity

---

96 ⊙ Track 27

Try imitating these examples from Ewe, a three-tone language spoken in Ghana and Togo. Note the marking system commonly used for such African languages: (ˊ) indicates high tone, (ˋ) indicates low tone; mid tones are left unmarked.

tsí tsí [‾ ‾] 'ladle'		*kú kú* [‾ ‾] 'hat'	
tsì tsì [_ _] 'growth'		*kù kù* [_ _] 'digging'	
		kù kú [_ ‾] 'dying'	
àtá [_ ‾] 'thigh'		*tó* [‾] 'ear'	
atá [– ‾] 'you will draw'		*tò* [_] 'buffalo'	

Languages like these, which use a tone system of two or three significant pitch levels, are called **register tone** languages. In the Far East, **contour tone** languages are more common. These chiefly employ falling and rising pitches; examples are to be found in the languages of China, including the most widely spoken variety, Mandarin Chinese.

---

97 ⊙ **Track 28**

Say the following words in Mandarin Chinese. The pitch pattern is indicated:

han	[ˉ]	'foolish'	*han*	[ˇ]	'rare'
han	[ˊ]	'cold'	*han*	[ˋ]	'perspiration'

The tones of a tone language may be analysed in a way comparable to the segmental phonemes, giving **tonemes** and **allotones.**

It is thought that most of the world's languages employ tone, and certainly, the vast majority of African, Far Eastern and American Indian languages are tonal. Europe in fact is rather odd in having few tone languages. Nevertheless, these do to an extent exist: Serbian, Croatian, Norwegian and Swedish all have in part a tonal element.

Intonation variation

Most European languages do not use pitch to indicate dictionary meaning. For instance, you can say the English word *yes* on a number of different pitch patterns:

╲	╱	╲╱
yes	yes	yes

Yet it continues to mean *yes* and can't be made to mean anything else. Moreover, we can't distinguish homophones, such as English *hare, hair*; French *foi, foie, fois* 'faith, liver, time'; or German *Rat, Rad* 'advice, wheel' by means of pitch. In English (and the vast majority of European languages), pitch variation is confined to **intonation.**

Intonation tunes operate over an extent greater than a single word, usually over complete clauses or sentences. Intonation is crucial to human communication, adding types of meaning additional to what is supplied by the words themselves. Think how often you hear people come out with statements like: 'It wasn't so much *what* he said – it was more the *way he said it.*'

Intonation works differently in different languages. One of the first things one notices about a French person speaking English is that the intonation sounds very characteristically French (and therefore non-English). A classic TV series (*The Muppet Show*) frequently featured a comic character, the 'Swedish cook', where the whole joke rested on stereotypical mock-Swedish intonation. Furthermore, each accent of a language has its own particular intonation. If you are at all familiar with the British Isles, you'll probably already be aware that accents such as Welsh English, Birmingham English, Geordie (North East) and Irish English all have different and easily recognisable types of intonation. Worldwide, we find the same thing over and over again. To give just two examples: many people are aware that the English of the southern states of the USA differs strikingly from General American in terms of intonation; less well known perhaps is that in New Zealand English there are distinct intonation differences between some South Island varieties.

Obviously we can't deal with all this variation in a single section. Fortunately, there is no real need to. You already know that there are obvious differences between the vowels and consonants of different English varieties, and yet there is also great overall similarity so that there are normally no problems of intelligibility. In the same way, although there are notable differences in the detail of different English intonation systems, there is enough overall similarity for people to be able to 'tune in' to a new system and recognise many – if not all – of its implications. The tuning-in process is sometimes termed 'normalisation'. We shall concentrate on describing some of the most important aspects of the intonation of British NRP, and mention other varieties only in passing (in Sections C1–C4).

The structure of intonation patterns in English

Marking systems for intonation

We employ the following **interlinear** marking system for intonation. Pitch patterns are indicated between an upper and lower line corresponding to the highest and lowest normal pitch range of the voice. (We are ignoring an effect known as *declination*, i.e. the tendency for pitch patterns to compress towards the end of each utterance.) Stressed syllables are shown by lines (—) and unstressed syllables by dots (•). Thicker lines (▬) can be used to show stressed syllables with particular prominence. The interlinear system is useful because it conveys a fairly clear impression of the rise and fall of pitch.

He insisted on cooking an omelette.

The complementary **in-text** marking system is a much more economical means of notation. In this case, as the name implies, the pitch information is conveyed by little marks placed within the actual text. By picking out the essential intonation features and ignoring the rest, the pattern becomes clearer and is easier to write and quicker to read.

He in˚sisted on cooking an ˋomelette

Intonation group division

The basic unit of speech melody is the **intonation group**, which is a complete pattern of intonation. As stated in Section A3, intonation group boundaries are indicated by single bars |; a double bar || can be used to indicate the end of a sentence.

I'd obviously broken my leg | so I needed to see a doctor.||

Intonation groups often correspond to a grammatical clause. However, much variation is possible. For instance, a noun phrase may have a complete group to itself. The longer the noun phrase, the more likely this is to happen.

(1)   This particular part of Pembrokeshire | is at its most beautiful in the spring.||

Or an adverb, or adverbial phrase, may have its own group:

(2)   Regrettably | paedophiles are unlikely ever to reform.||

The presence of an intonation group boundary can occasionally be crucial for meaning:

(3a) (Do you really want to leave home?)   I don't know.‖
                                             /aɪ ˈdəʊnt ˈnəʊ/ ‖

(3b) (Do you really want to leave home?)   I don't. ‖ No. ‖
                                             /aɪ ˈdəʊnt ‖ ˈnəʊ/ ‖

Where an intonation group boundary occurs, it is possible to pause – although in the flow of speech these pauses are often omitted. Intonation group boundaries are often (but not always) indicated in the writing by punctuation, e.g. full stops, commas and dashes.

The nucleus and nucleus location

In any complete intonation group, one stressed syllable will stand out as being more prominent than the rest. The syllable often has a marked change in pitch, and is usually longer and louder. Take this example:

Sophie adored her gorgeous   new motorbike.

The marked pitch fall on /ˈməʊ/, combined with its extra duration and loudness, high-lights the syllable, giving the whole word *motorbike* prominence in the sentence. We call this most prominent of the stressed syllables the (intonation) **nucleus**. (Be sure not to confuse this use of 'nucleus' with the obligatory element in syllable structure; see Section B1.) From now on in our examples we shall indicate the intonation nucleus in bold. Anything occurring after the nucleus follows the pitch pattern established already by it, i.e if the nucleus is falling the subsequent syllables will be low level; if the nucleus is rising they will continue to rise.

The nucleus is frequently (though not always) the stressed syllable of the last con-tent word in the intonation group – this is often (not always) the direct object, as in the example above. If the nucleus is part of an earlier word this usually indicates a special *focusing* effect. This focusing function of **nucleus location** is examined below (p. 124).

The pitch pattern carried by the nucleus is termed **nuclear tone** (not to be confused with 'lexical tone' in the sense of tone languages). Unlike the variables considered so far, nuclear tone shows considerable differences both between one language and another, and often between different accents of the same language. Let us consider the possible tones carried by the nucleus in NRP English, using the monosyllable *green* as an illustration.

Falls

High fall   ⟍   Low fall   ⟍
            ˋGreen   ˎGreen

Falls have been found to be by far the commonest type of nuclear tone. Research has shown that falling patterns account for roughly 70 per cent of all types used in conversation. We symbolise the high fall thus: (ˋ). A high fall is a swoop down from high to low (you can sometimes hear a tiny rise in pitch at the start before the fall). A low fall (ˎ) has much less pitch movement.

Any syllables after the nucleus (sometimes called the **tail**) follow the pitch pattern established by it. In the case of falls, these syllables are all on a low pitch.

Activity

98 ☺ Track 30

Say the following words on a high fall:

`Love `Lovely `Lovingly       `Bit `Bitter `Bitterly
`Sum `Summer `Summary       `Wart `Water `Watery

Now on a low fall:

‚Love ‚Lovely ‚Lovingly   ‚Bit ‚Bitter ‚Bitterly
‚Sum ‚Summer ‚Summary   ‚Wart ‚Water ‚Watery

Activity

99 ☺ Track 31

Say the following words on a high fall. Cue sentence: *What was Samantha's food like?*

`Great. `Fine. `Dire. `Lousy. `Dreadful. `Wonderful. `Miserable. Su`perb. Truly a`bysmal.

Now on a low fall:

‚Great. ‚Fine. ‚Dire. ‚Lousy. ‚Dreadful. ‚Wonderful. ‚Miserable. Su‚perb. Truly a‚bysmal.

Rises

Low rise ⟋   High rise ⟋
   ‚Green   ′Green

Rising patterns are much less common than falling ones. The most frequent rise has a pitch movement from low to mid, and is symbolised thus (‚). If there are syllables following the nucleus, the rise in pitch will be spread over all of them, i.e. following the pitch pattern established by it. The less common high rise begins mid and rises to high.

Activity

100 ☺ Track 32

Say the following words first on a low rise and then on a high rise. Cue sentence: *Guess what we're having for dinner!*

‚Lamb? ‚Soup? ‚Stew? ‚Fish? ‚Salmon? ‚Chicken? ‚Curry? ‚Pizza? ‚Hamburgers?
′Lamb? ′Soup? ′Stew? ′Fish? ′Salmon? ′Chicken? ′Curry? ′Pizza? ′Hamburgers?

In addition to simple falls and rises, we also find two 'broken' tones, i.e. the fall-rise and the rise-fall.

Fall-rise

Fall-rise $\vee$

ᵛGreen

The **fall-rise** nucleus, symbolised (ᵛ), moves from high to low to mid. Syllables after the nucleus continue the rise.

⭐ **Activity**

101 ☉ Track 33

Say the following words with a fall-rise. Cue sentence: *Jack speaks fluent French.*

ᵛRussian. ᵛSwedish. ᵛDanish. ᵛGerman. ᵛPolish. Swaᵛhili.

Rise-fall

Rise fall $\wedge$

ᐱGreen

The **rise-fall** involves a pitch movement from mid to high to low, and is symbolised (ᐱ). Syllables after the nucleus continue low. It is the least common of the nuclear tones mentioned here and indeed is absent from some varieties of English (e.g. certain of the accents of northern England).

⭐ **Activity**

102 ☉ Track 34

Say the following words and phrases on a rise-fall. Cue sentence: *Was that wine any good?*

ᐱGreat. ᐱFine. ᐱSuper. ᐱLovely. Fanᐱtastic. Aᐱstonishing. Unbeᐱlievable. Quite aᐱmazing. Out of this ᐱworld.

Syllables before the nucleus

The nature of the nucleus is the crucial factor in intonation. But there are often syllables which come *before* the nucleus, and we also have to take some account of these. Many intonation patterns in English either (1) begin on a fairly high-pitched syllable or (2) after a very few low-pitched unstressed or weakly stressed syllables have a jump up to a high-pitched syllable, as illustrated below. The portion between the high-pitched syllable (the **commencement**) and the nucleus is called the **head**. The commencement is marked with a high circle.

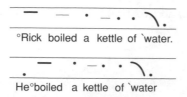

Although not as prominent as the nucleus, the commencement is usually relatively strongly stressed. After the high-pitched commencement, any other syllables before the nucleus usually fall slightly in pitch. Sometimes, but less commonly, the pre-nuclear pitches are all low-pitched, or may rise slightly from a low pitch. We shall for the most part ignore these differences, concentrating our attention on the far more important nuclear pitch pattern.

Functions of intonation in English

Intonation has four important linguistic functions:

(1) **Focusing function**, by which the speaker focuses on the most significant information by means of the location of the nucleus. As stated above, the nucleus is typically at the end of the intonation group. Shift to an earlier syllable is often used to highlight some information elsewhere in the utterance. This can easily be demonstrated (nucleus shown in **bold** type).

Sophie adored her gorgeous new **mo**torbike. (Neutral.)
Sophie adored her gorgeous **new** motorbike. (Not the old one.)
Sophie adored her **gorgeous** new motorbike. (Not the horrid one.)
Sophie adored **her** gorgeous new motorbike. (Not anybody else's motorbike.)
Sophie a**dored** her gorgeous new motorbike. (She didn't hate it.)
Sophie adored her gorgeous new motorbike. (It was Sophie – not Delia or Nigella.)

Activity

> **103**
>
> Although all the above are possibilities, some are perhaps more likely than others. Take a number of sentences out of an English novel and try moving the nucleus around. What sort of words are difficult to focus on in this way?

Nucleus location functions as a focusing device, not only in English but also in many other languages, e.g. German, Spanish, Italian and many more. However, some languages make relatively little use of this feature; French regularly has prominence on the last syllable of the intonation group, and consequently greater use is made of grammar and vocabulary as a means of focusing.

A similar focusing effect is to be found in the location of the commencement syllable. Once again, this stands out from the other syllables to be found at the beginning of the intonation group, and normally serves to focus on what is, for the speaker, the second most significant word in the utterance.

(2) **Attitudinal function** is what allows speakers constantly to superimpose an attitude on top of the bare semantic content of what is being said. This is one of the most important functions of intonation and why any written text must be deficient in at least one respect to the spoken word. When reading out loud, the reader automatically superimposes a series of attitudes on the author's words (not always necessarily those intended by the original writer). This is one of the most important factors in allowing different interpretations of prose, drama and poetry.

We can only broadly connect attitudes to the nuclear tones since so much depends on context and on the basic semantic content of the words in the intonation group. Nevertheless, two tones – **fall-rise** and **rise-fall** – seem noticeably attitudinally marked, i.e. these tones are inherently laden with certain implications:

Fall-rise: doubt, correction, reservation, appealing to the listener to reconsider.
Rise-fall: impressed, arrogant, confident, self-satisfied, mocking, putting down.

It is also possible to make the following broad distinctions:

Two tones – **high fall** and **low rise** – can be regarded as neutral.
Two tones – **low fall** and **high rise** – have a strengthening function. These tones tend
    to add to, emphasise or exaggerate a speaker's basic attitude.

(3) **Grammatical function**, which permits speakers to distinguish certain syntactic relationships, e.g. phrase and clause boundaries, question versus statement. One occasional example of the grammatical function of intonation in English is where a grammatical statement is converted to a question. Compare:

> You're °going to `Canterbury.
> You're °going to ˌCanterbury?

In some languages (notably French) a rising intonation pattern is probably the most frequent way of producing questions in colloquial speech (although it is possible to produce questions by other means):

> (Falling intonation) Vous allez à Dijon. ('You're going to Dijon.') ☻ Track 35
> (Rising intonation) Vous allez à Dijon? ('Are you going to Dijon?')

Perhaps rather more common in English is the reverse effect where a grammatical question takes on the meaning of an emphatic statement or exclamation. Compare:

> (We might be able to go to Brazil.) °Wouldn't that be exˌ**pen**sive? (question)
> (We might be able to go to Brazil.) °Wouldn't that be `**won**derful! (emphatic statement)

What might also be considered a further grammatical function of intonation is illustrated in the section on English tag-questions below.

(4) **Discourse function**, which covers such diverse matters as the organisation of conversation between two or more speakers (e.g. signals for turn-taking), the indication of speaker/listener relationship (e.g. in relation to power and authority) and the

indication of new versus old information. In this context, we can broadly allocate the nuclear tones to two categories on the basis of whether they are (terminally) falling or rising:

Falling tones (i.e. high fall, low fall and rise-fall) suggest: (a) finality, (b) unloading of information.

Rising tones (i.e. high rise, low rise and fall-rise) indicate: (a) non-finality, (b) information is sought or anticipated, rather than unloaded.

Consequently, we usually find that completed statements and commands involve falling tones, whereas *yes–no* questions and introductory non-final clauses more typically have rising nuclei, e.g.:

Statements:	Fanny °carefully repeated the in`structions.
Commands:	`Tell me about it.
Yes-no questions:	°Will it be ready by ‚Friday?
Wh-questions:	°What's the best way to roast a `goose?
Non-final clauses:	Al°though Oliver promised to ᵛhelp | (he let us `down).

However, these are broad categorisations and there are notable exceptions, often reflecting a combination of discourse and attitudinal function.

To take one example, *wh*-questions (beginning with a *wh*-word like *what*, *why*, *where* and also *how*) may be said with one of two patterns: either with a rising pattern, which makes them sound friendly, engaging and leading on to more; or with a falling pattern (sounding more distant, business-like and as if there is a conclusive answer to the question). Compare the same set of sentences, firstly with falling patterns:

°What's your `name?
°Where do you `live?
°What were you thinking of `doing this evening?

This tends to sound distant and businesslike. It would not be inappropriate for a policeman interviewing a suspect.

And now the same sequence with rising patterns:

°What's your ‚name?
°Where do you ‚live?
°What were you thinking of ‚doing this evening?

This sounds far more friendly, as opposed to interrogation, and could quite easily be a stage in making a date!

The overall correlation of rises with non-finality and falls with finality can be shown by an intonation pattern often heard in lists, e.g.:

We've invited ‚Delia, \| ‚Fanny, \| ‚Jamie \| and °all the `neighbours.

Below we shall look at different types of utterance – statements, commands, *wh*-questions, *yes–no* questions – and outline which type of intonation pattern tends to be associated with them.

Statements

Unmarked (default) pattern

Falling tunes are most frequent with **statements**.

(1) °Delia's bought a turkey from some guy in `Swindon. ☺ Track 29

(2) It's really °well worth a `visit. ☺ Track 29

(3) (When did Keith leave?) A `month or so ago. ☺ Track 29

Note that a low fall could also be used in each of these cases. However, the low fall is cooler and more distant.

(4) A ˌmonth or so ago. ☺ Track 29

> **★ Activity**
>
> ### 104 ☺ Track 36
>
> Practise the following sentences with head + high fall. Cue sentence: *Why did old Grigson leave so early?*
>
> He °claimed he was `tired. He °wanted to go `home. He was as °drunk as a `skunk. He had aⁿnother ap`pointment. He °couldn't stand that awful `music.
>
> Now with head + low fall:
>
> He °claimed he was ˌtired. He °wanted to go ˌhome. He was as °drunk as a ˌskunk. He had aⁿnother apˌpointment. He °couldn't stand that awful ˌmusic.

Other patterns

If a rising rather than a falling tune is used with a statement (often with no head), an element of non-finality is imposed on the utterance. Sometimes it will imply that the speaker is questioning a statement:

(5) It's °well worth a ˌvisit? (Well, I don't think so.) ☺ Track 29

(6) °Delia's bought a turkey from some guy in ˌSwindon? (How could she be so gullible?) ☺ Track 29

Statements said on a fall-rise add reservation, doubt, disagreement. They are used as a polite means of contradicting or correcting a speaker:

(7) (Floyd arrived this morning.) ᵛYesterday. A ᵛmonth aₒgo (all implying disagreement or doubt). ☺ Track 29

(8) (Did you finish the report?) I've °finished writing the introᵛduction . . . (implying 'but I still need to do the rest'). ☺ Track 29

If the statement consists of several intonation groups, usually only the last will have a fall (i.e. completed utterance). The remainder will be said on a rise or a fall-rise (implying non-finality, 'more to come'). (See further below on intonation sequences (non-finality).)

(9) If you °want a ᵛgood job | it's im°portant to possess `management skills. ☺ Track 29

Commands

Unmarked (default) pattern

Commands are often said with a falling pattern. This is particularly the case if a superior is talking to an inferior (e.g. teacher to student, parent to child, boss to employee) and if there is no possibility of discussing the issue.

(10) °Shut the `window. ☺ Track 29

(11) °Stack the books on those `shelves. ☺ Track 29

Other patterns

Commands said on a rising nucleus express a gentler, warmer tone, with a kind of deference to the other person's feelings. The discourse effect given is one of non-finality, i.e. that something will soon follow:

(12) °Meet us on ‚Thursday. (And then we can sort it out later.) ☺ Track 29

(13) °Don't ‚worry. (It'll be alright.) ☺ Track 29

Wh-questions

Unmarked (default) pattern

If the utterance is neutral or business-like, the most common pattern for *wh*-questions is a fall – often a low fall:

(14) How can we °possibly pay this ‚bill? ☺ Track 29

(15) Who on °earth can we ask to ‚help? ☺ Track 29

Other patterns

Wh-questions frequently have rising tunes. As in the case of commands, a rise makes the utterance friendlier and more intimate. More account is taken of the other person's feelings than is the case with a fall:

(16) °How can I ‚help you? ☺ Track 29

(17) °When shall we next ‚meet? ☺ Track 29

Yes–no questions

Unmarked (default) pattern

The commonest pattern for *yes–no* questions is a rise:

(18) Has °Prue booked her flight to ‚Paris? ☺ Track 29

Activity

105 ☺ Track 37

Practise the following sentences with low rises. Cue sentence: *We saw Jim the other day*.

°Has he ‚changed? °Is he still married to ‚Lisa? °Did he eventually get a new ‚job? °Had he cut his ‚hair? °Has he moved to ‚Denmark? °Is he still playing ‚football?

Other patterns

If *yes–no* questions are said on a falling pattern they give the impression of being more like exclamatory statements.

(19) Do we °have any `**choice**? (It doesn't look as if we have.) ☺ Track 29

Table B6.1 Patterns of intonation

Utterance type	Default pattern	Other patterns
Statements	Fall	(1) Rise (adds non-finality or questioning) (2) Fall-rise (adds non-finality with an implication of an additional but unspoken message)
Commands	Fall	Rise (turns command into request)
***Wh*-questions**	Fall	Rise (adds warmth, interest)
***Yes–no* questions**	Rise	Fall (turns question into exclamation)

Summary

Table B6.1 summarises the main patterns found in various types of utterance.

Intonation group sequences

Up till now we have concentrated mainly on the isolated intonation group. In this unit, the types of pattern employed in certain *intonation group sequences* are discussed.

Non-finality

As has already been stated, rising nuclei (i.e. low rise, high rise, fall-rise) have a discourse implication of non-finality. Consequently, such patterns are often used as lead-ins to further information:

(20) Ken was °driving home from ˌ**work**, | when he °suddenly had this great iˌ**dea**. ☺ Track 29

(21) On the ˅**other** hand | it would be °wrong to conclude that Elizabeth was in any `**danger**. ☺ Track 29

Lists

As mentioned earlier, lists provide a very clear illustration of the discourse divide of finality versus non-finality. Here, one common pattern is for all the items, except the last, to have a series of low rises. The last is said on a fall.

(22) You can have ˌ**pasta**, | ˌ**rice**, | boiled poˌ**tatoes** | or `**chips**. ☺ Track 29

(23) (What did Alan buy?) A ˌ**book**, | a ˌ**pen**, | and ten `**minidiscs**. ☺ Track 29

Parenthetic intonation

Another discourse effect is parenthetic intonation. Certain intonation groups may be said on a sustained low pitch, if they contain information which could be regarded as additional and possibly enclosed in brackets (parentheses). The intonation pattern frequently used in these cases is a low rise preceded by low-level syllables:

(24) After having °watched the ‚play | something I didn't do very ‚willingly | I'm con°vinced of Marguerite's `talent. ☺ Track 29

Parenthetic intonation is especially common in more formal registers, e.g. speeches, lectures, broadcast talks, and in reading aloud.

Tag-questions and tag-type responses

We shall examine this area in somewhat greater detail since it is something peculiar to English and follows regular patterns. It is typical of all varieties of native English, and so the advanced non-native learner needs at least a passive knowledge of what is implied by these.

System of tags

Tag-questions are short yes–no type questions attached to the main statement. They repeat the information through an appropriate auxiliary verb plus a pronoun, e.g.

Peter's seen a jaguar, hasn't he?

No other major language appears to possess corresponding structures. Their equivalents are stylised exclamations, mostly said on a rising tune, e.g.

French *n'est ce pas?*
Standard German *nicht?*
Southern German *gel?*
Spanish *verdad?*
Dutch *hè? niet?*
Danish *ikke? vel?*

These set phrases lack both the syntactic and intonational complexity of the English tags.

Balanced and unbalanced tags

The typical pattern for a tag-question is that if the main statement is positive, the tag is negative and vice versa. These we term **balanced tags**.

Peter's seen a jaguar | hasn't he?
   (positive)   (negative)

Peter hasn't seen a jaguar | has he?
    (negative)   (positive)

A less common type is the **unbalanced tag**, i.e. either positive/positive:

Fiona's offered to pay, | has she?

or, more rarely, negative/negative (often preceded by 'so'):

So Rick wouldn't acknowledge his mistake, | wouldn't he?

Nucleus location in tags

In all tags, the nucleus *invariably* falls on the verb – *never* on the pronoun. An intonation pattern such as the following, with the pronoun as the nucleus, is completely unacceptable in English, but is sometimes produced in error by non-native learners:

* °Peter's seen a `jaguar, | hasn't ˏhe?

Intonation in balanced tag-questions

Unbalanced tags are typically (not invariably) uttered with rising patterns. Balanced tags are regularly said on one of two main intonation patterns, giving two different meanings which can be viewed as an example of the grammatical function of intonation. If the tag rises, as in example (25) below, the implication is that the speaker is not really certain of the statement (perhaps 60 per cent). It is, in meaning terms, equivalent to *a true question*.

(25) °Peter's seen a `jaguar, | ˏhasn't he? ☻ Track 29

If the tag has a fall pattern, as in example (26) below, this indicates a far greater confidence in what the speaker is saying (perhaps 90 per cent). Despite the conventional question mark, the falling tag is here not so much a true question as a request for confirmation of the statement.

(26) °Peter's seen a `jaguar, | `hasn't he? ☻ Track 29

 ✪ Activity

---

106 ☻ **Track 38**

Say the following tag-questions using first a fall and then a rise.

He missed the train, `didn't he?
We don't owe them any money, `do we?
Nicola wouldn't do that, `would she?

He missed the train, ˏdidn't he?
We don't owe them any money, ˏdo we?
Nicola wouldn't do that, ˏwould she?

Tag-type responses

A very frequent feature of native-speaker conversational English is the occurrence of brief responses of a similar structure to the tags just discussed, but in this case a positive sentence requires a positive response and vice versa. These **tag-type responses** are of special interest since, because they lack any real semantic content, they allow the significance of intonation to be displayed most clearly.

(27) (Mrs Beeton's moved to France) ˏ**Has** she? (Oliver couldn't have written this book) ˏ**Couldn**'t he? ☻ Track 29

(28) (Mrs Beeton's moved to France) `**Has** she? (Oliver couldn't have written this book) `**Couldn**'t he? ☻ Track 29

Tag responses with falling nuclei indicate acceptance of what has been said. High falls give a far more sympathetic acceptance than low falls, which may have undertones of hostility and lack of interest. Compare the responses in (29) with those of (28):

(29) (Mrs Beeton's moved to France) ˏHas she? (Oliver couldn't have written this book) ˏCouldn't he? ⊙ Track 29

The broken tones have an inherent heavily laden attitudinal function. The fall-rise is employed to indicate doubt, correction or polite disagreement:

(30) (Mrs Beeton's moved to France) ᵛHas she? (Oliver couldn't have written this book) ᵛCouldn't he? ⊙ Track 29

Activity

107 ⊙ Track 39

Try to hear whether the tag-type response in the examples below is on (1) high fall, (2) low fall, (3) low rise, (4) fall-rise.

(Rebecca said she's moving in with David.) Did she?
(Mrs Craddock's a silly old fool.) Is she?
(The neighbours will look after your hamsters.) Will they?

Activity

108

Transcribe phonemically, showing intonation groups and sentence stress, and using weak and contracted forms wherever possible.

Transcription passage 12
Soon her eye fell on a little glass box that was lying under the table: she opened it, and found in it a very small cake, on which the words 'Eat me' were beautifully marked out in currants. 'Well I'll eat it,' said Alice, 'and if it makes me grow larger, I can reach the key; and if it makes me grow smaller, I can creep under the door: so either way I'll get into the garden, and I don't care which happens!' She ate a little bit, and said anxiously to herself, 'Which way?', holding her hand on the top of her head to feel which way it was growing; and she was quite surprised to find that she remained the same size. To be sure, this is what generally happens when one eats cake; but Alice had got so much into the way of expecting nothing but weird things to happen, that it seemed quite dull and stupid for life to go on in the common way. So she set to work, and very soon finished off the cake.

Section C
EXPLORATION

C1 ACCENT VARIATION – GENERAL AMERICAN

Types of variation found in accents

The basic set of NRP reference vowels (Section A2) is not adequate to deal with all the features encountered in other English varieties. For this purpose, we've used five additional keywords: BATH, JUICE, FORCE, NORTH, *happy*. Our full list of keywords is printed in Table C1.1.

It has become common practice to classify pronunciation variation between accents along the following lines (cf. Wells 1982: 72–80).

Systemic variation: where one accent possesses more or fewer phonemes than another accent in a particular part of the sound system.

❑ Northern English lacks the contrast /ʌ – ʊ/ in STRUT/FOOT; such varieties have no phoneme /ʌ/ as found in other types of English.
❑ South Wales English has an additional contrast in GOOSE/JUICE with an extra phoneme /ɪu/ not found in other accents.
❑ Scottish, Irish and some General American have an extra /ʍ – w/ contrast: e.g. *which – witch*.

Distributional variation accounts for cases where two accents may have the same system but where environments in which a particular phoneme may occur differ. Note that distributional variation is not restricted to a particular set of words but operates 'across the board' as an integral part of the phonological system of the accents concerned. There are (in principle) no exceptions to the rule.

Examples of distributional variation are:

❑ In rhotic accents (see Section B2), **r** is pronounced wherever it occurs in the spelling. In non-rhotic accents, it is pronounced only before a vowel.
❑ In the *happy* words, e.g. *happy, pretty, Julie, committee* etc., Scots, Northern Ireland, Yorkshire, Lancashire (except Merseyside) and traditional RP select KIT; most other accents (e.g. London, Birmingham, General American, Australian and most NRP) select FLEECE.

Table C1.1 Keywords for reference vowels

KIT	FLEECE	FACE
DRESS	SQUARE	GOAT
TRAP	PALM	PRICE
LOT	THOUGHT	MOUTH
STRUT	NURSE	CHOICE
FOOT	GOOSE	NEAR
BATH	JUICE	CURE
bonus	NORTH	
happy	FORCE	

Source: Table adapted from Wells (1982: 120); the keyword JUICE is additional to Wells's categorisation.

Lexical variation: where the phoneme chosen for a word or a specific set of words is different in one accent as compared with another. This can affect either a very large group of words (such as our first two examples below), or a very small group (as in our third example), or even a single word (our fourth example).

❑ In the BATH words, e.g. *bath, pass, dance,* etc. (see Section B3), northern England and Midland accents generally select the TRAP vowel; so do most other varieties worldwide, e.g. American. Cockney and NRP, however, select the PALM vowel. Australians vary.

❑ In words spelt **or**, most varieties of English select the THOUGHT vowel. However, some accents retain what was formerly a widespread distinction between two groups known as the FORCE and NORTH words. The FORCE category contains words like *force, store, sport* and also *hoarse, course* spelt with an extra letter. The NORTH words include *north, cork, absorb, horse.* The manner in which these groups are differentiated varies, but in Scottish English, for example, FORCE words have the GOAT vowel while NORTH words have the same vowel as in LOT, giving /fors/ and /nɔrθ/.

❑ In parts of Lancashire, words spelt *-ook* such as *book, took, look* have the GOOSE vowel. In other English varieties, GOOSE only occurs in a few examples of this type (e.g. *snooker, spook*). Otherwise FOOT is found.

❑ For the second vowel in *tomato*, North American (including General American) selects the FACE vowel. Other varieties generally choose PALM.

There is no easy way of predicting which words will be susceptible to lexical variation. Furthermore, speech habits may vary within one accent. For example, NRP speakers vary in their choice of vowel for orthographic **o** in words such as *constable, accomplish*. Most people use the STRUT vowel, but some choose LOT. The distinction between lexical and distributional variation is not always clear-cut. A good example of this is the case of what can be termed '/j/-dropping' in American varieties. Even though it is in principle possible to state a clear rule for the occurrence of this feature, there is in fact much variation on an individual speaker level.

Realisational variation: all variation which is not covered by any of the categories above will relate to the realisation of phonemes:

❑ FACE and GOAT are narrow diphthongs or steady-state vowels in Scots, Irish, Welsh and Northern English accents, but wide diphthongs in Cockney, Birmingham, Australian, New Zealand and most of the accents of the southern USA.

❑ Initial /p t k/ are aspirated in most accents (including NRP and General American) but are unaspirated in Lancashire, South African and most Indian English.

Once again, some realisational variation will occur even within a specific accent. Notoriously, even within NRP, glottalisation varies tremendously, as do realisations of vowels such as GOAT and GOOSE.

Patterns of realisational variation often affect more than one phoneme in similar ways, as is the case with both examples above. Such variation frequently shows interesting patterning, for instance in the symmetry of the vowel system, or modifications to articulations determined by specific phonetic contexts which affect a whole range of consonant or vowel phonemes.

In our brief overview of General American (as compared with NRP) below, we mention all four types of variation. Systemic, distributional and lexical variation are structurally the most significant types, since in their different ways they involve phonemic change. Realisational variation (the commonest type, but less significant since it involves no phonemic change) is regarded as the default.

British and American compared

In this and the following sections we are going to discuss some of the important varieties of English spoken worldwide. We shall begin with a comparison of the two major models of English – British NRP and General American. Although we shall be concentrating here on the differences between these two varieties, in fact they are most notable for their great similarity. It may be worth emphasising again (see Section A1) that educated British and American speakers communicate with ease, and rarely experience any problems in understanding each other's pronunciation.

Consonants

The consonant system of General American is in essentials the same as that of British accents and can be represented with the same phonemic symbols. Note, however, the following differences.

1   GA is rhotic, e.g. *worker* /ˈwɜrkər/; /r/ often functions as a syllabic consonant (see Section A2), e.g. /ˈwɜrkr̩/. (Distributional variation.)

2   GA /t/ is voiced in medial position. For the vast majority of Americans, in anything other than careful speech, the contrast /t – d/ is neutralised in this context, so that /t/ and /d/ in *writer* and *rider* may be identical. This is termed **t-voicing** and is indicated in transcription by the addition of a voicing diacritic 'ţ', e.g. *pretty* /ˈprɪţi/, *better* /ˈbeţr̩/, *battle* /ˈbæţl̩/, *thirty* /ˈθɜrţi/. Note that we are dealing here with an allophone of /t/ and not a phoneme. Nevertheless, because of its high frequency in American English, we have decided not to use square brackets whenever this sound occurs. (Distributional variation.) Medial /nt/ is regularly reduced to /n/, e.g. *winter* /ˈwɪnr̩/. Word-final /t/ often lacks any audible release.

3   A minority use an extra phoneme /ʍ/ for words spelt with **wh**, e.g. *whale, wail* /ˈʍeɪl, weɪl/ (systemic variation.). In England, /ʍ/ died out many hundreds of years ago and its use is often considered an affectation.

4   Most Americans (not all) have /j/-dropping following the dental and alveolar consonants /θ t d s z n l/, e.g. *studio* /ˈstudioʊ/, *nude* /nud/, *duke* /duk/. The modern NRP alternative /tʃ dʒ/ (see Section B2) is regarded as substandard in America. In NRP some words have a less common alternative form without /j/. In American, this is the *normal* form. (Lexical variation, with noteworthy patterning.)

	GA (normal form)	NRP (normal form)
enthusiastic	/ɪnθuzɪˈæstɪk/	/ɪnθjuːziˈæstɪk/
assume	/əˈsum/	/əˈsjuːm/
presume	/prəˈzum/	/prəˈzjuːm/

5   Some American speakers have dark *l* in all contexts, e.g. *level* [ˈɫevɫ̩]. To British ears the initial [ɫ] can sometimes sound similar to /w/, so that *life* sounds rather like *wife* (Realisational variation.)

Table C1.2 The vowels of General American

Checked	Keyword	Free steady-state	Keyword	Free diphthong	Keyword	Pre-r	Keyword
ɪ	KIT	i	FLEECE	eɪ	FACE	ɪr	NEAR
e	DRESS	ɑ	PALM	oʊ	GOAT	er	SQUARE
æ	TRAP	ɔ	THOUGHT	aɪ	PRICE	ɑr	START
ʊ	FOOT	u	GOOSE	ɔɪ	CHOICE	or	NORTH
ʌ	STRUT			aʊ	MOUTH	or	FORCE
ə	*bonus*					ʊr	CURE
æ	BATH					ɜr	NURSE
i	*happ*ʏ					ər	*lett*ᴇʀ

Notes

NORTH and FORCE may both be NORTH

PALM and THOUGHT may both be PALM

Vowels

Compared with the consonants, there is less similarity between the vowel systems of GA and NRP. Nevertheless for the most part we can employ the same symbols. For GA varieties, the 'length mark' for free vowels has been omitted since American varieties do not show the close correlation of length with free vowels found in British NRP. Other important differences are listed below.

1 Since GA (like most American varieties) is rhotic, there are differences in words spelt with **r**, where in GA the counterparts of NRP /ɑː ɛː ɔː ɜː ə ɪə ʊə/ take the form of a vowel followed by /r/: see Table C1.2. (Systemic variation.) Note that the vowels have a special quality known as r-colouring (p. 140).

2 The GOAT vowel is typically more back and rounded; it is represented here by /oʊ/, e.g. *solo* /ˈsoʊloʊ/. Americans (especially of the younger generation) seem to be acquiring a more central unrounded beginning [ə] similar to its counterpart in NRP. (Realisational variation.)

3 In GA (and other American varieties), the TRAP vowel is closer and lengthened, often sounding rather like [ɛː], similar in quality to SQUARE in NRP. (Realisational variation.) Furthermore, TRAP is used in all BATH words except *father* (see Section B3), instead of NRP PALM /ɑː/, e.g. *bath* /bæθ/, *laugh* /læf/, *chance* /tʃæns/, *ask* /æsk/. (Lexical variation.)

4 In American English many foreign names and loanwords spelt with **a** are said with LOT /ɑ/ rather than TRAP /æ/, e.g. *pasta* /ˈpɑstə/, *Mafia* /ˈmɑfiə/, *macho* /ˈmɑtʃoʊ/, *Picasso* /pɪˈkɑsoʊ/. (Lexical variation.)

5 Many Americans (in areas other than the East Coast) make no difference between words such as *merry*, *marry* and *Mary* – pronouncing all three as /ˈmeri/. (Distributional variation.)

109

Say this sentence: *Hairy Harry married merry Mary.* Unless you're American, you'll probably have three vowels (in NRP they come in this sequence /ɛː æ æ e ɛː/). See if you can find some Americans willing to say the same sentence. Note how many vowels they have in their various idiolects.

6 The STRUT vowel is generally closer (realisational variation) – more like /ə/ than in NRP. Before /r/, in words where NRP has /ʌ/, American uses /ɜ/, e.g. *hurry* /'hɜri/, *courage* /'kɜrɪdʒ/. (Distributional variation.)

7 For most present-day GA speakers, LOT and PALM are the same (i.e. [ɑ]). For certain GA speakers (mostly East Coast), the NRP LOT words are split into two different sets depending on the following consonant. (Lexical variation, but with strong patterning.)

   (a) Before /g ŋ s f θ/, the THOUGHT vowel /ɔ/ (similar to NRP /ɔː/) tends to be used, e.g. *log* /lɔg/, *song* /sɔŋ/, *lost* /lɔst/, *coffee* /'kɔfi/, *moth* /mɔθ/.

   (b) Elsewhere, PALM /ɑ/ (similar to NRP /ɑː/) is employed, e.g. *top* /tɑp/, *job* /dʒɑb/, *shock* /ʃɑk/.

   This type of patterning is particularly common in the New York conurbation and other eastern areas, but is also found to a degree elsewhere especially in high-frequency items such as *dog, wrong, cost, off,* etc.

8 Many GA speakers (particularly of the younger generation) do not have a contrast between LOT and THOUGHT, so *cot* and *caught* are pronounced identically. This is a trend which seems to be developing rapidly in the United States and is already established in Canada. (Systemic variation.)

9 Many words ending in *-ile* have /əl/ or /l̩/ in GA compared with /aɪl/ in NRP, e.g. *fertile* /'fɜrtl̩/, *missile* /'mɪsl̩/. For most words, alternative pronunciations with /aɪl/ also exist. (Lexical variation.)

10 A number of GA speakers (particularly of the older generation) still maintain the NORTH – FORTH contrast discussed above. (Lexical variation.)

Stress and stress-related features

There are some significant differences between British and American in (1) allocation of stress, (2) the pronunciation of unstressed syllables.

(1) Words ending in *-ary* and *-ory* take a secondary stress on that syllable, and the vowel is neither reduced to /ə/ nor elided.

	GA	NRP
military	/'mɪlə,teri/	/'mɪlɪtəri/ or /'mɪlɪtri/
arbitrary	/'ɑːrbə,treri/	/'ɑːbɪtrəri/ or /'ɑːbɪtri/
mandatory	/'mændə,tori/	/'mændətəri/ or /'mændətri/

(2) Words borrowed from French are generally stressed on the first syllable in British English but they often have final-syllable stress in American.

	GA	NRP
ballet	/bæ'leɪ/	/'bæleɪ/
Bernard (first name)	/br̩'nɑrd/	/'bɜːnəd/
blasé	/blɑ'zeɪ/	/'blɑːzeɪ/
brochure	/broʊ'ʃʊr/	/'brəʊʃə/
buffet	/bə'feɪ/	/'bʊfeɪ/
baton	/bə'tɑn/	/'bætɒn/
garage	/gə'rɑʒ/	/'gærɑːʒ/
perfume	/pr̩'fjum/	/'pɜːfjuːm/
Tribune (newspaper)	/trɪ'bjun/	/'trɪbjuːn/

Frequent individual words

The following is a short list of individual words showing lexical variation not covered above. The pronunciations cited are those which appear to be found most commonly either side of the Atlantic. Note that in some cases a minority of American speakers may use forms which are more typical of British speakers and vice versa. Words of this type are indicated by arrows (→ and ← respectively).

Stress shift	GA	NRP
address (n.)	/'ædres/ →	/ə'dres/
cigarette	/'sɪgəret/ →	← /sɪgə'ret/
detail	/dɪ'teɪl/ →	/'diːteɪl/
inquiry	/'ɪŋkwəri/ →	/ɪŋ'kwaɪəri/
laboratory	/'læbrətɔri/	← /lə'bɒrətri/

Consonant variance		
erase	/ɪ'reɪs/	/ɪ'reɪz/
figure	/'fɪgjər/	/'fɪgə/
herb	/ɜrb/	/hɜːb/
Parisian	/pə'rɪʒn̩ pə'riʒn̩/	/pə'rɪziən/
puma	/'pumə/	/'pjuːmə/
schedule	/'skedʒul/	← /'ʃedʒuːl/
suggest	/səg'dʒest/	/sə'dʒest/

Vowel variance		
anti-	/'æntaɪ/ →	/'ænti/
ate	/eɪt/	← /et/
borough	/'bɜroʊ/	/'bʌrə/
thorough	/'θɜroʊ/	/'θʌrə/
clerk	/'klɜrk/	/klɑːk/
depot	/'dipoʊ/	/'depəʊ/
dynasty	/'daɪnəsti/	/'dɪnəsti/
docile	/'dɑsl̩/	/'dəʊsaɪl/
either	/'iðər/ →	← /'aɪðə/
multi-	/'mʌltaɪ/ →	/'mʌlti/

neither	/ˈniðər/ →	← /ˈnaɪðə/
leisure	/ˈliʒər/	/ˈleʒə/
lever	/ˈlevər/ →	/ˈliːvə/
process (n.)	/ˈprɑses/	/ˈprəʊses/
progress (n.)	/ˈprɑgrəs/	/ˈprəʊgres/
record (n.)	/ˈrekərd/	/ˈrekɔːd/
semi-	/ˈsemaɪ/ →	/ˈsemi/
shone	/ˈʃoʊn/	/ˈʃɒn/
simultaneous	/saɪməlˈteɪniəs/	/sɪməlˈteɪniəs/
tomato	/təˈmeɪt̬oʊ/	/təˈmɑːtəʊ/
vitamin	/ˈvaɪt̬əmɪn/	← /ˈvɪtəmɪn/
what	/wʌt/ or /wɑt/	/wɒt/
z (in alphabet)	/zi/	/zed/

Names

The pronunciation of similarly spelt names frequently varies between Britain and the USA, with a tendency for American versions to reflect spelling more closely. Some of the more familiar examples are the following:

	GA	NRP
Berkeley	/ˈbɜrkli/	/ˈbɑːkli/
Birmingham	/ˈbɜrmɪŋhæm/	/ˈbɜːmɪŋəm/
Burberry	/ˈbɜrberi/	/ˈbɜːbri/
Derby	/ˈdɜrbi/	/ˈdɑːbi/
Warwick	/ˈwɔrwɪk/	/ˈwɒrɪk/

Differences in setting, intonation and rhythm

Setting

One of the most noticeable differences between GA and NRP setting is that American vowels are influenced by **r-colouring**, affecting adjacent consonants as well as vowels. For example, in *partner*, not only the vowels are affected but also the /t/ and the /n/. The body of the tongue is bunched up to a pre-velar position and the root of the tongue is drawn back in the pharynx. As compared with NRP, American English also appears more coloured by semi-continuous **nasalisation** running throughout speech. Many Americans, particularly of educated varieties, have noticeable creaky voice (see Section A4).

Intonation

Much of what has been said about British intonation applies to GA intonation with this important difference: American intonation tends to have fewer of the rapid pitch changes characteristic of NRP, and rises and falls are more spread out over the *whole* tune. A very typical pattern, for instance, is this sort of rising tune for questions:

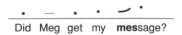

Did Meg get my **mes**sage?

Perhaps because of these differences, American English is sometimes claimed to strike a British ear as 'monotonous'. On the other hand British English intonation is said to sound 'exaggerated' or 'affected' to Americans.

Rhythm

A second difference concerns rhythm. American English, because of a tendency to lengthen stressed checked vowels (e.g. TRAP) and an apparently slower rate of delivery, is stereotyped by the British as 'drawled'. British English, because of the general tendency to eliminate weakly stressed vowels, together with an apparently more rapid rate of delivery, seems to strike many Americans as 'clipped'.

Sample of general American ☺ Track 40

Well – being a – semi-geek – in high school – I – was also in the marching band – and – basically – we had to – perform at football games – at the 4th of July Parade of course – and we had to wear these horrible uniforms – that were – in our school colours of course – red white and blue – made of 120 per cent polyester – and – we had to march in formation out on the football field – before the games and during half time – and one time we were marching – doing our little – kind of – sequence of movements on – the field – right before a game and the football players were – warming up – and I played the flute – and – at one point some guy from the opposing team – kicked the ball – out of control – and – the ball came flying towards me and hit me in – the mouth – which – hit my flute as well – luckily I didn't have any broken teeth but I had a broken flute – and – a bloody lip – anyway – there was mass panic – the whole formation kind of fell apart – and – all these – you know – panicking women were running out onto the field to see what was wrong – and I was holding my – hand to my mouth – and – some woman from the – I don't know – what do you call it – the – what is it called – it's kind of sports – this group of people who raise money for sports and kind of you know distribute the money and stuff for school activities – came over and started yelling at me to not get blood on my white gloves – that those white gloves cost ten dollars a pair or something – here I am – blood streaming from my mouth – my thousand-dollar flute in pieces – on the ground – and lucky to be alive – and she's screaming at me about getting blood on my – gloves – anyway I quit marching band after that

Notes

geek = a socially inept person

Description

Our informant, Kathy, is a translator from the American Midwest. General American displays a degree of variation, so many, but not all, of the features described above can be identified in this small sample of Kathy's speech. Her pronunciation is rhotic (☺ *marching, warming, started*) with noticeable **r**-colouring. She has consistent **t**-voicing (☺ *little, started, getting*). There is no **h**-dropping (☺ *high, holding*). In words like ☺ *during*, Kathy has [j]-dropping. She uses TRAP in BATH words

(☺ *half*). Her THOUGHT vowel is open, rather like NRP PALM (☺ *also, ball, called*). Kathy doesn't exhibit all the American features we have mentioned; for instance, initial /l/ isn't noticeably dark, and her TRAP vowel is more open than average GA. Kathy (not being an Easterner) doesn't split LOT words up into THOUGHT and PALM sets (see above) (☺ the vowels in *dollar* and *wrong* are the same), nor does she have any evidence of a NORTH–FORCE split. Like most younger GA speakers, she doesn't contrast words spelt with **w** and **wh** (☺ *white, what, which* are all said as /w/).

C2 **ACCENTS OF THE BRITISH ISLES 1: ENGLAND**

Introduction
This section discusses the regional accents (concentrating on the largest cities and conurbations) of England. The remainder of the British Isles (together with Liverpool, which is in many ways a special case) is covered in Section C3. The accompanying audio CD provides samples of the types of speech discussed. The recorded material for this and the two subsequent sections have all been provided by genuine speakers of the variety of English concerned (nobody here is 'putting on an accent').

Salience and stigmatisation
In discussing local accents of a basilectal type, it is useful to introduce two concepts which are often of significance in determining people's reactions to the speech concerned. **Salience** is a term used to pick out a feature which outsiders notice, and may also be known and remarked upon by local members of the community. Well-known examples of **salient** features are:

❑ the uvular [ʀ] of traditional Geordie;
❑ the 'lilting' intonation of Welsh English;
❑ rhoticism in the English of the West Country;
❑ fronted /ɑː/ in Australian English PALM.

Certain salient features may also suffer **stigmatisation**. A stigmatised accent characteristic is one which has low status, and accordingly is the subject of social disapproval. Such disapproval can range from correction by parents or teachers to the feature being the butt of humour or ridicule. Given this scenario, the linguistically upwardly mobile will ensure that their first step is to drop any such feature from their idiolects and substitute an alternative socially approved pronunciation.

Figure C2.1   Map of British and Irish accent locations

Some significant features of the selected accents

1 *TRAP or PALM vowel in the BATH words (lexical variation)*

NRP, Cockney and other south-eastern accents have the PALM vowel in a set of words which have been termed the BATH words (most of which are spelt with the letter **a** followed by a fricative or nasal, e.g. *craft, bath, pass, chance, plant*). Here, most other accents have the TRAP vowel (see also Sections B3 and C1).

2 Final vowel in happʏ *(distributional variation)*

The *happʏ* vowel (see Sections B3 and C1) has FLEECE in some accents and KIT in others.

3 Vowel /ʊ/ or /ʌ/ in the *STRUT words (systemic variation)*

All northern and some Midland accents in England lack the STRUT vowel. In these varieties, STRUT is replaced by FOOT in *rush, bus, blood*, etc. See Sections B1 and C1.

4 *FORCE–NORTH (lexical variation)*

Certain accents divide words spelt **or** into two sets: NORTH words (e.g. *north, cord, form, cork*) and FORCE words (e.g. *force, port, more, four*). In Scottish, words

Figure C2.2 Regional variation in British and Irish accents showing approximate geographical distribution of eight accent features. A question mark (?) indicates where occurrence is variable, or where data is unreliable)

in the NORTH set have the vowel [ɔ] found in LOT/THOUGHT, while the FORCE words have the vowel in GOAT (realised as [o]), i.e. [nɔrθ] vs. [fors]. (See Section C1.)

5 Narrow or wide diphthongs in the FACE and GOAT words (realisational variation)

The FACE and GOAT vowels can be realised either as narrow diphthongs, possibly steady-state vowels, e.g. [eː oː] (as in South Wales English) – or as wide diphthongs, e.g. [æɪ æʊ] (as in Cockney).

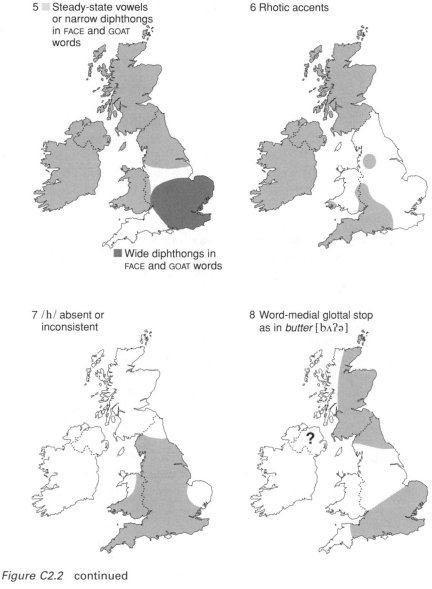

5 Steady-state vowels or narrow diphthongs in FACE and GOAT words

6 Rhotic accents

■ Wide diphthongs in FACE and GOAT words

7 /h/ absent or inconsistent

8 Word-medial glottal stop as in *butter* [bʌʔə]

Figure C2.2   continued

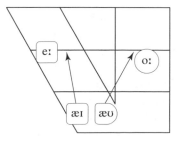

Figure C2.3   The FACE and GOAT vowels realised as (1) steady-state vowels (South Wales), (2) wide diphthongs (Cockney). See map 5 above where dark shading indicates wide diphthongs

6 Rhotic or non-rhotic distribution (distributional variation)

NRP and most English and Welsh varieties are non-rhotic. Scots, Irish, West Country and parts of Lancashire are rhotic (see Section B2).

7 h-dropping (systemic variation)

Most urban accents in England and Wales are **h**-dropping, thus potentially levelling contrasts such as *hedge – edge*. A totally **h**-less accent would mean the lack of the /h/ phoneme and hence systemic variation. In reality, because **h**-dropping is one of the most frequent and best-known phonetic social markers in English and is severely stigmatised, virtually all **h**-droppers strive, with varying degrees of success, to produce /h/ in more formal situations. Consequently, in the descriptions this is labelled 'variable **h**-dropping' (examples quoted from the CD recording will normally refer to /h/ deletion).

8 Medial /t/ realised as glottal stop [ʔ] (realisational variation)

Many British accents have more extensive glottalisation than that described for NRP (see Section B2). Most noticeably, these varieties have glottal replacement of medial /t/, e.g. *letter, bottle* [ˈleʔə ˈbɒʔl̩].

Details of individual accents

In the transcripts contained in this and the following section we have followed the normal practice in linguistic work of removing most punctuation and also capitalisation at the beginning of sentences. Breaks in the flow of speech corresponding roughly to intonation group boundaries are shown with a dash, thus – . Hesitation markers ('ums' and 'ers') have been omitted. Sections which are garbled or difficult to interpret are indicated by a question mark in brackets (?). Italics are used (sparingly) to indicate particularly emphatic speech. In the accent descriptions, slant brackets have been used where appropriate for individual phonemes, but the transcription of connected speech has been placed in square brackets. The sign ☺ indicates that a specific feature is exemplified on the audio CD. Brief explanations have been offered in the notes for words and phrases which might puzzle readers who are non-native English speakers.

Some of the English varieties have nicknames which are in common use, e.g. 'Cockney, Geordie, Scouse, Brummie' and we have noted and explained these. The location of the sample taken is shown in brackets. Population figures are approximate estimates. Names of informants have been changed.

1 Cockney (Greater London) ☺ Track 41

Steve: there was one of our blokes – one of his family – like cousins or uncles – or you know – in that range – had had an accident – and been taken to hospital – so he spent – I think most of his weekend without any sleep at all – at this hospital like – until he knew – that the person was going to be OK – anyway – come Monday morning – he decides to go straight to work – and – he comes to work – and say he has had no sleep at all and he's got a job to do in this house to provide – an extension phone – you know – and usually – it's – you run the cable upstairs into a bedroom – it's the usual place to have the phone – and – the bed – was fitted into slots in the floor – so he couldn't sort of – move it over. I mean – he could only get two legs out of the hole in the floor and he couldn't – he needed two people to actually lift it and move it – so he laid across the bed – to – finish the cabling – and screw the – terminal box on the wall – and – not having had any sleep – he just sort of drifted off – and the thing is – the gentleman who let him in – but said he was going to work – and his wife would be in shortly – and *she's* come in – and not knowing the telephone man was there – I mean – to see a van outside – but she didn't – you know – sort of put two and two together – she's come in – she's gone upstairs – into the bathroom – and she's – taken her clothes off like – you know – and gone into the bedroom to get her housecoat – she was going to have a bath – and there's a strange man laying on the bed – snoring his head off – needless to say – our bloke spent about six hours in the nick – trying to explain what had happened – yes – spent six hours in the police station

Notes

bloke (colloquial) = *man*
laying = *lying*. Many southern British varieties conflate the two verbs *lie* and *lay*.
the nick (general slang) = *police station, prison*

Description

The traditional word for the broad accent of London is 'Cockney'. The origins of the word, which go back at least 700 years, are uncertain; one attractive theory is that it may come from an old tale of the fool who believed in a 'cocken ey', a cockerel's egg. A Cockney is allegedly someone born 'within the sound of Bow Bells' – that's to say where you can hear the bells of St Mary-le-Bow church in the East End of London. That definition would cut the number of Cockneys down to a few thousand, but 'Cockney' is generally used to refer to all London, and to the speech of the Greater London area, which has a population of nearly seven million. Outer London, where most people speak with accents similar to London, covers a huge area and takes in 12 million inhabitants. Our speaker, Steve, is a telephone engineer from Lewisham in south-east London.

Cockney is non-rhotic with variable **h**-dropping. Steve, for instance, pronounces /h/ in *hospital* on two occasions but drops /h/ in *hole*. Syllable-final stop consonants are strongly glottalised. In medial and final position, Steve often replaces medial /t/ by glottal stop [ʔ] (e.g. ☺ *without any, move it over*). Post-vocalic /l/ is very dark, sounding rather like [ʊ] (e.g. ☺ *usual, terminal, wall*). Many speakers replace /θ ð/ by /f v/, e.g. *three feathers* = ['frəi 'fevəz] (not heard in this sample). /j/-dropping can be heard in ☺ *knew*.

Londoners use virtually the same vowel system as NRP, but the realisations of the vowels are very different. The STRUT vowel is front and open [a] (e.g. ☺ *come Monday*). FLEECE and GOOSE are extended glides [əi əu] (e.g. ☺ *needed, move*). The diphthongs FACE, PRICE and GOAT (e.g. ☺ *straight, like* and *phone*) sound like NRP diphthongs PRICE, CHOICE and MOUTH. The Cockney MOUTH vowel (e.g. ☺ *house*) is fronted and often raised ([aː] or [ɛə]), sounding rather like NRP SQUARE. Front checked vowels DRESS and TRAP (e.g. ☺ *bed, van, family*) tend to be closer. Like NRP, but unlike most other British accents, Cockney has the PALM rather than the TRAP vowel in the BATH words (e.g. ☺ *bathroom*).

2 West Country (Bristol) ☺ Track 42

Joe: well I think all these – countries are – are like that – now this Saudi Arabia and all – they got – high rise flats or whatever they call them – they got the finest hospitals in the world see

Interviewer: they're rich now

Joe: oh – millions – millions – I was listening to a man on the wireless here one day this week – when they come over these princes – 'cos of course there's about three thousand princes – in Saudi Arabia – like – on account of the – king or prince – Mohammed – and look he can have three wives – that's why they've got so many children – isn't it – this prince had a house in a well-known street in London and the window cleaner used to call there – this man was saying this on the wireless the other night – and – the prince come out to him and – said to the window cleaner – how much is that 'cos he cleaned all the windows in the front of the house – and of course the – window cleaner said two forty – and – this prince give him a cheque for two hundred and forty pound

Linda: did he

Joe: aye

Linda: cor – I wish that would happen to me

Joe: ooh – that's what I thought

Notes

aye = yes

cor is a mild expletive.

Description

The West Country (in Britain this means only the *south*-west of England) is often thought of as being essentially rural in character, but it also takes in some very large, densely populated urban areas, such as Bristol–Bath, Plymouth, Bournemouth and Torquay. West Country accents are spoken by perhaps as many as four and a half million people in total. As a result of a long seafaring tradition, many of the original English immigrants to other countries hailed from the south-west so it is thought likely that this English accent has had considerable influence on the English speech of America, Canada, the Caribbean and possibly elsewhere. Our speakers come from Bristol, the largest city in the west of England, which with its suburbs has a population of about three quarters of a million.

The accent is consistently rhotic (☺ *world, forty, course*), with /r/ often realised as a retroflex approximant [ɻ] and with strong vowel colouring (in some ways reminiscent of General American). There is variable **h**-dropping (☺ *high, Mohammed*) and extensive glottalisation; as in Cockney, /t/ may be replaced by [ʔ] (e.g. ☺ *whatever*, second rendering of *forty*). Joe frequently replaces initial /ð/ by /d/ (☺ *this (week)*, *these (princes)*), but this is not true of all Bristolians. Connected speech exhibits a great deal of consonant assimilation and elision.

STRUT is close (☺ *countries, much*). A number of BATH words are said with the TRAP vowel. The PALM vowel is very front, giving a contrast with TRAP which is of length rather than of quality. The starting-point of PRICE is closer (☺ *rise, wives, wireless*). Much of the West Country has many features similar to those just described, but the city of Bristol is unique in that words ending in orthographic **a**, **ia** have a very close final allophone of /ə/. This sounds almost like FOOT [ʊ] and is interpreted by non-Bristolian ears as a kind of dark *l* (☺ *Saudi Arabia*), giving rise to what has come to be known as 'Bristol-*l*'.

3 Midlands (Birmingham) ☺ Track 43

Interviewer: well she's trying to get an exchange back – is she

Joyce: well you see – they want to come back – but she's got a daughter – twenty-one – and she doesn't want to come back – so what can you do – got to study the kids I suppose

Gran: and yet er's courting and er's going to get married

Joyce: – and yet er's courting – and I suppose er'll get married one of these days and her mother will be left there – 'cos er's twenty-one in January – but our Margie wants to come back because she's epileptic you know – my sister – she has been for a few years since the bombing – isn't she – and of course er suffers badly you know – and

Gran: er lives right away from all of us

Joyce: er lives right away from all of us – and he's like my chap – he works at the same firm as him – and they had to work seven days a week – well I mean – if my – she was here I mean we could see more of her – 'cos I mean we can't go unless her husband takes us in the car

Gran: and then stop the night

Joyce: and then you have to stop the night – well I mean it's our babby

Interviewer: yes

Joyce: they've got no cot for her to sleep in or anything – and

Gran: the other boy's fifteen and the girl's twenty-two – her boy's fifteen and her girl's twenty-one

Joyce: I mean if I want to go over there I got to go from here to Lichfield – and then from Lichfield to Rugeley – and I think the buses only run about once a fortnight

Interviewer: it does seem silly doesn't it – you know – it's all very well but they need to put buses and trains and things on

Gran: I mean they ask the people to go on these housing estates – to leave their houses here in Birmingham – but they don't cater for them

Interviewer: no

Gran: no

Notes

my chap: Joyce is referring to her husband.
study the kids = *consider the needs of the children*
babby = *baby, young child*

Description

Birmingham is the largest city (one million) in the West Midlands conurbation, which in total has a population of about two and a half million people. The inhabitants often call it by the nickname of 'Brummagem' – actually derived from an older form of the name. Consequently, people from Birmingham are called 'Brummies', and Midlands speech is often informally referred to as the 'Brummie accent'. Our two informants, Joyce and her mother – 'Gran' in the family circle – come from Small Heath, an inner city district of Birmingham. The interviewer is also from Birmingham, but has a much modified form of the accent.

The accent is non-rhotic (☺ *courting, our Margie*) and has variable **h**-dropping. Joyce and Gran delete /h/ very consistently (☺ *here, houses*). A frequent realisation of /r/ is a tap [ɾ] (☺ *married, January*). Medial (and sometimes final) **ng** has sounded /ɡ/ (☺ *anything*). Lexical variation is found in BATH words, which generally have the TRAP vowel (☺ *ask*). A lexical variation feature found in almost all Midland and northern English is that LOT rather than STRUT is used in the common words ☺ *one* and also *none*.

The realisation of the front checked vowels KIT and DRESS is closer than in other varieties. KIT in fact sounds as close as FLEECE in other accents (☺ *sister, Lichfield*). The FLEECE and GOOSE vowels are both extended glides (☺ *sleep, do*). Many dialectologists have claimed that in this accent there is no STRUT – FOOT contrast. In fact, although these vowels sound very similar (at least to a non-Midlander), a contrast certainly exists. STRUT is similar to an unrounded [ʊ] (☺ *study, suffers*), whereas FOOT is closer and more rounded than in most other types of English (☺ *could*). LOT is unrounded [ɑ] and sometimes fronted (☺ *cot, bombing*). NURSE is close, front and may have a degree of lip-rounding [øː] (☺ *work, firm*). There are wide glides (like Cockney) in FACE, GOAT (☺ *away, days, over*). As in Cockney, the PRICE diphthong starts further back, sounding like the CHOICE of most varieties (☺ *right, night*). The *happy* vowel is FLEECE realised with a wide glide. Broad Birmingham English is notable for extended intonation patterns with frequent sharp falls, sustained low pitches or rise-falls, and there are plenty of examples of these in the speech of Joyce and Gran.

'Er' in our text represents the all-purpose (*he, she, it*) 3rd person pronoun /ɜː/ (weak form /ə/). Interestingly, this seems to be a relic of what Shakespeare (also a Midlander!) frequently indicates by '*a* or *a* in the speech of his 'low' characters. It occurs frequently, for instance, in *Henry IV, Parts 1* and *2*. It is also to be found in *Hamlet* coming from the lips of the Prince of Denmark himself: 'Now might I doe it, now *a* is a-praying' (Act III, Scene ii, l. 73; *Arden Shakespeare*, H. Jenkins 1982).

4 North (Lancashire) ☺ *Track 44*

Dave: another instance – I was on a – I was at Romiley – that's in – near Marple – and I give the driver the sign – I was going for a Jimmy Riddle – I had all my machine on and my bag of money on – and I gets in – was having a wee there in t' toilet – and I heard the ding ding – I thought – oh it can't be – and I heard the bus set off – so I thought oh Christ – what can I do now – so I saw this motorbike – which was coming up – so I stopped him – and he gave me a lift – down to Woodley – and I found out – that it was a bloke who were drunk on the back seat – as always – wanted to leave the guard so he decided to ring the bell and leave me stood at Romiley . . . we had another incident – I had a driver called Brian Craven who suddenly phoned an inspector up at Stalybridge Garage – to say that he'd lost a guinea pig – left a guinea pig on the bus on the 330s went from Hyde to Ashton which in them days you had three corporations – you had Stockport corporation – Ashton corporation – and you had SHMD – and we said to this driver – this inspector – if the guinea pig's *not* found it'll die – so he had a look in the lost property office – and he come back – he says – well – he says – there's no guinea pig here – and then he asked us – very sarcastically – was it on a *blue* bus – a *red* bus – or a *green* bus – so he said a *red* bus – so he put the phone down on us

Notes

incident: the speaker mispronounces this word.

Jimmy Riddle: one of many colloquial expressions for *urinate*. This is what is known in Britain as 'rhyming slang' where a rhyme is used for another word – in this case, *piddle*, also a slang word meaning *to urinate*. Rhyming slang is mostly associated with Cockney, but is also heard elsewhere.

a wee (general colloquial): another word for *urination*

guard = bus conductor. The word is used in this sense only in this part of the north of England.

leave me stood (general non-standard) = *leave me standing*

them days (general non-standard) = *those days*

Stockport corporation, Ashton corporation, SHMD: all public transport companies.

a red bus: all the various bus companies had their buses painted different colours. Once the inspector heard it was a *red* bus, he knew it had nothing to do with his particular bus company, so he just abruptly stopped speaking and hung up.

Description

The phrase 'northern accent' is popularly used for the kind of speech heard over a large area of England, more especially in the populous counties of Yorkshire and Lancashire (not so often for Merseyside or the north-east). Perhaps as many as ten million people speak English of this type, making it the second most widely spoken variety in Britain. This is a region of great contrasts, taking in the huge industrial conurbations of Greater Manchester, the Yorkshire West Riding (Leeds–Bradford) and South Yorkshire (Sheffield–Rotherham), but also having large stretches of sparsely populated hills and moorland in between, where rural populations maintain distinct forms of local dialect speech. Our speaker, Dave, is a bus conductor from the Lancashire town of Dukinfield in Greater Manchester, and there are some features in his speech which are characteristic of that particular area.

Northern English has variable **h**-dropping (☺ *having, Hyde*). One salient feature is to replace the definite article *the* by /t/, which is often glottalised or elided (☺ *in t' toilet*). /p t k/ tend to have weak aspiration. There are many noticeable differences in the vowels. PRICE vowels have a very narrow glide (or even a steady-state vowel), sounding rather like a long [aː] vowel (☺ *motorbike, Hyde*). The FACE and GOAT vowels have little or no glide (☺ *say, days, bloke*). DRESS is more open (☺ *left, bell*) and TRAP is retracted (☺ *Ashton, back*). Systemic variation is found in the lack of a STRUT vowel, FOOT being used where other varieties have STRUT (☺ *coming, up, bus*). The TRAP vowel is used in most BATH words, e.g. ☺ *asked*. The *happy* vowel is clearly KIT rather than FLEECE (☺ *guinea (pig)* ['gɪne]). Southerners often accuse Northerners of having 'flat' intonation, and certainly Dave tends to have less variation in the pitch of his voice than many of the other accents in our sample.

There are distinct differences between Lancashire and Yorkshire. Some areas of Lancashire (but not normally Yorkshire) have sounded /g/ for medial **ng**, i.e. /ŋg/, e.g. *singer* = [ˈsɪŋgə]. Moreover, even though this does not emerge in Dave's speech, quite an extensive area of Lancashire adjacent to Manchester (but not the city itself) is rhotic. Yorkshire English is notable for frequent lenis to fortis energy assimilation, e.g. *Bradford City* [bratfət ˈsɪte] – which is something a Lancastrian like Dave wouldn't say.

 Activity

110

Explain the phonetic features and comment on the social judgements contained in this extract from Stephen Fry's novel *The Stars' Tennis Balls* (2001: 30).

> Slowly you have become infected by a northern accent. Not obvious, just a trace, but to your sensitive, highly attuned ears as glaring as a cleft palate. You began to pronounce 'One' and 'None' to rhyme with 'Shone' and 'Gone' instead of 'Shun' and 'Gun', you gently sounded the g's in 'Ringing' and 'Singing'. At school you even rhyme 'Mud' with 'Good' and 'Grass' with 'Lass'. Fair enough, you would be beaten up as a southern poof otherwise, but you have trailed some of that linguistic mud into the house with you.

---

5 Geordie (Newcastle) ☉ Track 45

Kathleen: last Sunday – come right out of this wind – and I'm sure that it'd been open – he would have been (?) been in – well – he went away – I put one or two crumbs on that side – and he came back a few times back and forward – but we haven't seen him since – you want a bag of grain here every morning for the starlings and the sparrows and the what (?) little

Dora: blue tits

Kathleen: blue tits – I have nowt to say

Peggy: have you not

Kathleen: I've run out of words

Peggy: hardly – are they still – are they still getting all the – cows and things down there

Kathleen: no they haven't been out – just – I think – last Sunday was it – they were in that field – just one or two of them – but there's no small – but there's no calves aren't out just now

Peggy: but what did they do – what did they do when all that snow was on the ground –

Kathleen: they weren't out

Peggy: were they not

Kathleen: no they weren't out – not in neither of the fields – I just seen in the latter end there was one or two out in yon field – but that's the lot – I wonder where – where Elaine's gone and

Peggy: they went down – they went down Nobby's – oh there they are – they're just coming back up from down the Mill Road there – you can just see them

Kathleen: oh – they're making a lump of difference on there – the big turn they have – at the corner

Peggy: it's a bad road though coming up there

Kathleen: up there – up the Mills

Peggy: you get your tree cut

Kathleen: I hope

Peggy: it's a pity because it spoils our view doesn't it really – you know if we had a little bit more –

Kathleen: when it's fuller – the foliage and the green leaves – it makes this very dark – you see – but still we've got compensations – we can see the other part of the valley – beautiful

Peggy: still – you got a nice – you've got a nicer view here than what you've got – or had down home – I mean – down the back yard

Kathleen: what – looking at the chimney pots

Peggy: uh-huh (?) before – the back yard – the back wall

Kathleen: the back wall

Peggy: I know – my Dad used to sit and he used to look – across the – the – roof didn't he – to tell the weather

Kathleen: oh aye – he was a cold weather man – he used to sit around and they used to have lays

Peggy: oh dear – I suppose he'd be here watching all the traffic going along the road

Kathleen: oh – he would have seen nothing – nothing at all

Notes

nowt = nothing

yon = that over there (now archaic in most English varieties)

lays = naps

Description

The most northerly conurbation of England is Tyneside in the north-east, dominated by the city of Newcastle-upon-Tyne. This region has nearly a million inhabitants of whom nearly 300,000 live in Newcastle itself. The popularity of the name 'George', locally modified to 'Geordie', is the reason for the nickname applied to both the Tynesiders and their mode of speech. Our two main speakers are Kathleen, who grew up in Blaydon, a suburb to the south-west of the city, and has a conservative form of speech; her daughter Peggy, being younger, speaks a more modified form of the accent.

Geordie has considerable phonetic/phonological differences from other England varieties and is in some ways closer to Scottish accents (see Section C3). It is, for instance, the only large conurbation in England (or Wales) where the accent shows no **h**-dropping (☺ *home*). But, unlike Scots, it is non-rhotic (☺ *other part*). Most Tyneside speakers reinforce medial /p t k/ with glottal stop, e.g. *better, paper* [ˈbɛʔtɑ ˈpeːʔpɑ], but this isn't noticeable with our informants; but note Peggy's glottalised [ʔt] in for example ☺ *get your tree cut*. For both Kathleen and Peggy, /l/ is invariably clear in all contexts (☺ *still, little*). Broader speakers (only of the older generation and usually outside Newcastle itself) sometimes realise /r/ as a uvular fricative or approximant and Kathleen, but not Peggy, regularly pronounces it in this way (☺ *grain, green, very*).

The STRUT vowel is absent from the system (see above) (☺ *crumbs, run*). Both final /ə/ and the second element of the centring diphthongs NEAR and CURE are very open, e.g. *better* ['bɛtʔɑ], *beer* [biɑ], *cure* [kjuɑ]. The PALM words spelt **ar** (e.g. *start*) have a very back vowel. An extra vowel /aː/ is used for THOUGHT words spelt with **al**, e.g. *walk* = [waːk] so that *talk* and *yawn* contain different vowels /taːk – jɔːn/. In broad accents, NURSE and THOUGHT words are merged so that ☺ *word* is pronounced as [wɔːd] and, in some words, MOUTH may be replaced by /uː/, e.g. *house* /huːs/ (cf. Scots). PRICE has a narrow glide, e.g. *Tyneside* ['tɛɪnsɛɪd]. FACE and GOAT are steady-state vowels [eː oː] (☺ *away, snow*). Tyneside is renowned for its extended 'lilting' intonation with many final rising patterns, and in this respect Kathleen and Peggy are both typical Geordies.

Activity

> ### 111 ☺ Track 71 (Answers on website)
>
> Listen to the extracts on your audio CD (track 71). In each case, there is another voice speaking with one of the accent varieties discussed and which you have already heard. Try to locate the speaker geographically and state which particular phonetic features enable you to do this.

C3

ACCENTS OF THE BRITISH ISLES 2: CELTIC-INFLUENCED VARIETIES

Introduction

This section deals with the regional varieties of English in the United Kingdom and the Republic of Ireland which are in some way Celtic-influenced. There are samples of Belfast, Dublin, Edinburgh, South Wales and also the English city of Liverpool. The last-mentioned may seem a bit surprising but Liverpool is actually strongly influenced by Irish and North Wales Welsh, as we shall see below.

1 Scottish (Edinburgh) ☺ *Track 46*

> *Alison:* when I was a psychiatric nurse – when – when I was training to be a psychiatric nurse – I think I was about eighteen or – nineteen or something like that – and I can remember going in to like what was the – the dayroom where everybody sat – and everybody had their meals and stuff like that – and – used to try and sort of facilitate various – pieces of conversation with people – you're trying – find out what

was going on – and and whatever – and I remember we took the dinner trolley in one day – and – the food was disgusting – there was absolutely no doubt about it that the food was absolutely disgusting – and this guy started going absolutely bananas about the food – do you know – you cannot possibly expect me to eat this – this is absolutely disg[usting] – no – it was an Essex accent you had actually – because I trained to – used to call everybody Jock – I was a Jock – anyway I've lost part of the story – anyway aye – I'm bringing in the dinner trolley – and him going on about the food being disgusting and whatever – and this guy went absolutely bananas in the dinner hall – he tried – started sort of chucking stuff around – I was really frightened – I think – no no what was going on here – eventually I moved out of this sort of dinner hall place to go and get some sort of help to find out what should happen – 'cos I was just a student – I did not understand any of this – and this guy chased me out of the dayroom – with – what I thought was a big stick – or – I thought he'd broken a chair – or something like that – and I thought he was chasing me up a corridor with this piece of wood or something like that – and at one point I looked behind me and I had to – just burst out laughing because he had this huge big cucumber – he had this huge big cucumber in his hand – and he just looked absolutely ridiculous – and it was fine – it was fine – I sort of went – *hah.*

Notes

Essex: the speaker had undergone her nurse's training in the south-east of England.
Jock: traditional Scottish form of 'John'. Used as a nickname for all Scots – even females!
aye = yes

Description

Scottish accents are in many ways the most conservative varieties of English and preserve many features which have been lost elsewhere (see Section C5). Scottish English is spoken by nearly all of Scotland's five million population. It is very different from the English spoken in England, being the direct descendant of a quite separate language called Scots (this was the language of Robert Burns's poetry and the characters in Walter Scott's novels and not to be confused with Scots Gaelic, a Celtic language related to Irish, and still spoken mainly on the islands off the western coast). This speaker, Alison, is a nurse from the capital, Edinburgh, in the densely populated central lowlands which also include Glasgow, Scotland's largest city.

Perhaps the most noticeable feature of Scottish English is that it is rhotic (☺ *burst, dinner hall*) and that /r/ is realised with a strong tap (☺ *remember*). Scottish is **h**-pronouncing and voiceless /ʍ/ occurs in words spelt **wh** (e.g. ☺ *what*). There is systemic variation in the form of an extra consonant phoneme /x/, used for **ch** in a small number of specifically Scottish words, e.g. *loch, och!* /lɔx ɔx/ (not to be heard in this sample). Plosives /p t k/ are only weakly aspirated and there is considerable glottalisation of final/medial /p t k/, with glottal replacement of /t/ (e.g. ☺ *eat this, started*). Like many Scots, Alison has a relatively dark variety of /l/ in all contexts (e.g. ☺ *absolutely, looked, trolley*).

The vowels of Scottish English are quite dissimilar in their patterning from other kinds of English. Vowel length also operates on very different principles. A major systemic variation is the lack of a FOOT–GOOSE contrast. Words like ☺ *wood*, *took* are pronounced with the GOOSE vowel, exactly the same as ☺ *food, looked*. Like the vowels of Northern English and Welsh English, Scottish FACE and GOAT are steady-state vowels and not diphthongs (☺ *dayroom, chased, going*). TRAP is retracted (☺ *sat, absolutely*).

The LOT vowel is very close and similar to THOUGHT in England varieties (☺ *Jock, trolley*). In fact, many speakers have no LOT/THOUGHT contrast and *cot – caught* are homophones. On the other hand, the NURSE words may be represented by /ɪr/ as in *sir*, /ʌr/ as in *burst, word* (☺ *burst*), /ɛr/ as in *heard*. The KIT vowel is very open, sounding rather similar to [ə] (☺ *think, big, stick, dinner*) and is used instead of FLEECE in *happy* words (☺ *everybody*). In broader varieties, the incidence of many vowels may be radically different from the norm, e.g. *good* = KIT [gɪd]; *home* = FACE [hem]; *dead* = FLEECE [did]. The NORTH–FORCE distinction can be heard in Alison's speech in ☺ *sort* vs. *story*. The PRICE and MOUTH vowels have very close starting-points [əɪ, əu] (☺ *frightened, fine, around*). In a few high-frequency words (e.g. *round, about, house, out*) the MOUTH vowel may even be replaced by GOOSE (☺ *find out*) in more relaxed styles of speech.

Within the speech of the Scottish lowlands there are interesting 'east–west differences' as they are known. This is particularly true of intonation; for instance, Glasgow (in the west) is noteworthy for terminal rising patterns but these are largely absent from the speech of our Edinburgh (eastern) informant.

2 Irish Republic (Greater Dublin) ☺ Track 47

Paul: this one girl that I was with when I – when I saw that – don't know – Mrs White we used to call her – afterwards anyway – because it was all white – and – in *her* house – they have a fireplace yeah – and it's small tiles – marble tiles – and on one tile – it's about the third one across – and about the fourth one down or something like that – if you look at it – (*alarm clock rings*) shut up – if you look at it

Ray: time to get up

Paul: If you look at it – you can see – the shape of a head – and it's like our Lord's head – you know like you see in the holy pictures and that – but there's only two people that can see that – and that's me and her – and the rest of our family don't believe her – and they can't see it – so she never talks about it – and nobody else ever saw that in the house – in Gerry's house – O'Leary's – yeah – I had a look at it when I was at home

Sean: it's still there

Paul: it's still there

Sean: hasn't followed you to Holland

Paul: I said it to her – she says 'don't say that' – they think I'm going mad . . . yes but it's funny though – it's – it's like – a vision of our Lord's head – like you know – just see that head there like it's – just like that – it's almost as plain – but it's in kind of brown tiles – you know – oh it's clear really clear to me anyway – and *she* sees it clear

Interviewer: are there colours – are there colours – or is it black and white

Paul: yeah well the tiles are in – a kind of brownish tiles – d'you know you get streaks going through them like

Sean: yellow streaks

Paul: yellow – you know it's really a low yellow one kind of dark yes – kind of black – not really black black – white black – but that's – I was really amazed at that

Notes

Mrs White: the speakers are talking about a white ghost of a woman, which one of them claims to have seen.

hasn't followed you to Holland: the recording was made in the Netherlands.

Description

Irish English is of two distinct kinds – southern Irish English spoken in most of the Republic of Ireland, and northern Irish English which is spoken not only in the British province of Northern Ireland but also in the adjacent parts of the Irish Republic.

Ireland has its own Celtic language, Irish. Although there are relatively few every-day users of Irish now left, in 1850 well over a million people had it as their mother tongue. Consequently, Irish has had an important influence on much present-day Irish English, especially in rural areas. Our sample is from Dublin, which with nearly a million speakers in the surrounding region is by far the largest Irish urban area. The speakers, Paul and Sean, are two young men from Sallynoggin, near Dublin.

Dublin has no **h**-dropping (☺ *her house*) and has variable use of /ʍ/ in *wh*-words (listen to Paul's inconsistent pronunciations of ☺ *white*). The accent is variably rhotic (☺ *her (house), marble*). Non-final /r/ is frequently realised as a strong tap (☺ *Gerry*), especially in clusters (☺ *brown*), varying with an approximant (in realisations of ☺ *really*). /θ ð/ are replaced regularly by dental [t̪ d̪] (☺ *think, third, fourth, the, that*) or affricated [t̪θ, d̪ð] (cf. Liverpool) and with many speakers the contrasts /θ – t/ and /ð – d/ are lost. Word-final /t/ may be realised as a weak dental fricative or approximant (e.g. in the frequent repetitions of ☺ *that* [daθ]). Sequences such as /rm/ and /lm/ may be realised with /ə/-insertion, e.g. *arm, film* = ['arəm 'filəm] (does not occur in this sample).

The Dublin vowel system lacks the links to Scottish English found in Northern Ireland (see below), but there is nevertheless much significant variation compared with most England accents. FLEECE is used in *happy* words rather than KIT (☺ *holy, family*). FACE and GOAT are narrow glides (or steady-state vowels) (☺ *say, holy*). The TRAP vowel is more open (☺ *black*), while NURSE is more back, sounding a little like NRP THOUGHT (☺ *her*).The STRUT vowel is close and back, similar to FOOT to non-Irish ears (☺ *funny*). Furthermore, for some speakers, the contrast LOT/FOOT may also be uncertain with a vowel of an [ɔ] type being employed. Broader speakers (of the older generation) may replace the vowel in certain FLEECE words by the FACE vowel, e.g. *feet, tea* = [feːt teː] (not to be heard in the present sample). The contrast CHOICE/PRICE may be absent (☺ *tile*). GOOSE is a wide glide (☺ *two*). MOUTH begins fronted [ɛʊ] (☺ *about, brown*).

Rural southern Irish English has an extended 'lilting' intonation range, and this is one of the main features of what is sometimes referred to by English people as an 'Irish brogue', i.e. a stereotypical Irish accent. Nevertheless this is not so much a part of Dublin speech, and Paul and Sean (who both grew up in the Dublin urban area) lack the Celtic-influenced intonation of their country cousins.

3 Northern Ireland (Belfast) ☺ Track 48

Interviewer: was there more country when you were younger

Martin: oh yes oh yes – there was more country – more – in fact all that Springfield
Road – well there weren't houses at all – there was no houses there at all – all fields
– lovely fields – big rivers – you could even have went up and had a swim in them
– in the summer – instead of going away out – out of Belfast at all – could have
went up there – and five or six of us – went in their boat (?) and had a swim – we
even picnicked out in it and all – but now you see you can't do all that – all houses
were all built in it – now they're all wrecked – you know

Interviewer: no it's terrible

Martin: isn't terrible – shut in altogether – it used to be great round here – you know
– you used to say to your mummy – I'm away up – away up the fields – away up
– forget the name – up the Forth river for a swim – and then your mummy would
have knew where you were like you know instead

Interviewer: there was no worries

Martin: – there was no worries – because you knew it was safe enough

Interviewer: d'you get people now – you know kind of going out into the country
for outings – because it is very close still – you know you got the mountains at
the back of the Falls or

Martin: but you see – that's very funny – you can't because it's very dangerous – you
see – you can't leave your own district hardly now – you know – because if you
do you're taking your – your – life in your own hands – going out – you see – unless
you went in a car during the day – and just keep driving – or something – out
there right round the countryside – but to go for a walk – can't – you can't – you
wouldn't guarantee you'd come back again

Notes

Falls: district in Belfast.

Description

As a result of massive immigration from Scotland in previous centuries, the accents
of Northern Ireland sound quite different from those of the Irish Republic, being
similar to Scots in many ways. Many rural accents in Northern Ireland, some of
which are commonly called 'Scotch-Irish', show even more Scottish features. In
fact, overall there is a vast range of variation in Northern Irish speech. Our speaker,
Martin, comes from West Belfast and has the speech more typical of the older
generation. The information below therefore applies particularly to Belfast and the
surrounding area.

Northern Ireland English has no **h**-dropping (☺ *houses, hands*). Many rural
speakers have /ʍ/ in **wh** words (but this is not true of Martin, or indeed of most
Belfast speakers, ☺ *where*). The accent is rhotic (☺ *rivers*). Fortis stops are sometimes
glottalised. Older speakers (like Martin) may have dental /t/ before /r/ (☺ *country*).
Medial /ð/ is either a very weak approximant or may be elided. Many Northern Irish
speakers have clear *l* in all positions (☺ *fields*).

KIT is very open and central [ɛ] (☺ *picnicked, built, big, district*), and is used instead
of FLEECE in the *happy* vowel. DRESS and TRAP are also very open, TRAP in addition being
retracted (☺ *hands*). STRUT is more back (like an unrounded [ɔ] vowel) (☺ *country*).

The PRICE vowel has a much closer starting-point [ɛi] (☺ *kind, life, driving*). The MOUTH vowel is fronted and lip-rounded [œy] (☺ *houses, now, out*). The GOOSE vowel is also fronted but unrounded (☺ *do*). FACE has a centring diphthong (☺ *dangerous, safe*). Broader varieties have considerable lexical variation in vowels, as compared with most accents of England, e.g. *bag* = DRESS [beg]; *doll* = THOUGHT [dɔːl]. Northern Irish speech is notable for its characteristic intonation in which there are more rising than falling tunes, and Martin is very typical in this respect.

4 South Wales (Glamorgan, Carmarthenshire) ☺ Track 49

Gwen: do you know – remember I was telling you – about – that I – played and spoke outside school in Welsh – inside school it was all English – but you'd – once we were in the playground we played in Welsh – but that my sister who is nine years younger than me – by the time she came – they were – they were – it was English – now I was reading a piece about Gwyn Thomas – the writer – the novelist

Owen: oh yes

Gwen: he was the youngest of a family of about six children – all his brothers and sisters were Welsh-speaking – but by the time *he* came along – you see to go to school – he was English-speaking – he didn't speak Welsh – that might – but you know that might be psychological because he was the only one in the family who was not brought up to speak Welsh

Owen: it probably *was* a psychological thing – yes – but what you say now has amazed us quite often – you'll get certain members of the family speaking Welsh – and then in a matter of years – it's lost

Gwen: I only spoke Welsh at home – you know – we weren't allowed to speak English – my father wouldn't let us – but by the time she came to school – the school had changed – the classroom had changed – she used to play in English – all the children were speaking English – you know

Owen: yes, that's it

Gwen: it was in that short space of time – it's always amazed me

Interviewer: what do you put this down to

Gwen: well – a lot of it was put down to parents thinking it was posher to speak English to their children than to speak Welsh – you know – you'd often find a father and mother speaking Welsh to each other – and they'd turn round and speak English to their children

Owen: that's true

Gwen: specially in the Valleys

Owen: that's always been to the detriment of the Welsh language – yes they've always thought too you know

Gwen: it was more the thing – my mother-in-law was like that – *she* was Welsh-speaking – brought up Welsh-speaking – but she spoke English to her children

Notes

Gwyn Thomas (1913–81): a Welsh author (who wrote in English).

the Valleys: the densely populated mountainous area of South Wales where over a million people live in strings of small towns and villages built along the river valleys in between steep hillsides.

posh(er) (general British colloquial) = *upper-class, smart*

Description

Welsh certainly is the liveliest of the Celtic languages. It was spoken by the majority of Welsh people until the beginning of the twentieth century and still survives as the everyday language in many areas – over half a million people claim to speak it. So it is not surprising that Welsh English often has an echo of the old language about it. There are several distinct varieties of Welsh English. North Wales English is very different from the accent of the south; within South Wales, the Cardiff–Newport area is quite unlike the rest.

South Wales English is spoken by well over two million people. Our informants are of the older generation and are both native Welsh speakers. Gwen is a retired teacher from Aberdare in Glamorgan, and Owen is a language researcher from Carmarthenshire. Having academic backgrounds, they speak Welsh English with a modified form of the accent.

Broad South Wales accents have **h-dropping**, but this stigmatised feature is not found in the speech of our informants. Welsh English is non-rhotic (except for some older-generation native Welsh speakers). /r/ is realised as a tap [ɾ]. Plosives lack glottalisation. /l/ is clear in all contexts, e.g. ⊙ *Welsh, children.*

Most Welsh English has extra vowel contrasts. The GOOSE vowel splits system-ically into GOOSE words /uː/ (e.g. *goose, blue, mood,* ⊙ *too*) and JUICE /ɪu/ (e.g. *juice, blew, nude, include,* ⊙ *used*). This means that words like *through – threw* [θruː – θrɪu] form minimal pairs. As in Scottish English, there is a NORTH/FORCE split /ɔː – oː/, although there is no FORCE word in this sample. The STRUT vowel is often more front than open, while NURSE is sometimes closer and rounded. TRAP is retracted (⊙ *family*) and differentiated from PALM mostly by length (⊙ *matter, father* ['matə 'faːðə]). Many BATH words have TRAP rather than PALM (⊙ *classroom*). FACE and GOAT are usually narrow glides or steady-state vowels [eː oː]; notice how the vowels in words like ⊙ *came, amazed* and *home, spoke* are pronounced by Gwen with hardly any glide. But in FACE and GOAT words spelt **ai**, **ay** and **ow** (⊙ *played, know*) glides are used. PRICE and MOUTH have centralised first elements [əi, ʌu] (⊙ *writer, allowed*).

Gwen's English has extended 'lilting' intonation patterns, reflecting those of the Welsh language with abrupt falls and rise-falls being particularly common; these are less obvious in Owen's speech. Another salient feature is the rhythm of Welsh English which gives the impression of lengthening of consonants (e.g. ⊙ *lot of*).

5 Scouse (Liverpool) ⊙ Track 50

Pete: I was working on an – see for these people here

Interviewer: yes – coincidence

Pete: Rainford's Demolition – on a place up by the Bullring I think it was an old tannery – it was the first job after I left school – can lad

Interviewer: yes

Pete: and the floor collapsed – you know – the place we were – demolishing – you know – one fellow got killed – but only three of us went through – you know – but I fell clear – to the others like – and what was you saying – what was I think-ing like

Interviewer: uhm

Pete: well I – I found out that – every – every – see I was on like a slab – and what
– when I went down – have you ever thrown a plate in the water – and it goes
Interviewer: yes
Pete: sinks to the bottom and – and well that's the way this flag seemed to go as I
was going down – it was only a matter of about – twelve feet
Interviewer: oh dear
Pete: but there was heavy stuff falling round us – you know – these – other two
were buried alive – for – the first thing that – what I was thinking of down there
– I never went to mass on a Sunday – you know what they say what happens
when you drown
Interviewer: that's right yes
Pete: that was the first thing I thought of

Notes
can lad = teaboy
flag = flagstone

Description
Liverpool is the centre of the Merseyside conurbation (population about one and a half million) and it has a long history as a major port with a long seafaring tradition. It was the popularity of 'lobscouse' – a stew made of cheap meat, potatoes and ship's biscuit – which gave rise to the inhabitants' nickname of 'Scousers', and led to their speech being dubbed 'Scouse'. Merseyside English (spoken by about one and a half million people) sounds strikingly different from other types of Northern English, probably as a result of a massive influx of in-migrants over the last three centuries from two Celtic countries – southern Ireland and neighbouring North Wales. Our speaker, Pete, is a building worker who was asked to describe a dangerous moment in his life.

Scouse is non-rhotic and has variable **h**-dropping. Like most Scousers, Pete has virtually no glottalisation, but /p t k/ are heavily aspirated or affricated (☺ *collapsed*) (possibly an influence of North Wales Welsh where the same effect is heard). Medial /ŋ/ is followed by sounded /g/. Typically, /r/ is realised as a strong tap [ɾ] (found in Welsh and Irish) (☺ *buried*). Medial /t/ often shows **t**-voicing and may also be realised as a tap [ɾ], e.g. ☺ *matter* ['maɾə]. Many speakers (including Pete) frequently replace /θ ð/ by /t d/ (☺ *think, that's*) (this is probably an Irish influence, compare Dublin).

Like other northern England varieties, Scouse has no STRUT vowel, this being replaced by FOOT (☺ *others, stuff*). Furthermore, there is another notable systemic variation in that there is no SQUARE/NURSE contrast (☺ *first, there*). PALM is very fronted [aː] (no occurrence in sample). The starting point of PRICE is retracted (☺ *like*).

The intonation of Scouse is characterised by rise-fall intonation patterns. Liverpool is often noted for its velarised setting (an effect sometimes pejoratively called 'adenoidal'). Despite popular fantasies about this being the result of the damp climate and adenoidal infections, a more likely source is the similar pharyngealised setting characteristic of North Wales Welsh.

Activity

112 ☉ **Track 72 (Answers on website)**

Listen to the extracts on your audio CD. In each case, there is another voice speaking with one of the accent varieties discussed and which you have already heard. Try to locate the speaker geographically and state which particular phonetic features enable you to do this.

C4

WORLD ACCENT VARIETIES

Introduction

In this unit we shall examine three more types of North American English and three southern-hemisphere accents (Australia, New Zealand and South Africa). Second-language varieties are represented by Singapore and Indian English. Finally, Caribbean and Sierra Leone illustrate creole-influenced speech.

1 Southern USA (Texas) ☉ Track 51

Gary: Nacogdoches people look down their noses at Lufkin people – we think we're – we think we're – far superior to Lufkin – 'cos they're

Interviewer: do they make bad jokes about them

Gary: yeah – and they always beat us at football – we – we haven't beat them since 1941 – no – well that's not true – but – but – we our smashing football victory over Lufkin was in 1941 – when Lufkin was to be – Lufkin was – destined to be the state champs – state champions in their district – and Nacogdoches was not supposed to beat 'em – and I was only six years old but Daddy – took me to the ball game I remember – and we beat Lufkin seven to six

Interviewer: all right

Gary: and I could remember – I wasn't but six years old – and but I remember – after the game – Daddy going to town – took me to town – in the car – and we drove around the – square – around the – what's now the library – used to be the post office – and Daddy was honking the horn – honking the horn – and I said 'Daddy, why are you honking the horn?' – he said "cos we beat Lufkin' – but we have *not* beat Lufkin at football many times since that time – we *have* beat them a few times – but – anyway – but Lufkin has some – some nice areas and Lufkin has a lot of industry

Interviewer: OK

Gary: that we do not have over here – it's sort of a blue collar – it's sort of a working-class – town – and Nacogdoches – we've always thought we were a little – little above Lufkin – of course actually we're just jealous of Lufkin because they have all the good industries now – and our main – the best thing Nacogdoches has going for *it* – is the college – is the university – that's our main source of – income

Description

The English of the southern United States sounds quite different from that of the north of the country. Traditionally, the southern states have always been regarded as the poorer, more backward parts of the USA but they have been catching up rapidly since the mid-twentieth century. But perhaps because of the long-standing economic differences, Northerners have tended to look down on the accents of the south, and stereotype them as sounding amusing and uneducated. As a result, some Southerners try to modify their speech and make it sound closer to the language of their northern neighbours.

Gary is a lawyer with an educated, but quite distinctly Texan, accent. Nacogdoches and Lufkin are two towns, situated about 30 kilometres' distance from each other in Texas in the south-east of the USA. As Gary explains, there has always been a friendly rivalry between the neighbouring communities.

Unlike General American (GA), some southern USA English is variably non-rhotic. Notice how Gary deletes /r/ in ☺ *horn, years* and *remember*, but pronounces it in *far superior*. There is **t**-voicing (☺ *forty, heat 'em, little*). Unlike Kathy (see Section C1), Gary, from an older generation, uses /ʍ/ in *wh*-words (☺*what's*). A salient feature is the replacement of fricative /z/ by a stop /d/ preceding nasal /n/ in ☺ *wasn't* [wɒdn̩t]

Much of what we have said about the vowels of General American also applies to southern USA English. But southern USA English has several distinctive characteristics – notably in the vowel system. For instance, the PRICE vowel often lacks any glide, sounding like a long vowel [aː] (☺ *times, I, library*). Another noticeable feature is the phenomenon called 'breaking', which involves inserting [ə] between a vowel and the following /r/. Notice, for instance, how the vowels in ☺ *square, ball, old* become [ɛɪə, ɔːə, əʊə].

The absence of contracted forms with *not* is also characteristic of southern speech (☺ '*Nacogdoches was not supposed to beat 'em*', '*that we do not have over here*').

One of the most striking things about southern USA English is its rhythm and intonation. It is often described as 'drawling', implying that it sounds slow and drawn out to other Americans. Intonation tunes also appear more extended than in GA. Notice how high-pitched the syllable ☺ *Luf-* is in '*but Lufkin has some . . .*', '*Lufkin has a lot of industry*').

2 Kentucky ☺ Track 52

Bill: well I'm – right now we're living in Louisville – Louisville Kentucky, which – we don't have accents in Louisville any more but – that – I went – I was raised about two hours east of here in the – Appalachian Mountains in Irvine Kentucky – which is a town of thirty-five hundred – and now if you want to hear accents we just call Jobie – he lives there in Irvine – and I guess that – you get a sampling of what – what the dialect would be up that way – but – usually when I call home I really get my old – accent back in a hurry – and then when I call California I lose it so – but – I've been trying to get Jacob to come up there and spend a couple of days on the farm and relax a little bit – but – he's got another two thousand miles to go – here you're gonna have to go up there – Mike and Barb – Mom's sister has a – farm up there – they have like – seven horses – and it's up in – near Red River Gorge – which is just one of the prettiest parts of the state – and we go horseback riding up there – and when you come we're gonna have to hop on one of those things – I guess you ride horses don't you – but – it's beautiful up there and you put – especially here in two weeks when the leaves will have turned – it's gonna be nice

Description

Bill would also regard himself as a middle-class speaker but is proud of his country origins. Kentucky is geographically a south midland state but, at least in its rural forms, has many affinities with the south. Nevertheless, one exceptional feature (heard clearly in Bill's speech) is consistent rhoticism (☺ *farm, horseback*). Final -ing is pronounced as /ɪn/ rather than /ɪŋ/ (☺ *riding*). The FLEECE, GOOSE, FACE and GOAT vowels are extended (☺ *leaves, lose, raised, home*), whereas the PRICE vowel is steady-state (cf. Texas) (☺ *dialect, riding, miles*). A feature characteristic of many American varieties is the neutralisation of the KIT and DRESS vowels before /n/, KIT being used for both (☺ *spend* [spɪnd]). The final syllable in *accents* shows no vowel reduction. Bill also has extended intonation patterns similar in some ways to southern varieties (☺ 'which is a town of thirty five hundred', 'and spend a couple of days on the farm and relax a little bit').

3 Canadian ☺ Track 53

Anne: the set-up of the university is very different than what I found here – I mean – there's – all the buildings are in one location – and there's probably – well at least fifty different buildings – all – centred right there – I mean and then there's the residences – so – first-year students usually stay in residences – and then once you've met a couple of friends in second year and – up until fourth year you usually live in a house – with a couple of your friends right around – the – all the buildings of – of campus – we like to call it the student ghetto – so I mean we still only have a five-minute walk to class or so – so it's very different – than here – because here you find you only have to bike from building to building – and from your house to – and everything is so much more spread out here – . . .

It's the most beautiful place – like in Canada that I've really ever been to – it is *so* pretty – it's along the Ottawa river – and so I mean – the whole town is on the river – so there's beaches everywhere – and it's a very outdoorsy outdoorsy – kind of – nature town – and – I mean if you enjoy skiing – like cross-country skiing is very big there – and just all kinds of water sports like – canoeing – or fishing – even biking – just anything outdoors – you know you'll find it in my town – it's very active – outdoorsy town – yeah

Description

Canada has a population of 29 million people, but a sizeable minority of these are French speakers while many recent immigrants don't have English as their mother tongue. Nevertheless, this still leaves perhaps as many as 18 million English native speakers. The overwhelming influence on Canadian pronunciation (uniquely amongst the major countries of the former British Empire) is USA English, but Scottish and

Irish influences are also claimed. In fact, Canadian English, although recognisably a distinct variety, is much closer to General American than are many regional varieties of the USA itself. Within Canada, there is considerable variation on the Atlantic seaboard, notably the 'Newfie' speech of Newfoundland.

The speaker, Anne, grew up in a rural area (the Ottawa Valley) 200 kilometres west of Ottawa and was an exchange student in a European university at the time of recording. Like most American English, Anne's Canadian accent is **h**-pronouncing (☺ *house*), rhotic (☺ *river, water, fourth*) and has **t**-voicing (☺ *Ottawa, water, beautiful*). BATH words have the TRAP vowel (☺ *class*).

Anne's /l/ is dark in all positions (☺ *along*). Her front vowels, KIT, DRESS and TRAP are all rather open (☺ *river, residence, Canada*). The THOUGHT and LOT vowels are merged and sound like British NRP PALM (the vowels in ☺ *cross* and *walk* sound the same). Perhaps the most recognisable feature of Canadian is the central starting-point of the diphthongs MOUTH and PRICE before fortis consonants (☺ *house, out, right, like*). Note the **upspeak** terminal rise intonation patterns in *of* ☺ *campus, walk to class or so, just anything outdoors*. See p. 182 and pp. 222–34.

4 Australian ☺ Track 54

Helen: university is a lot different from school – do you want to know about that – it's a little bit just – the holidays – because – university – now have holidays in semesters – whereas the schools still have them in terms – and schools are really trying to get their holidays in semesters – because that's what you work in – and it seems strange having term holidays when you're working in semesters – but at university we have – three – well it all depends on when your exams finish – there's – you have two weeks of holidays – but – most exams – you have three weeks of exams – and then – say two weeks of holidays – but – not many people have exams – towards the end of those three weeks – most people will be finished with their exams within the first – what – at least two weeks – so you'll have probably at least three weeks' holiday – and you can go home as soon as you've finished your exams – and so – well I – I had over – I had three and a half weeks' holiday – this year – that was in the middle and – you really need the break – and we also have mid-semester holidays – which – this year – in the semester that I had the first semester before I came over here – it wasn't – it wasn't in the middle of semester – it was – I suppose they shouldn't be really called mid-semester because it was just a week off – and the week was two weeks before we started swot-vac

Notes

swot-vac: a non-teaching period (vacation) which allows students to work intensively for their examinations.

Description

Australia, with a present-day population of over 20 million and growing, appears set to become one of the chief standard forms of English of the future. Until recently, most of its population came from the British Isles, with a majority from southern England, and this is reflected in the nature of Australian speech today. Australian is a relatively young variety of English, and there are as yet no distinct regional accents in Australia;

all over this vast country, people sound surprisingly similar. However, as mentioned in Section A1, there are distinct social differences. This speaker, Helen, is a university student, and speaks what would be classified as 'General Australian' English (i.e. neither 'Broad' nor 'Cultivated', see p. 6).

Australian English is non-rhotic (☻ *working, semesters*). Broad accents have some **h**-dropping, but this is much less common than in England, and there is no trace of this in Helen's speech (☻ *holidays, home*). Helen has regular medial **t**-voicing similar to that found in much General American (☻ *university, started*). Her /l/ is noticeably dark. Systemically, the Australian vowel inventory is identical to that of NRP. Lexical variation is found in some BATH words, where the TRAP vowel rather than PALM is found in words like *dance*. There is considerable realisational variation. DRESS and TRAP vowels are close (☻ *semesters, exams*). Wide glide realisations are found in FACE and GOAT (☻ *break, go home*). The PALM vowel (☻ *started*) is very fronted [aː] while NURSE is close and fronted, sometimes with rounding [øː] (☻ *work*).

Helen's speech provides some good examples of one very well-known feature of Australian English, namely 'upspeak' terminal rise intonation (in fact another term occasionally used is 'Australian question intonation'). Note the terminal rises in ☻ *'so you'll have probably at least three weeks' holiday – and you can go home as soon as you've finished your exams'.*

5 New Zealand ☻ Track 55

Simon: Thursday night we decided to go down to the pub – and that made me feel quite good because I really wanted to have a beer – and so – we went down there and we had a beer – and then on the way home – we were there for a couple of hours – we got back to the flat – and – we saw that the back door was open – and – some people thought that maybe – there was – other flatmate had got home – forgotten to close it – but I had this sinking feeling in my stomach – that maybe – maybe that something dodgy was going on – because the lights were on and the door was open – and I had this bit of a sick feeling in my stomach – and so as we walked in the door – we saw that all the cupboards – the food cupboards – were all opened – and that's when we knew that something wasn't right – and I thought to myself – oh no – this is very bad – and so we walked through the house – we came down to – Rachel and I came down to *her* room – and everything had been turned out on to her bed – the desk was trashed – some money was stolen – you know – things were all rifled through – and – it was a very very bad scene – it's not – it's makes – you know – it makes you feel really bad when you see that your stuff's been gone through – and – it turns out that – one of the flatmate's cars had been stolen as well – to carry all the stuff – and – one of the other flatmate's – all his guitars – heaps of – thousands and thousands of dollars worth of stuff was stolen – everybody felt really – unhappy about the whole situation I have to say – and – the police came around – and we told them what had happened – but nobody was insured – and so everybody felt a bit sick – and I felt really sorry for everybody – even though I didn't have that much stuff here – and – the next day – the crime scene investigator guy came but – they're not very confident of catching anyone – so – I feel a bit let down by society in – in this respect – that we don't live in a safe place – and my – and my faith in humanity has been – severely knocked –

Description

Most of New Zealand's four million people speak English as their first language – even though there are still a significant number of Maoris who are bilingual. Located geographically nearly two thousand miles from Australia, New Zealand nevertheless shares many cultural ties with its closest neighbour, so it isn't surprising that we find similarities between these two antipodean varieties. Our speaker, Simon, is a post-graduate student at Canterbury University in the South Island and speaks an educated variety of New Zealand English. His speech, like that of most New Zealanders (all except those from the extreme southern portion of South Island), is non-rhotic (☺ *hours, insured*).

Although New Zealand English resembles Australian English in many ways, there are some interesting differences, and the pronunciation of the KIT vowel is a sure-fire way of picking out a New Zealander. KIT is noticeably central for Simon as for most New Zealanders, and is levelled with /ə/ (☺ *sick, live*). DRESS and TRAP are both even closer than in Australian English (☺ *desk* (sounding very like *disk* in most other varieties), *everybody; flat, bad*). The SQUARE vowel is often very similar to English NRP NEAR (there are no instances of SQUARE on this recording).

Other features are indeed very like Australian. Simon's NURSE vowel is front and rounded (☺ *Thursday, turned*) and PALM is extremely front (☺ *cars, guitars*). The NEAR vowel is often disyllabic (☺ *here, beer* [hiːə biːə]). A feature of the consonant system is a noticeably dark *l* (☺ *police, feeling*). Medial /t/ is often a tap (☺ *investigator*). As with Australian speakers, rising terminal upspeak intonation patterns frequently occur (☺ . . . *to carry all the stuff,* . . . *were all opened*). Simon's educated variety lacks the extended diphthongs of FACE and GOAT found in broader New Zealand accents.

6 South African ☺ Track 56

Nicolo: it depends – English schools in South Africa are far more formal – especially the school I went to – which is the Pretoria High School for Girls – an only girls' school – an Anglican school at that – so it was quite formal – and – I didn't really enjoy my time there – the Afrikaans school was *much* more fun – not as posh and la-di-da as the – as the – English school – but – the people were much warmer – they loved the idea of having an English person wanting to learn *their* language – that was a whole new idea to them – since they were usually the ones having to adapt – and there was there was lots of fun . . . *Bobotie* is very – OK it's actually a mince dish – with raisins and cloves in it – and – some special kinds of leaves – what are they called again – I can't remember what the leaves are called – funny name – bit of an exotic name – and it's – it's eaten with rice – which you – that yellow kind of rice also with raisins – and you basically bake it in the oven – so it's a very spicy meat dish – South Africans eat a lot of meat by the way – a lot of meat – they're real carnivores – and they also like eating potatoes and rice together – so a typical South African dinner – would be meat potatoes rice and a vegetable – something else that's – is eaten in South Africa very often – especially among the black people – is what they call *putupap* or *mealiepap* – it's basically – crushed – crushed corn – and that's really ground into a into a sort of a powder – and then cooked up – and then you get this type of white porridgy substance – and that's very filling – although not very nutritious – so – many poorer black people eat that – very often

– but – are malnourished because of it – so – those things are eaten quite often – and what the black people also love eating – is – you know the intestines and brains and eyes and those things – those really are delicacies among the amongst the black people so

Interviewer: but you don't eat them

Nicole: no – I couldn't – I couldn't really

Description

Some people may still be surprised to hear that mother-tongue English speakers are very much in the minority in South Africa, numbering no more than about three and a half million speakers. The English of South Africa has been very much influenced by the other major South African language of European origin, Afrikaans (with perhaps as many as five million speakers). It has been said that South African English ranges all the way from broad accents strongly influenced by Afrikaans to upper-class speech which sounds very similar to British traditional RP (Crystal 1997: 40). In the new South Africa many black south Africans who speak African languages, such as Zulu, Xhosa and Sotho, now speak English as a second language.

Our speaker, Nicole, is a student who had spent one year at an Afrikaans-speaking school, but had the rest of her schooling from English-speaking institutions. Although Nicole's speech is very recognisably South African, hers is a middle-class variety lacking many of the potentially stigmatised features (such as voiced /h/ and unaspirated /p t k/).

There is no **h**-dropping (☺ *high, having*) (but broad South African accents have voiced /h/) and the accent is non-rhotic (☺ *are far more formal*). The distribution of clear vs. dark *l* is as in NRP and many other varieties, but dark *l* has a hollow pharyngealised quality (☺ *else, school, people*). /t/ is strongly affricated (☺ *wanting, eating, a lot of*), perhaps a slight over-compensation for the lack of aspiration in much South African English. Nicole has very little glottalisation (☺ *went to, it was, much*).

DRESS and TRAP are close (☺ *together, went, black, adapt*). In certain words, the KIT vowel is central resembling [ə] (☺ *dinner, mince*, cf. New Zealand). STRUT is relatively front (☺ *much, fun*). LOT is open and unrounded (☺ *wanting, not*). The *happy* vowel is said with a close short FLEECE vowel (☺ *really, funny, basically*). The PALM vowel is very back (e.g. ☺ *far, carnivores*). PRICE and MOUTH have relatively narrow glides (☺ *time, kinds, rice, ground, South, powder*). SQUARE is very close (☺ *their*). The weak form of *the* is consistently /ðə/ whether it occurs before a vowel or a consonant (☺ *the idea, the English, the oven*). The PALM vowel is used in BATH words (☺ *can't*).

7 Indian English ☺ *Track 57*

Rajiv: and of course the politics – they keep on going on with all stupid things I think – I don't know why – but – that is the reason I think because the rest I don't understand because – India and Pakistan used to be – they were in the beginning like – let's say – before the partition – were in a – yeah – it was a big country – and half of them were in India and the other half was in Pakistan – I don't know how come the friction came but – why we have this friction I think maybe – both

countries want to prove that I'm better than another – that is the reason I think –
but the rest yeah – if you talk to the Pakistani like – Wasim the other guy – if you
talk sometime about the politics (?) – why we have problem – then I say because
of the politics – the politician they – they look for their own interest – and he say
– absolutely the same thing – the politics – the politician they look for their own
interest – that they – just – this way they keep – they keep their own their seats –
if you ask the people – maybe people don't allow – they don't want any – this kind
of a nonsense – because life itself is pretty hard

Description

In terms of numbers, Indian English is without doubt a major world variety; estimates
vary, but it could have as many as thirty million speakers. 'Indian English' is used loosely
to include the English spoken in all the southern Asian area, i.e. that part of Asia which
includes India, Pakistan, Bangladesh and Sri Lanka. The chief languages, including
Hindi, Urdu, Bengali and Punjabi, are all spoken by many millions of people. Because
there are so many different languages all over southern Asia, English is recognised as
an official medium which all educated people can use. Consequently, in India, as in
all the countries of Southern Asia, English means essentially second-language English.
Our speaker, Rajiv, comes from Delhi and is a Hindi speaker but from his schooldays
onwards has been speaking English on a day-to-day basis.

One of the most striking things about much Indian English, and this is true of
Rajiv's speech, is that many consonants are retroflex (see Section A5); this is true
of /t d s z l n r/ (☺ *better, hard, pretty*). The dental fricatives /θ ð/ are often replaced
by /t d/ (☺ *think, both, that, they*). The consonants /v/ and /w/ are not consistently
distinguished (☺ *why, we*), or a compromise (a labio-dental approximant) is used
for both. As with most Indians, Rajiv's English is rhotic (☺ *hard, partition*); initial
and medial /r/ are generally strong taps (☺ *reason, rest*). /p t k/ are unaspirated
(☺ *politics, talk, keep*) and /b d g/ are voiced throughout (☺ *because, guy, big*).

Most types of Indian English use the vowels of the local Indian language and these
will sound quite unlike those of native English. Note also that some Indian words are
said differently in English from the way they are pronounced in India itself. For instance,
the name *Gandhi* has a long PALM vowel in Indian languages but a short vowel in
British English.

Indian English is notable for its syllable-timed rhythm, a feature it shares with
many Indian languages (☺ *'life itself is pretty hard'*). In many Indian languages stress
does not appear to fall on any particular syllable, resulting in unexpected stress patterns in Indian English (☺ *beginning*). These effects can cause intelligibility problems
for non-Indians trying to understand these Indian varieties of English.

8 Singapore ☺ Track 58

Ben: everybody has to go through national service in Singapore – I mean not
everybody – every – every male citizen has – have to go through national service
in Singapore – from – I think after sixteen you can – you can enlist – but you have
to do it from within two to two and a h- – you have to do it – you have to – you
have to serve – in the army – I mean – you have to join the national service for
two to two and a half years – so you have some – you're just trained as a soldier

and – I think basic training – they have lots of accidents and – dangerous stuff like live firing – live explosives and – yeah – and – lots of military training – so I think – I think the rate of – I think this is – I've seen – I've – of I've heard stories that people get killed – and they're reading – I'm not really sure if it's real but – maybe it's a story to scare all of us – but I've seen – people – I've think I've seen – people – one person commit suicide before – because uh – it's quite – pressurising in – in the army – of course – I mean – I mean the – your – I mean most people can take it but some people – are not suited to do military service – but they're still forced to because it's – it's by law that you have to do it – so – they can't really – probably can't take the pressure and kill themselves – so – yeah I've seen – once – someone just jumped down a building – and – there was a huge commotion – everyone surrounding him – and they had uh – they had to get a helicopter from somewhere – and carried him off to a stretcher – I don't know if he's still alive – but I mean he jumped from the fifth floor I think – so yeah

Interviewer: not a good thing

Ben: yeah and – yeah we – we didn't like – we do – grenade throwing – live firing – everything – and uh – we do – obstacle courses where – they actually fire live rounds two metres from the ground level – but I mean – unless we – unless you jump up you get hit – so for that obstacle course we all just on our – on our hands there – I mean we are crawling on the ground – through barbed wire and everything and – yeah

Description

Singapore is a truly multicultural country. Most of its inhabitants are of Chinese origin, but a variety of languages are spoken by the two and a half million people crowded onto this small island. English is only one of four official languages, but it has a special position since most Singapore children go to English-language schools. They understand English well and speak their own variety – sometimes called 'Singlish' – fluently. Our speaker, Ben, is typical of many educated Singapore people. Although he is fluent in two types of Chinese, he regularly speaks English both for his work and in conversation with his friends. He can move with ease between more formal English for work to something much closer to Singlish when relaxing with friends.

Ben has no **h**-dropping (☻ *has to, helicopter*) and his speech is non-rhotic (☻ *heard, barbed wire, person*). The dental fricative /θ/ is variably replaced by /t/ (☻ *through, throwing*). Final dark *l* is regularly completely vocalised sounding like an [u] vowel (☻ *killed, level*). Final stops are typically unreleased. There is extensive glottalisation, with complete replacement of /t/ even in intervocalic position or before pause (☻ *quite, rate of*). Ben regularly reduces consonant clusters to a single consonant (☻ *ground, think, jump*).

LOT is tense (☻ *lots*). The *happy* vowel is said with a short FLEECE vowel (☻ *actually, stories, army*). THOUGHT and PALM are very tense and somewhat shorter (☻ *forced to, before, half*). BATH words typically have the PALM vowel (☻ *after, half*). FACE and GOAT lack a glide (☻ *rate of, commotion, most*).

Ben's speech is also characterised by patterns of stress and intonation which are typical of Singapore English. Many of these are traceable to the influence of his Chinese origins. Note the high level tones in ☻ *everybody, I've seen, but some people, we do.* There is little reduction of unstressed syllables, giving a syllable-timing effect, ☺ *military training.*

9 Caribbean (West Indian) ☺ Track 59

Gregory: old fellow in Golden Rock – they call him Jim – and it seems as if the estate owner of the land was Mr Moore – had some grudge against him – and he always want to whip Jim – the whip man was Hercules – so any time he's finished eat – and he having a smoke he would sit – I remember the old window that he used to sit in – he showed me – and it was a big tamarind tree right outside there – the house close this window and he used to sit there and smoke – they say you see all those holes there – in that window in tho sill there – that's where he spit his tobacco out – spit – and he said (?) rotten holes like that – he say now – when he want fun – and he finish eating – he want a smoke he light a cigar – and he call the whip man to bring Jim – he say – bring Jim – and they would bring old Jim – and they would tie him – a rope up in the tree and it would come down and tie Jim around his waist – and he can't go no further than where that rope would let him go – and they would keep whipping – so when they – he start whipping him – asked well – how many lashes to give him – some time he say ah – give him a round dozen – a round dozen meaning twelve times twelve – is one forty four – hundred and forty-four lashes – say give him a round dozen – some time he would say – well – give him as much as I take a puff – each puff he take from his cigar is a lash for Jim

Interviewer: he could get away with that – just that – like that

Gregory: well he was the slave own[er] – he was the owner of the slave

Notes

Hercules: slaves were frequently given names from classical mythology. (Note the pronunciation ['haːkləs] conserving the probable eighteenth-century pronunciation: see p. 177).

round dozen: in fact this phrase means 'twelve' and not what Gregory believes.

Description

Caribbean English in one form or another stretches across a large area of the Pacific throughout the West Indies and over Guyana on the mainland of South America. There are also sizeable numbers of first- and second-generation speakers with some competence in Caribbean creoles in Britain and the USA.

Our sample comes from one of the smallest speech communities, St Eustatius in the Leeward Islands, more commonly known by its nickname of 'Statian'. Here just over 2000 people live on a tiny island which is still a colony of the Netherlands. Dutch is the official language that everyone learns in school, and many islanders also have a knowledge of Spanish. Nevertheless, the main language of daily communication is a variety of English. Because of the official status of Dutch, there is no continuum from an acrolectal form of English through to a basilectal creole variety (as is true of Jamaica or Trinidad, for example). Our speaker, a member of the older generation, Gregory, is retelling stories that he has heard concerning one of the most notorious of the nineteenth-century slave owners.

Caribbean English divides along rhotic and non-rhotic lines, and Statian English is of the latter type (☺ *further*). A salient feature is the simplification of consonant clusters, which is to be heard throughout this sample, often eliminating the past tense /t d/ or third person /s z/ markers of verbs (☺ *waist, finish, start*). One common word with a typical Caribbean pronunciation is ☺ *asked* [akst]. Unlike Caribbeans in, for example, Jamaica, Gregory is not a regular **h**-dropper. The only indication here of the frequent Caribbean uncertainty concerning the occurrence of this consonant is the hint of epenthetic /h/ in the emphatic pronunciation of ☺ *owner*. The realisation of /w/ is at times a labiodental approximant (☺ *whip*). Replacement of dental fricatives by stops /t d/ is heard throughout the Caribbean, and Gregory is typical in this respect (☺ *further than*).

Like most Caribbean speakers, Gregory has an open TRAP vowel (☺ *land*) – more like British than American realisations. The PALM vowel is very fronted (☺ *start, cigar*). The FACE and GOAT vowels are narrow diphthongs or steady-state vowels [eː oː] (☺ *take, smoke*). Final /ə/ is open (☺ *owner* [oːna]). In ☺ *forty*, THOUGHT is open and retracted. The PRICE and MOUTH vowels consistently have the typical central starting-points of Caribbean English (☺ *light, round*).

10 West African (Sierra Leone) ☺ Track 60

Aminata: To him what happened was – he went – a Dutchman in Sierra Leone – I call it – he went to Sierra Leone – he make appointment with the police – and he has appointment for one o'clock – he was there ten to one or quarter to one – and he found out the person he has appointment with was sleeping – so he was standing there – waiting – he was – he has been sleeping for two hours – and he's still sleeping – I say – look I have an appointment one o'clock and it's now three o'clock – I say – yes I know – I know I'm coming – so he went in – into another room – he came after forty-five minutes – so my husband has been there for – since one o'clock – didn't (?) – his appointment was actually four o'clock – so he become so irritated he blushed and so – I said now – take it easy – this is Sierra Leone – they say one o'clock – they mean three o'clock – it's African time – that's what we call it – African time – never you go again when they say one o'clock – make sure you're there three o'clock or ten past three to be precise – he says oh OK – yes and when he goes to the market – now that's what I find terrible – he can't buy in the market because then he has to pay three times the real price – when he goes – one day I was sick so I sent him – I said please go buy some pepper and onions and I want to make soup – so he went – he bought pepper onions tomato – and he came to me – he says it's about fifty thousand leones – and fifty thousand leones is about twenty-five dollar – I said what – fifty thousand leones – he says yes – for onions tomato and pepper – yeah yeah – I said now – now what we're going to do we go back – so I went with him – I was sick in my night's (?) dress and so I – I went to the market – everybody was looking at me (?) as if I am a mad woman – I said where did you buy this – show me – because I know – well actually this man – is a white man with a black woman – so now you people sell give to me what I want for the normal price – so I end up pay five thousand leones – so he pay fifty – forty-five thousand leones extra – so I end up pay five thousand leones for a few things and I come home – yeah – since then when he went to the market – then he say my wife says – then he buy normal – otherwise

Notes

Dutchman: Aminata's husband is Dutch.
leones: Sierra Leone's unit of currency.

Description

Sierra Leone has its own creole language, Krio, derived originally from English. Some Sierra Leonians are only able to speak Krio and indeed have grown up speaking it exclusively as their mother tongue. Others, like Aminata, although able to speak Krio, also speak English as a second language. They can switch easily between Krio and English, and indeed constantly vary their use of Krio and English according to the circumstances and the persons with whom they're conversing.

Aminata has much in her English which is common to many West African countries, but some features are peculiar to Sierra Leone. Unlike most West African varieties, there is variable **h**-dropping (⊙ *he, his*). /p k/ are unaspirated and there is no devoicing of /l/ following the fortis plosives (⊙ *appointment, o'clock, coming*). The dental fricatives /θ ð/ are replaced by stops /t d/ (⊙ *three, thousand, with, there, this*). An unusual Sierra Leone feature compared with other varieties of African English is that /r/ is uvular (⊙ *irritated, dress*). The accent is non-rhotic (⊙ *quarter, forty-five, market*).

Aminata's realisations of vowels are typical of Sierra Leonian English. TRAP vowel is open (⊙ *mad, back, black*) while STRUT is back (⊙ *onions, Dutch, coming*). NURSE is a back vowel rather like NRP THOUGHT (⊙ *person*). The *happy* vowel is said with a short steady state FLEECE vowel (⊙ *forty, actually*). Syllables which are unstressed in most other varieties of English are pronounced with a degree of stress and not reduced to /ə ɪ ʊ/ (⊙ *market, African, police, woman*). The BATH words are said with the PALM vowel (⊙ *after, past, can't*). FLEECE and GOOSE are noticeably short (⊙ *sleeping, soup*).

Activity

113 ⊙ Track 73 (Answers on website)

Listen to the extracts on your audio CD (track 73). In each case, there is another voice speaking with one of the accent varieties discussed and which you have already heard. Try to locate the speaker geographically and state which particular phonetic features enable you to do this.

C5 PRONUNCIATION CHANGE: PAST, PRESENT, FUTURE

Pronunciation change in the past

Speech habits vary not only geographically but also chronologically. Changes take place not only from one area to another but also from one generation to another. You are probably aware that you don't speak in quite the same way as your parents do and that your grandparents speak or spoke differently again. And you may have noticed that if you watch old films, or see extracts from newsreels on TV, the pronunciation of, say, fifty or sixty years ago is in many ways different from that used today.

If we move further back in time, then the differences become much more obvious. When reading Shakespeare (sixteenth century) you have undoubtedly noticed the changes that have taken place in grammar and vocabulary between his English and ours. But it is not perhaps as immediately apparent that Elizabethan pronunciation would also have been quite different from ours. The English of Chaucer's time (fourteenth century) strikes us as being very far removed from modern English, while Old English (sometimes called Anglo-Saxon), which was spoken in England before the Norman Conquest in 1066, looks like – and certainly would have sounded like – a totally alien language, as just a couple of lines from a famous poem, *The Battle of Maldon*, will indicate:

Old English: The Battle of Maldon (anon., tenth century) ☺ Track 61

> *Hiʒe sceal þe heardra, heorte þe cenre,*
> *mod sceal þe mare, þe ure mæʒen lytlað*

> 'hiːjə ʃæl ðə 'hæərdrɑ, 'heərtəðə 'keːnrə.
> 'moːd ʃæl ðə 'maːrə, ðeː uːrə 'mæjən 'liːtlɑθ

> *(Thought shall be the harder, heart the keener,*
> *courage the greater, as our might lessens.)*

Although, obviously, we can't dig up our ancestors and get them talking, nevertheless it's possible to reconstruct their pronunciation from the historical evidence that's available. We can do this in a number of ways. For instance, we can derive a great deal of information from the orthography: the current spelling of *knight* indicates that this word was probably originally pronounced as [kniçt]. In addition, we can examine poetry to see how certain words in previous eras rhymed where they don't rhyme today (for example, Shakespeare rhymed *love* and *prove* while Pope rhymed *tea* and *obey*). In some cases, present-day regional accents still preserve older pronunciation forms which have been lost in the majority of English varieties. And, finally, a very important source of information are books written by the phoneticians of previous eras, who published either works on elocution for native speakers or books to help non-natives acquire English (one of the earliest and best examples was produced in 1550 by a Welshman, William Salesbury, in an attempt to persuade the Welsh to learn English, and the English to learn Welsh). Assembling and analysing information from these various sources has enabled historical linguists to construct patterns of sound change and apply these to many areas of pronunciation.

Let's now have a look at the changes which took place in English over a period of several centuries from about 1350 to 1750 by examining the reconstructed English pronunciations of three famous writers – Geoffrey Chaucer, William Shakespeare and Alexander Pope.

English pronunciation in the fourteenth century

Middle English: Geoffrey Chaucer (1345–1400) ☉ Track 62

> *Whan that Aprille with hise shoures soote*
> *The droghte of March hath perced to the roote*
> *And bathed every veyne in swich licour*
> *Of which vertu engendred is the flour*
> *Whan Zephirus eek with his sweete breeth*
> *Inspired hath in euery holt and heeth*
> *The tendre croppes and the yonge sonne*
> *Hath in the Ram his half cours yronne*
> *And smale fowules maken melodye*
> *That slepen al the nyght with open eye*
> *So priketh hem nature in hir corages*
> *Thanne longen folk to goon on pilgrimages*
> > (*from the* Prologue *to* Canterbury Tales)

> 'ʍan ðat 'aːprıl wıθ hıs 'ʃuːrəs 'soːtə
> ðə 'drʊxt ɔf 'martʃ haθ 'pɛrsəd toː ðə 'roːtə
> and 'baːðəd 'ɛːvrı 'væin ın 'swıtʃ lıˈkuːr
> ɔf 'ʍıtʃ vərˈtiu ɛnˈdʒɛndərd ıs ðə 'fluːɪ
> ʍan 'zɛfırʊs 'ɛːk wıθ hıs 'sweːtə 'brɛːθ
> ınˈspiːrəd 'haθ ın 'ɛːvrı 'hɔlt and 'hɛːθ
> ðə 'tɛndər 'krɔppəs and ðə 'jʊŋgə 'sʊnnə
> 'haθ ın ðə 'ram hıs 'halvə 'kʊrs ıˈrʊnnə
> and 'smaːlə 'fuːləs 'maːkən mɛlɔˈdiːə
> ðat 'sleːpən 'aːl ðə 'nıçt wıθ 'ɔːpən 'iːə
> sɔː 'prıkəθ 'hɛm naːˈtiur ın 'hır kʊˈraːdʒəs
> ðan 'lɔːŋgən 'fɔlk toː 'gɔːn ɔn pılgrıˈmaːdʒəs
> > (*Adapted from Cruttenden 1994: 73–4*)

Even though the grammar was somewhat different and certain vocabulary items like *eek* 'also' and *holt* 'wood' may strike us as strange, the Middle English of the fourteenth century was perfectly recognisable as the forerunner of the language we speak today.

As you can see from the transcription above, the basis of the modern consonant system was already present in Chaucer's day. The most noticeable differences were the existence of the voiceless velar and palatal fricatives [x ç] (spelt **gh**) in words like ☉ *droghte*, *nyght* and the consistent use of voiceless /ʍ/ in *wh*-words (e.g. ☉ *whan* or *which*). In addition, the English language is at this period rhotic. (You'll find all these features still present today in Scottish English varieties, which are the most conservative of modern regional accents. See Section C3.)

The fourteenth-century vowel system, however, would seem less familiar to us. Shortly after Chaucer's time, a massive change, known as the Great Vowel Shift, was to take place in the pronunciation of English vowels. Up till the fourteenth century, for example, many present-day FLEECE words (e.g. ☉ *sweete*) had the vowel [eː], while GOOSE words (e.g. ☉ *roote*) were said as [oː]. Modern FACE words (like ☉ *Aprille*, *bathed*) contained the [aː] vowel; MOUTH words (e.g. ☉ *flour* 'flower') were pronounced with [uː]; and PRICE words (e.g. ☺ *inspired*) with [iː]. All this was to change in the space of a century or so.

English pronunciation in the sixteenth century

Elizabethan English: William Shakespeare (1564–1616) ☺ *Track 63*

> *Friends, Romans, Countrymen, lend me your ears:*
> *I come to bury* Caesar, *not to praise him:*
> *The euill that men do, liues after them,*
> *The good is oft enterred with their bones,*
> *So let it be with* Caesar. *The Noble* Brutus,
> *Hath told you* Caesar *was Ambitious:*
> *If it were so, it was a greeuous Fault,*
> *And greeuously hath* Caesar *answer'd it.*
>
> *(from* Julius Caesar, *Act III, Scene ii, original spelling*
> *and punctuation as in 1623 Folio edition)*

ˈfrɛndz | ˈroːmənz | ˈkʏntrɪmɛn | ˈlɛnd miː juːɹ ˈiːɹz ||
əɪ ˈkʏm tə ˈbɛrɪ ˈseːzəɹ | ˈnɒt tə ˈpreːz hɪm ||
ðɪ ˈiːvɪl ðət mɛn ˈduː | ˈlɪvz ˈæftəɹ ðɛm ||
ðə ˈguːd ɪz ˈɒft ɪnˈtaːrɪd wɪð ðɛːɹ ˈboːnz ||
ˈsoː lɛt ɪt ˈbiː wɪð ˈseːzəɹ || ðə ˈnoːbl ˈbrjuːtəs |
həθ ˈtoːld juː | ˈseːzəɹ wəz æmˈbɪsɪəs ||
ɪf ɪt ˈweːɹ soː | ɪt ˈwaz ə ˈgriːvəs ˈfɒlt |
ənd ˈgriːvəslɪ kəθ ˈseːzəɹ ˈænsərd ɪt ||
([ʏ] *indicates unrounded* [o], *secondary CV 7. See IPA chart, p. 258).*
(Adapted from Jones 1956: 210)

Even though in modern times Elizabethan theatres have been reconstructed with close attention to minute detail (the Globe in London is perhaps the most famous example) few amongst the present-day audience probably ever stop to consider how the actors' words would have sounded in the Elizabethan era. In fact, Shakespeare's own pronunciation would have been very different from the English of modern actors like Judi Dench or Ian McKellen.

As you can see from the transcription, Shakespeare's English, like Chaucer's, was rhotic (☺ *ears*). By this time, the velar fricative [x] had disappeared from the consonant system, although [ʍ] lived on. With the advent of the Great Vowel Shift, the vowel system had become much closer to that which we know today. Sixteenth-century English had a STRUT–FOOT contrast (even though STRUT, as in ☺ *come*, was not yet as open as it is now). The pronunciation of GOAT (e.g. as in ☺ *bones*) would be recognisable to the present day, even though the vowel was steady-state and not a diphthong. Certain modern FACE words were now pronounced with an open [ɛː] vowel, sounding similar to present-day SQUARE. PRICE (☺ *I*) and MOUTH were by now diphthongs but with central starting-points [ə]. There was no separate set of BATH words; all were said with TRAP (e.g. ☺ *after, answer'd*).

English pronunciation in the early modern period

Eighteenth-century English: Alexander Pope (1688–1744) ⊚ Track 64

> *True ease in writing comes from art, not chance,*
> *As those move easiest who have learnt to dance.*
> *'Tis not enough no harshness gives offence,*
> *The sound must seem an echo to the sense.*
>   (*from* An Essay on Criticism)

truː 'eːz ɪn 'rəɪtɪn 'kʌmz frəm 'æːt | nɒt 'tʃæːns |
əz 'ðoːz muːv 'eːzɪəst | hʊ əv 'læːnt tə 'dæːns ‖
tɪz 'nɒt ɪ'nʌf | 'noː 'hæːʃnɪs 'gɪvz o'fɛns |
ðə 'səʊnd məst 'siːm ən 'ɛkoː tə ðə 'sɛns ‖

By the eighteenth century the pace of change slowed down somewhat. This was the result of greater literacy and a new respect for spelling forms. The efforts of lexicographers (culminating in 1755 with Dr Samuel Johnson's dictionary) had by now fixed the modern English spelling system with all its shortcomings and inconsistencies.

Pope's English had both the consonant and the vowel systems much as we have them today. London speech was by now non-rhotic (⊚ *art*), and few people bothered to say /ʍ/ in *wh*-words. Final -*ing* was said as [ɪn] (⊚ *writing*) – a feature (sometimes loosely called **g**-dropping) still found today in non-standard English worldwide. In educated pronunciation, /h/ was dropped in many words, not just as today in *hour* and *honour*, but also in, for example, *hospital, humble, herb* (the last word is still h-less in American English).

The modern NURSE words spelt **er, ear** (⊚ *learn*) at this point contained [æː], not [ɜː]. Certain FLEECE words, e.g. ⊚ *ease*, had the vowel [eː] (as they still do today in some southern Irish varieties).

Vowels differed from modern English mainly in terms of realisation. Much had been retained from Shakespeare's time: FACE and GOAT (⊚ *those*) were still steady-state vowels, and MOUTH (⊚ *sound*) and PRICE (⊚ *writing*) retained their central starting-points, but STRUT (⊚ *comes*) was now moving towards its modern central open quality. Perhaps the most significant change was taking place with the TRAP vowel, which was lengthening before certain consonants. This had already affected TRAP before /r/ (as in *harsh*). The final /r/ was then dropped leaving a lengthened vowel [æː] as its only trace. In many words, a similar change was now taking place before fortis fricatives /f θ s/ (e.g. *draft, pass, path*) and nasal + consonant (e.g. ⊚ *dance, chant, demand, branch*). During the nineteenth century, the new long front vowel [æː] then retracted to become the modern back [ɑː], thus giving rise to the complex vowel distribution in the BATH words in southern British varieties. But this process was not completed in the Midlands or north of England nor, crucially, in the USA and Canada.

A corresponding effect took place with LOT words before fricative consonants, where a long vowel similar to present-day THOUGHT developed in words like *cost, off, cloth*, giving /kɔːst ɔːf klɔːθ/. It survives in much American English (see Section C1) and was until recently also a feature of traditional RP and certain southern regional varieties (notably Cockney). See below for the current situation.

Change in recent times and in progress

Regularly in the newspapers you will come across journalists deploring the changes taking place in the English language. Or you may find members of the public complaining in letters to the editor on the lines of: 'Will the younger generation totally destroy our beautiful language? Will it ever stop? Is there anything we can do about it?' The answer in each case is in all probability 'no'. Even if you wanted to, there's nothing you can do to stop linguistic change; it has always taken place and always will. Nevertheless, although linguistic change must, by definition, alter certain aspects of our language, English will survive. One cannot charge the upcoming generation with ill-treating their linguistic inheritance any more than one can accuse the people of Pope's or Shakespeare's time of destroying the English that had gone before them.

To take a more positive view, linguistic change is always interesting to explore and analyse – and especially so when it is change in progress happening all around us. So let's move on to examine how speech has developed in relatively recent years: changes which have taken place in your parents' and grandparents' lifetimes, and also some changes which are going on at the very moment.

Activity

114

This satirical poem appeared in 2002 in a British magazine aimed at the older generation. How accurate are the phonetic observations made by the authors of young people's speech habits? What influences do they appear to believe are at work? Can you yourself think of any personal experiences which demonstrate the irritation of older people with the way the younger generation speak?

> She's barely twelve, and Hayley Howells
> Has virtually abandoned vowels.
> Her teachers say she's over-text,
> Which makes her ma and pa perplexed.
> Now they find their Hayley drops
> Her aitches, and her glottal stops
> Are so pronounced, she speaks in code –
> This makes her Mum and Dad explode.
> Although they pay the highest fees
> To educate their daughter, she's
> Already fuelled by the hopes
> Of a long career in soaps.
> When Hayley's daily on our screens
> They'll know what modern living means:
> That kids today must show forbearance
> With their over-cautious parents.
> (Paul Evans and Bernadette Evans, The Oldie, September 2002)

Changing consonants

Listening to early twentieth-century recordings of British English speakers, one is struck by the clearer quality of syllable-final /l/. The present-day 'vocoid l', i.e. a dark *l* with a back vowel quality of an [ʊ] type, is especially noticeable following back vowels, e.g. in *doll* [dɒʊ], *ball* [bɔːʊ], etc. Until recently such pronunciations would have been regarded as 'Cockney', and they may indeed have come into late twentieth-century speech from London English.

The same London influence may be at work in the spread of glottal stop – a feature which is often thought of as a 'slipshod Cockneyism' that has invaded young people's speech in the last few years. In fact, glottalisation in one form or another is something which has been around in English for a long time. It can be heard in the speech of George V – born in 1865, and hardly a Cockney! The King's pronunciation provides evidence that, contrary to what is sometimes believed, glottalisation was actually to be found in traditional RP – even though it only occurred in pre-consonantal syllable-final contexts (and not medially or before dark *l*). See also Section B2.

Medial **t**-voicing, giving a rapid tap, with slight voicing carrying on through the articulation, is getting very common indeed. In colloquial speech, many speakers tap medial /t/, especially across word boundaries (e.g. *that I, not a bit, get it*) and medially in high-frequency words like *better, later, little*, e.g. *but I'd better get it a little later* [bət aɪd 'betə get ɪt ə 'lɪtl̩ 'leɪtə]. Nevertheless, there is no sign in British English of the medial /t – d/ contrast being lost in colloquial speech, as is true of much General American, e.g. *writing – riding*.

Even though /ʍ/ in *wh*-words has disappeared in many varieties, curiously, /hj/ in words like *huge, humour*, etc. is now universal. Not so long ago, one could still hear old-fashioned speakers who would pronounce /juːdʒ 'juːmə/, but this had died out in RP by the 1970s and has no place in modern NRP. It is still, however, to be heard from a minority of General American speakers, and is common in South African English.

Nevertheless, /j/-dropping is on the increase. After /l/, as in *lute* /ljuːt/, /j/ has effectively died out, although it is still shown in some dictionaries. It is rare nowadays to hear /sjuːt 'sjuːpə/ for *suit, super*, etc., and the vast majority pronounce /suːt 'suːpə/. On the other hand, /j/ lives on in *assume* and *presume*, where /ə'suːm prə'zuːm/ are minority variants. Furthermore, there's no tendency in NRP – or indeed in most British English – to remove /j/ from *duke, tune, news* /djuːk tjuːn njuːz/. Pronunciations such as /duːk tuːn nuːz/ (all of which are the majority form in America) are confined to regional accents, notably Cockney, East Anglia and parts of the West Country. In fact, /tj/ and /dj/ are increasingly replaced by /tʃ/ and /dʒ/, e.g. *tune* /'tʃuːn/, *duke* /'dʒuːk/; this has been true for many years, but still starts alarm bells ringing for many speakers of traditional RP.

Activity

115

Say these words: *suitable, supermarket, presume, consume, news, lute, avenue, revenue, Luke, enthusiastic*. Do you pronounce a /j/ before /uː/? Now try asking people from other English-speaking areas. Can you discover any geographical patterning – either within your own country, or worldwide?

Changing vowels

The only systemic change in the NRP vowel system from that of traditional RP is that /ɔə/ as in *shore* – still shown in most pre-1970 dictionaries – has disappeared. This, of course, does not take account of speakers of varieties which contrast words of the FORCE–NORTH type, common in Wales, Scotland, Ireland and much of northern England and the USA. Nor does it include Londoners who contrast *paws – pause* /ɔə - ɔː/. But in NRP, there is no longer any /ɔə - ɔː/ contrast, so that *oar/ore – awe* are homophones.

One possible systemic change that could take place in the near future is that NRP English will lose both of its centring diphthongs NEAR and CURE. Of these, NEAR /ɪə/ is the more stable, although it tends nowadays to have a closer starting-point [iə]. Some younger speakers replace it by a long steady-state vowel of a KIT type, e.g. *really* ['rɪːli]. In mainstream NRP, CURE /ʊə/ is nowadays more and more replaced by /ɔː/, especially in high-frequency words like *poor, sure, your* etc. In other – potentially two-syllable – words, e.g. *fewer, jewel*, a sequence /uːə/ is used instead of CURE /ʊə/. This may imply that many speakers regard these vowels as being sequences of /iː + ə/ and /uː + ə/. Traditional RP also had a third centring diphthong in SQUARE represented with eə. In NRP, this is now overwhelmingly a steady-state vowel – something which was noted as early as 1890. We have recognised this development by using a steady-state vowel transcription symbol ɛː.

> ### 116
>
> Say the following words. All traditionally had /ʊə/. Do you yourself pronounce /ʊə/, /uːə/ or /ɔː/? Ask your friends what they say. Can you think of any other words of this type?
>
> cure, sure, furious, cruel, insure, tourist, endure, reviewer

In terms of lexical variation there has been a change in THOUGHT replacing LOT before fricatives in words like *cost, off, cloth* (see above). This process, which began in the eighteenth century, seemed to have become almost universal by the early twentieth, but has now boomeranged. In this context, the THOUGHT vowel is retained only by a few traditional RP speakers of the 60-plus generation. All other speakers have reverted to LOT. In words such as *halt, malt, salt* the use of /ɔː/ is much more prevalent, but even so is diminishing. Another change is that the FOOT vowel, formerly used in words like *room, broom* /rʊm brʊm/, etc. is now generally replaced by GOOSE, i.e. /ruːm bruːm/. In *happy* words, the final vowel is now FLEECE – rather than the KIT of traditional RP – but most NRP speakers realise it as a short vowel with a quality between /ɪ/ and /iː/ (see Section B1 on neutralisation). Only regional varieties in Yorkshire, Lancashire and Scotland overwhelmingly keep the KIT vowel.

In endings such as **-ate, -less, -ness, -ity**, the KIT vowel has largely been replaced by /ə/. Words such as *obstinate, careless, softness, calamity* are now overwhelmingly said as /'ɒbstɪnət 'kɛːləs 'sɒftnəs kə'læməti/.

A notable realisational change has been that the TRAP vowel /æ/ is now much more open (similar to [a]). In traditional RP it sounded a little like present-day SQUARE, something which can be clearly heard in old British newsreels and feature films (Celia Johnson in *Brief Encounter* is a famous example). A close TRAP vowel is also found in most other world varieties (American, Australian, New Zealand and South African; see Section C4). And a small minority of traditional RP speakers (almost all now 60-plus – listen to veteran cricket commentator Henry Blofeld) retain the traditional closer quality of the vowel. Nevertheless, in twenty-first-century Britain old-fashioned RP realisations of TRAP as [ɛə ɛ:] are found comic by the younger generation. (Interestingly, as early as 1918 the phonetician Daniel Jones warned non-native learners against over-close /æ/, and cited possible confusion of *ballet dancer* and *belly dancer*.)

The FLEECE and GOOSE vowels (/i:/ and /u:/) are now typically diphthongal [ɪi ʊu] in all contexts except before fortis consonants. A much commented-on change in the speech of the younger generation is that the GOOSE vowel /u:/ is becoming front and losing its rounding. The effect is particularly striking following palatal /j/ and also palato-alveolar /tʃ ʃ/, as in *few, music, new, shoe, Tuesday*, etc., making a young person's *shoe* sound rather like *she* to older people. The FOOT vowel /ʊ/ is typically more central in NRP, markedly so with many younger speakers. In addition, it often lacks lip-rounding, especially in common words, e.g. *good, put* sounding almost like [gɪd pɪt]. See also Section B3 for more detail on all these changes.

The diphthongs MOUTH /aʊ/ and PRICE /aɪ/ have swapped their traditional RP starting-points. They are now either the same or – as with many younger speakers – /aʊ/ has a *front* starting-point while /aɪ/ starts *back*. This may be the reason for the frequent accusation that the older members of the Royal Family pronounce *house* as 'hice' and walk 'rind the tine' (i.e. *round the town*).

Of the diphthongs, GOAT /əʊ/ has moved from a back vowel [oʊ] – a quality which it still has in much American English – to a central starting-point [əʊ]. (A lot of American English seems to be going the same way.) With many younger NRP speakers the quality is further fronted to [eʊ]. This realisation may be confusing to older speakers, who interpret it as the FACE vowel, thus understanding younger-generation *road* as older-generation *raid*.

Activity

117

This is an extract from Stephen Fry's *The Stars' Tennis Balls* (2001: 32). Suggest some possible reasons why the character speaking might want to change his accent in these ways. Explain Fry's examples, using phonetic symbols for the purpose.

> But firstly, there must come the accent. When I arrive, the accent will be in place and they will never know. I have my exercises all written out:
>
> *Don't say good, say gid*
> *Don't say post, say paste*
> *Don't say real, say rail*
> *Don't say go, say gay*

Changing stress and intonation

Intonation

One striking intonation change which has occurred in the last few years is the increase in what has been dubbed 'upspeak' or 'Australian question intonation' referring to terminal rising patterns employed particularly for narrative. Since this is a well-known feature of Australian English, its popularity in British accents has been put down to the influence of Australian 'soaps' (see also Bradford 1997, Section D, pp. 229–34). But it's worth noting that very similar patterns existed in regional British English (e.g. certain West Country and South Wales accents) long before Australian English penetrated the airwaves. Whatever the origins, it is without doubt the most obvious instance of ongoing change affecting intonation.

Stress

In 1855, the writer Samuel Rogers complained about the way words were changing their stress patterns. 'The now fashionable pronunciation of several words is to me at least very offensive: CONtemplate is bad enough; but BALcony makes me sick' (quoted in Crystal 1988: 64). The stress patterns indicated seem pretty normal to us in the twenty-first century, but Rogers was regretting the passing of the pronunciations of his youth /kən'templıt bæl'koʊnı/.

Changes in stress have affected a number of words in the course of the twentieth century. Examples are:

> *exquisite*, formerly '*exquisite*, now instead *ex'quisite*
> *dispute*, formerly *di'spute*, now also '*dispute*
> *comparable*, formerly '*comparable*, now also *com'parable*
> *primarily*, formerly '*primarily*, now also *pri'marily*
> *laboratory*, formerly '*laboratory*, now instead *la'boratory*

There is a strong tendency for stress change in longer words (three syllables or more) to result in stress shifting to the antepenultimate syllable (two from the end). This will usually also affect the vowels in the word. *Primarily* shows this tendency. Other examples of this stress change are:

> *minuscule*, formerly *mi'nuscule*, now instead '*minuscule*
> *pejorative*, formerly '*pejorative* /'piːdʒərətɪv/, now instead *pe'jorative*
> *etiquette*, formerly *eti'quette*, now instead '*etiquette*
> *marital*, formerly *ma'rital* /mə'raɪt‖/, now mostly '*marital*
> *kilometre*, formerly '*kilometre*, now also *ki'lometre*
> *controversy*, formerly '*controversy*, now also *con'troversy*
> *lamentable*, formerly '*lamentable*, now also *la'mentable*
> *formidable*, formerly '*formidable*, now also *for'midable*

Ongoing change is to be observed in many of these items, in some cases with a strong rearguard action being fought by older-generation speakers against what they consider to be upstart pronunciations – *controversy* being a notorious example.

118

How do you stress the following words?

controversy, hospitable, contribute, applicable, lamentable

Certain compounds formed from verb plus particle, e.g. *make-up, breakdown, hold-up, lock-out,* have changed their stress pattern. Final element stress has been replaced by initial element stress so that what was formerly said as *make-'up* is now pronounced *'make-up.* This change, which appears to have taken place in the 1920s, is now completely established in the present-day language. It is interesting that certain European learners of English (for example, Germans, Dutch and Danes) tend, for whatever reason, to retain the outdated stressing, which now counts as a non-native learner's error.

Other influences

Spelling influences

A significant influence affecting ongoing pronunciation change is the regularisation of pronunciation to fit the spelling. A common phenomenon is the restoration of former 'silent letters', i.e. examples of historical elision, e.g. /t/ in *often,* /l/ in *falcon,* or a vowel changing to conform with its typical spelling. There are many examples, notable ones being:

waistcoat, formerly /ˈwəskɪt/, now instead /weɪstkəʊt/
landscape, formerly /ˈlænskɪp/, now instead /ˈlændskeɪp/
forehead, formerly /ˈfɒrɪd/, now generally /ˈfɔːhed/
nephew, formerly /ˈnevjuː/, now generally /ˈnefjuː/
portrait, formerly /ˈpɔːtrɪt/, now generally /ˈpɔːtreɪt/
retch, formerly /riːtʃ/, now generally /retʃ/
ate, formerly /et/, now also /eɪt/
covert, formerly /ˈkʌvət/, now also /ˈkəʊvɜːt/
fortune, formerly /ˈfɔːtʃən/, now also /ˈfɔːtʃuːn ˈfɔːtjuːn/
handkerchief, formerly /ˈhæŋkətʃɪf/, now also /ˈhæŋkətʃiːf/
often, formerly /ˈɒfən, ˈɔːfen/ now also /ˈɒftən/
towards, formerly /tɔːdz/, now also /təˈwɔːdz/

There are signs that more words may nowadays be going the same way. One candidate (by the way, do you yourself say /ˈkændɪdət/ or /ˈkændɪdeɪt/?) is the word *says* – traditionally /sez/, but people are starting to pronounce /seɪz/. Others are *solve, involve, proven,* traditionally /sɒlv ɪnˈvɒlv pruːvən/ but now sometimes /səʊlv ɪnˈvəʊlv ˈprəʊvən/.

American influences

It's a commonly heard moan from the older generation that American English is beginning to overwhelm British English, but it's actually very difficult to assemble any evidence to support this claim with respect to pronunciation. Although indeed much American vocabulary is streaming into Britain speech, pronunciation seems remarkably impervious to USA influences – apart from the mock-American assumed by the majority of popular vocalists. Curiously, clear-cut examples of straightforward Americanised pronunciation are in fact very difficult to find. An exception is *harass* and *harassment*: formerly pronounced as /'hærəs 'hærəsmənt/, an American-style /hə'ræs hə'ræsmənt/ seems now to be taking over.

In other cases where an American pronunciation has gained in popularity, there has probably also been influence from the orthographic form. A notable case is *ate* (formerly /et/ but increasingly /eɪt/). Another example is *schedule* (formerly only initial /ʃ/ but now increasingly with /sk/ as with other words beginning with **sch**, such as *scheme, school, scholar, schizophrenic*).

One further possible American influence is the pronunciation of certain nouns containing the prefix *re-*, e.g. *research, resource, relapse*, where the traditional British rendering with stress on the second syllable occurs side by side with forms commoner in American English stressed on the first syllable.

Ironically, American English, rather than being the source of new British pronunciations, frequently preserves traditional forms that were formerly common in British English but which are now extinct or going out of favour. Examples are stress on first syllable in *laboratory* and *controversy*, use of /aɪ/ rather than /ɪ/ in *privacy*, *vitamin*, and elision of /w/ in *towards*.

Place-names

The pronunciation of English place-names is often influenced by orthography, leading to a rendering closer to the spelling taking over from a traditional form. Examples are: *Romford* and *Margate* (formerly /'rʌmfəd 'maːgɪt/, nowadays more often /'rɒmfəd 'maːgeɪt/). Not all names are affected in this way – size matters. Big towns, like *Leicester* and *Worcester*, seem more stable – but smaller towns, suburbs and villages are much more likely to change.

Activity

119

Try to find out the traditional and the modern pronunciations of the places listed below. See if you can transcribe them phonemically.

Chesham, Cirencester, Coventry, Grantham, Lewisham, Pontefract, Romford, Todmorden, Uttoxeter, Walthamstow

Are there any place-names in an area you know where two pronunciations exist side by side? Is one an old pronunciation and the other a replacement closer to the spelling?

For many years now there has been a tendency for foreign words, particularly place-names, to trade their traditional English pronunciations for something more exotic.

Some names have altered totally, as is true of *Prague, Marseilles* and *Lyons* (formerly /preɪg mɑː'seɪlz 'laɪenz/ now /prɑːg mɑː'seɪ 'liːɒ̃n/). Interestingly, the new forms are also far removed from the original ['praxa maʁsɛj ljɔ̃]. In other cases, an ongoing battle carries on between, for instance, those who say *Copenhagen* as the traditional /kəʊpen'heɪgən/ and those who use the newer form /kəʊpen'hɑːgən/ (neither sounds much like Danish *København* [købən'hauʔn]). An interesting oddity is the holiday resort *Ibiza*. At one time most British visitors pronounced this /iː'biːtsə/. Nowadays a pronunciation /iː'viːθə/, not too far away from Spanish [i'βiθa], seems more popular – but it is rivalled by an upstart with a quite different initial vowel /aɪ'viːθə/.

120

Ask your grandparents (or other people you know of the same generation) to say these place-names and then say them yourself. Are there any differences in the way you and the older generation pronounce them?

Copenhagen, Hiroshima, Ibiza, Lyons, Majorca, Marseilles, Milan, Munich, Prague, Valencia, Ypres

121 ⊙ Track 65

On your audio CD you'll find a reading of the text below as it might have sounded in the early nineteenth century. Listen and then read through the text yourself. Note the words which have changed their pronunciations over the course of the last two centuries. See if you can produce two columns, using phonemic transcription, with what one might term (1) 'outgoing' forms (in some cases already extinct) and (2) 'incoming forms', reflecting respectively the characteristic pronunciations of previous eras, and pronunciations either established in the twentieth century, or those now coming into vogue in the twenty-first. Check by looking at the key on the website.

I was all set to go to the theatre in Coventry Street last Wednesday. I'd bought seats in the balcony for me and Sophia. Ate my supper, and was just putting on a waistcoat when I lost my footing and knocked my forehead on a picture – not the portrait of nephew Ralph but that huge landscape I got at the auction in Holborn. I contemplated my bruised profile. It was quite exquisitely odious. No easy cure to be sure – but off to the chemist to get some iodine. Even though it wasn't the result of a controversy, etiquette demands that I re-schedule all my plans. Truly lamentable. Shan't see the girl again either. Soon she'll be gadding off towards Prague – lucky thing! Via Marseilles, Lyons and Milan. And I'll have to stay in my rooms in Lewisham. And no peace or privacy – Aunt Maria's coming across from Cirencester.

C6 TEACHING AND LEARNING A FOREIGN LANGUAGE

Hierarchy of error

One of the most useful day-to-day applications of phonetics courses is learning the pronunciation of a foreign language. In this section we deal with (1) teaching English to non-native learners; (2) the problems native speakers of English have in learning a foreign language. We shall use the abbreviation **L1** (i.e. first language) to refer to the learner's mother tongue (also termed 'source language') and **L2** (i.e. second language) to refer to the language which is being learned (also termed the 'target language').

In learning a language it is necessary to have realistic goals. Unless you begin in your infancy, it is very unlikely that you will ever achieve a perfect command of a language. Nowhere is this more true than of pronunciation. Even if you start in your teens, and go to live in the country concerned, it is likely that you will have some traces of a foreign accent all your adult life. If perfect pronunciation is your target then you must accept that you will inevitably fall short of it. A realistic aim is therefore to speak in a way which is clearly intelligible to your listeners and which does not distract, irritate or confuse them.

So a major consideration when dealing with pronunciation is to discover which errors are the most significant. Not all deviations from native-speaker pronunciation are of equal importance (see Jenkins 2000). Some pass unnoticed whereas others may be enough to cause total lack of comprehension on the part of the listener. In trying to establish a hierarchy of error we must take into account the reactions of native speakers. In general terms we can rank errors in the following way:

1   errors which lead to a breakdown of intelligibility;
2   errors which give rise to irritation or amusement;
3   errors which provoke few such reactions and may even pass unnoticed.

Obviously, the first category of error is the most significant and requires the most attention from teacher and student. The second group can also be of great significance and are often those which draw attention to the foreignness of an accent. The third category is of far less significance. Below, examples will be given of each of the three types of error with an indication of speakers' L1. Note that 'widespread' implies an error that is likely to be made by people from a large number of language backgrounds.

Error rankings for English

Category 1: Errors leading to breakdown of intelligibility

1   Confusion of crucial phonemic contrasts in vowel system, e.g. /ɪ – iː/ (widespread), /e – æ/ (German, Dutch), /ɜː – ɑː/ (West African languages), /ɒ – ʌ/ (Danish).
2   Confusion of fortis/lenis, e.g. final fortis/lenis (German, Dutch, Danish, Russian), /f – v/ (Dutch).
3   Consonant clusters (widespread, e.g. Arabic, Spanish).
4   Crucial consonant contrasts, e.g. /b – v/ (Spanish), /v – w/ (German), /f – h/ (Japanese), /l – n/ (some Chinese), /l – r/ (Japanese, some Chinese), /ʃ – s/ (Greek).
5   Deletion of /h/ (widespread, e.g. French, Italian) or replacement by /x/ (Spanish).
6   Word stress, especially if not on initial syllable (widespread, e.g. French, West African).

Category 2: Errors which invoke irritation or amusement

1   Inappropriate /r/ articulations, e.g. uvular [ʀ] (French, German, Hebrew), strong alveolar trills (general).
2   Dental fricative problems ('**th**-sounds') (widespread), e.g. replacement of /θ/ by /t/ (Dutch) or /s/ (French, German, Danish); of /ð/ by /d/ (Dutch) or /z/ (French, German), etc.
3   Less significant vowel contrasts, e.g. /uː – ʊ/ (widespread), /ɒ – ɔː/ (widespread).
4   Incorrect allophones of /l/, especially replacement by dark *l* throughout (Portuguese, Russian), or by clear *l* throughout (French, German, Italian).
5   Weak and contracted forms (widespread).
6   Inappropriate rhoticism/non-rhoticism for particular models of pronunciation (widespread).
7   Strong retroflex setting (Indian languages).

Category 3: Errors which provoke few such reactions and may even pass unnoticed

1   Intonation errors (widespread).
2   Lack of syllabic consonants (widespread).
3   Compound stress (widespread).

Contrastive/error analysis

Errors made by language learners frequently reflect the sound systems of their L1. If we compare their sound system with that of the L2, we can often predict the nature of errors which they will make. Let's take as an example the case of a speaker of European Spanish (or *Castellano*, see below) learning English.

Spanish lacks a phoneme contrast similar to English /b – v/, the Spanish /b/ having a range of allophones similar to the *two* English consonants. There will be regular deletion of /h/ or replacement by the velar fricative [x]. On the other hand, unlike many languages, European Spanish has a voiceless dental fricative /θ/, and [ð] exists as an allophone of /d/, even though in the latter case English words containing /d/ and /ð/ will be regularly confused.

The syllable structure of Spanish is less complex than that of English. For example, there are no onset clusters with initial /s/, and the possibilities in coda position are far fewer (only final /n l r s d θ/ occur with any frequency). Final consonants and consonant clusters in general are a major problem area for Spanish speakers. This means that *spam* will be produced by learners as */espan/ (better not let a Spanish speaker loose on old Monty Python songs!).

European Spanish has a five-vowel system with a number of additional diphthongs. There is no equivalent to the checked/free vowel distribution in English, nor are there any central vowels similar to /ə ɜː ʌ/. From this one would predict that a Spanish learner would have considerable problems with the English vowel system, and that the checked/free vowel contrasts and the central vowels would be especially problematical. For example, vowel contrasts such as /ɪ – iː, ʊ – uː, æ – ɑː/ might pose difficulties.

Spanish has syllable-timed rhythm – very different from the stress-timed rhythm of English (see Section B5). A characteristic of Spanish English is the absence of vowel reduction in unstressed syllables. The range of intonation is less extended than in the English of native speakers. Spanish learners will not possess the elaborate systems of weak and contracted forms which characterise native-speaker English.

This scenario holds true for the vast majority of European Spanish speakers learning English – something which indicates that the main areas of difficulty can indeed be very largely predicted from contrastive analysis. Interestingly, not all learners' difficulties can be forecast in this way, while some expected problems do not materialise. It is, however, no exaggeration to say that a great many second language pronunciation problems can be traced back to the sound system of the learner's L1.

Other errors may arise through difficulties derived from confusing spelling systems – this is particularly the case for target languages like English, French or Danish which have archaic orthography incorporating many confusing sound–spelling relationships. In other cases, we may be faced with teaching traditions which are inaccurate or out of date – this may be the reason for the reluctance of Germans to distinguish TRAP and DRESS, when two perfectly adequate vowels for the contrast exist in their L1 (/a/ as in *acht* 'eight' and /ɛ/ as in *Bett* 'bed').

Hints on teaching pronunciation to non-native learners

It is essential to decide on a model for your students – this will normally be either British NRP or General American, for the reasons outlined in Section A1. Your own speech does not have to conform to the model but you should be aware of where you deviate markedly from it.

You should also make yourself aware of the problems your students have by giving them brief diagnostic tests. If you're based in a non-English-speaking country, and your students all have the same L1, you can assume that they will probably have a large number of pronunciation problems in common. If, as is generally the case when teaching in an English-speaking country, you're faced with students from many different language backgrounds, you have to approach the problems of each nationality separately.

In all cases, your task will be helped if you gain some phonetic knowledge of the L1s of the students in your classes. This can be done in three main ways:

❑   through English language courses directed at the nationality concerned;
❑   through courses directed at English speakers acquiring an L2;
❑   by discussing pronunciation problems with the students themselves.

How to learn a foreign language

How can phonetics help you if you're an English native speaker learning a foreign language? If you have acquired the language in school, perhaps the first thing to recognise is that you may need to do a lot of repair work. Many language teachers feel they do not have sufficient time to give their students prolonged pronunciation training. Some, indeed, devote no time to it whatsoever. All too often, language laboratories, where they exist, are locked up gathering dust whilst the students who should be allowed to use them plod away on written exercises.

Nevertheless, it's amazing how quickly great improvements can be achieved in your pronunciation by applying a few basic phonetic principles.

Table C6.1 Survey of errors for a selection of languages

Languages	Final Fortis/Lenis	Aspiration	/f, v, w/	/θ, ð/	/s – ʃ z – ʒ/	/h/	/r/ articulation	Consonant clusters	/ɪ – iː/	/e – æ/	Central vowels	Stress and rhythm
Arabic	✓	✓	✗	✓/?	✗	✓	✗	✗	✓	✗	✗	✓
Chinese	✗	✓	✗	✗	✗	✓/?	✗/?	✗	✗	✗	✗	✗
Danish	✗	✓	✗	✗	✓	✓	✓	✓	✓	✓	✓	✓
Dutch	✗	✗	✗	✗	✓	✓	✓	✓	✓	✗	✓	✓
French	✓	✗	✓	✗	✓	✗	✗	✓	✗	✓	✓	✗
German	✗	✓	✗	✗	✓	✓	✗	✓	✓	✓	✓	✓
Indian	✓	✗	✗	✗	✗	✓	✗	✗	✓	✗	✓	✗
Indonesian/Malay	✗	✗	✗	✗	✗	✓	✓/?	✗	✗	✗	✓	✗
Italian	✓	✗	✓	✗	✓	✗	✗	✗	✗	✓	✗	✗
Japanese	✗	✓	✗	✗	✗	✗	✗	✗	✗	✓	✗	✗
Norwegian/Swedish	✓	✓	✗	✗	✗	✓	✓	✓	✓	✗	✓	✓
Polish	✗	✗	✓	✗	✓	✗	✓	✓	✗	✗	✓	✗
Portuguese	✗	✗	✗	✗	✗	✗	✓/?	✗	✓	✓	✓	✗
Russian	✗	✗	✗	✗	✓	✗	✓	✓	✓	✗	✗	✓
Spanish	✓	✗	✓/?	✗	✗	✗	✓	✗	✗	✓	✗	✗
Turkish	✗	✓	✗	✗	✓	✓	✓	✓	✗	✗	✓	✗
West African	✓/?	✗	✗	✗	?	✓	✓/?	✗	✗	✓	✗	✗

Key

✓ indicates that the feature concerned is a prime source of error

✗ indicates that the feature concerned is, on the whole, not one of the major problem areas

? indicates variation between languages/language varieties

Notes

This table is intended only as a generalised overview. More detailed analyses for a variety of European and Asian languages can be obtained from Swan and Smith (2001). Deterding and Poedjosoedarmo is a useful source of information on the languages of south-east Asia.

1 Choose an appropriate variety as a model and stick to it.
2 Discover differences and similarities between the target language and English in terms of:
   □ consonant and vowel systems;
   □ sound and spelling relationships;
   □ stress, rhythm and other features of connected speech.

Here are three overviews of how to use your phonetic knowledge to acquire a better command of the European languages most commonly studied in Britain: Spanish, French and German. These summaries are all very brief and deliberately simplified.

Spanish ☉ Track 66

Model

It is worth noting that Spain not only has a number of regional varieties but also has several other languages spoken within its borders, e.g. Catalan, Galician and the non-Indo-European language Basque. *Castellano* /kaste'jano/ is the term used in the Spanish-speaking world for the educated variety spoken in northern Spain, including the capital Madrid and the provinces of Castile. This is the model of Spanish usually chosen by European learners, but an alternative is a Latin American variety, such as Argentine Spanish. European and Latin American Spanish are at variance in many respects, but the most significant pronunciation difference is the existence in Castellano of a phoneme /θ/ used for orthographic **z** (e.g. *zapata* 'shoe') and for **c** preceding front vowels (*cinco* 'five'). In all of Latin America, and also in Andalusia in the south of Spain, /s/ is employed in this context. As is always the case in language learning and teaching, it is best to be consistent – choose one model and stick to it. We shall assume in what follows that you are a British NRP speaker aiming at Castellano.

Spanish consonant system

p	*paso*	/ˈpaso/
b	*vaca, abeto*	/ˈbaka/ [aˈβeto]
t	*tapas*	/ˈtapas/
d	*dos, nada*	/dos/ [ˈnaða]
k	*casa*	/ˈkasa/
g	*gafas, amigo*	/ˈgafas/ [aˈmiɣo]
tʃ	*chico*	/ˈtʃiko/
f	*fino*	/ˈfino/
s	*seis*	/ˈseis/
θ	*cerveza*	/θerˈbeθa/
x	*jefe*	/ˈxefe/
m	*mucho*	/ˈmutʃo/
n	*noche*	/ˈnotʃe/
ɲ	*caña*	/ˈkaɲa/
l	*luna*	/ˈluna/
r	*rana, parra*	/ˈrana ˈpara/
ɾ	*para*	/ˈpaɾa/
w	*bueno*	/ˈbweno/
j	*yo, ciento, llave*	/jo ˈθjento ˈjabe/ [ˈjaβe]

Some speakers have an additional phoneme /ʎ/ in words containing orthographic **ll**, as in *llave* /'ʎabe/. The voiced plosives /b d g/ have fricative allophones [β ð ɣ] when occurring between vowels, as indicated in the list above.

Spanish vowel system

i	*si*	/si/
e	*este*	/'este/
a	*hasta*	/'asta/
o	*poco*	/'poko/
u	*tu*	/tu/
ei	*rey*	/rei/
ai	*hay*	/ai/
au	*aun*	/aun/
oi	*hoy*	/oi/

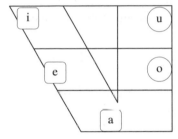

Figure C6.1   Basic Spanish vowels

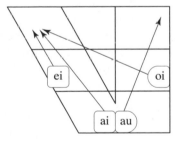

Figure C6.2   Frequent Spanish diphthongs

All vowels can combine to form diphthongs, but only /ei ai au oi/ commonly occur. Vowel sequences having initial /i/ and /u/ are regarded as semi-vowels /j/ and /w/. See below.

Description of consonants

A new sound which must be mastered by the English learner of Spanish is the velar fricative /x/ – spelt **j** or **g** (before **i** and **e**), as in *jefe* 'boss', *general* 'general'. Double **ll**, as in *paella*, was traditionally a palatal lateral but is nowadays overwhelmingly said as [j] (far easier for an English learner to copy).

Unlike non-rhotic English, Spanish /r/ is pronounced in all contexts; deleting /r/ is a common British learner's error. The Spanish sounds are also articulated very differently from English /r/, being typically a tongue-tip trill /r/ or tap /ɾ/. A major problem occurs in word-medial position where single **r** (alveolar tap) and double **rr** (alveolar trill) produce minimal pairs, contrasting, for example, *para* 'for' and *parra* 'grapevine'.

The *tilde* [˜] accent placed over **ñ** indicates a palatal nasal /ɲ/ as in *mañana* 'tomorrow'. Replacement by /nj/ similar to English *onion* is only an approximation, but it doesn't seriously affect intelligibility.

The voiced plosive consonants /b d g/ have weaker voiced fricative allophones [β ð ɣ]. The plosive allophones occur word-initially and following nasals; the fricatives are used elsewhere.

It is recommended, if you're imitating Castellano, that **c** (before front vowels) and **z** are pronounced as /θ/ rather than /s/. In Spain, using /s/ in this context is associated with particular regional varieties and may attract social comment.

Description of vowels

Standard Spanish has an attractively simple five-vowel /i e a o u/ system plus a number of diphthongs, the most significant of these being /ei ai oi au/. The two main problems are:

❑ to avoid diphthongisation of /o/ and /e/ (which will cause confusion with diphthongs /ei/ and /ou/);

❑ to avoid reducing unstressed vowels to [ə]. (Note that there is no central vowel of any kind in Spanish.)

Spelling

In general, Spanish orthography is highly reliable and efficient. Nevertheless, there are potential pitfalls. Note that **h** is invariably a 'silent letter' and either the letter **b** or **v** could be regarded as superfluous as they are exact equivalents, both representing /b/. The letter combination **qu** represents [k] *queso* 'cheese'; **c** represents [θ] before front vowels **i** and **e**: *cine* 'cinema', *cero* 'zero' but [k] elsewhere: *calle* 'street'.

Vowel spellings in Spanish are very straightforward with effectively no complications.

Connected speech

Word stress in Spanish operates on a basic rule system whereby stress falls regularly on the penultimate syllable if the word ends in a vowel, **n** or **s**, e.g. *ven'tana*, 'window', *'manos* 'hands', *'cantan* 'they sing'. Words ending in a consonant (other than **n** or **s**) are stressed on the final syllable, e.g. *ani'mal* 'animal', *co'ñac* 'brandy', *ha'blar* 'to speak', etc. All of the fairly large number of words which are exceptions to these rules have stress indicated by an accent placed over the stressed syllable, e.g. *volcán* 'volcano', *cámara* 'room', *compás* 'compass', *difícil* 'difficult'. Note that word stress is significant in Spanish and can change the meaning of words: *término* (noun) 'end', *termino* 'I finish', *terminó* 'he finished'.

There is no reduction of unstressed syllables to a fully central vowel. Rhythm is essentially syllable-timed, each syllable giving the impression of having roughly equal duration. English speakers accustomed to the stress-timing of their own language have to try to give every syllable in Spanish full value.

In Spanish, there is no clear separation of syllables across word boundaries. 'All the words seem to run into each other' is one of the commonest complaints of students attempting to acquire the language – and this feature is indeed one of the major listening comprehension problem areas for the non-native learner.

French ⊙ Track 67

Model
Although there are many French regional accents, only one variety of the language is normally chosen as a model for foreign learners. This is the educated standard variety of Paris and the north, which has no commonly used special name, but has been termed *français neutre* (Lerond 1980).

French consonant system

p	*pas*	/pa/
b	*bas*	/ba/
t	*tôt*	/to/
d	*dos*	/do/
k	*quand*	/kɑ̃/
g	*gant*	/gɑ̃/
f	*fer*	/fɛr/
v	*verre*	/vɛr/
s	*celle*	/sɛl/
z	*zèlc*	/zɛl/
ʃ	*choux*	/ʃu/
ʒ	*joue*	/ʒu/
m	*mont*	/mɔ̃/
n	*non*	/nɔ̃/
ŋ	*camping*	/kɑ̃piŋ/[1]
ɲ	*cygne*	/siɲ/
l	*lire*	/lir/
r	*rire*	/rir/
w	*oui*	/wi/
j	*yeux*	/jø/
ɥ	*huile*	/ɥil/

Note
1 /ŋ/ is a marginal phoneme (see Section B1) found only in loanwords ending in **-ing**.

French vowel system

i	*vie*	/vi/
e	*fée*	/fe/
ɛ	*crème*	/krɛm/
a	*patte*	/pat/
ɔ	*homme*	/ɔm/
o	*eau*	/o/
u	*cou*	/ku/
ə	*me*	/mə/

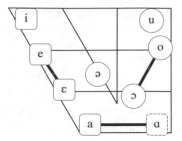

Figure C6.3 Basic French vowels. The lines joining pairs of vowels indicate close phonological relationships

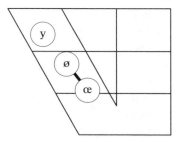

Figure C6.4 French front rounded vowels. The line indicates a close phonological relationship

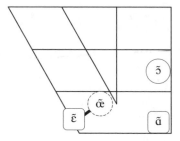

Figure C6.5 French nasal vowels. The line indicates a close phonological relationship

y	*rue*	/ry/
ø	*peu*	/pø/
œ	*bœuf*	/bœf/
ɛ̃	*bain*	/bɛ̃/
ã	*temps*	/tã/
ɔ̃	*pont*	/pɔ̃/

The bands in the vowel diagram indicate vowels where there is a close relationship of some kind. The vowels /ɛ/ and /ɔ/ occur in closed syllables, whereas /e/ and /o/ are found mostly in open syllables. Some speakers, mainly of the older generation, have an additional /œ̃/, as in *un*, *brun* /œ̃ brœ̃/. Others (especially older Parisians) make a distinction between two open vowels /a/ and /ɑ/ as in *patte* 'paw' and *pâte* 'paste'.

Neither of these extra contrasts is nowadays heard in the French of younger speakers of the standard language.

Further information is to be found in Fougeron and Smith (1999). A reliable French pronunciation dictionary is the Larousse *Dictionnaire de la prononciation* (Lerond 1980).

Description of consonants

While there is much overall similarity in the consonant systems of French and English, there are also some notable differences. Unlike English /p t k/, French voiceless plosives are unaspirated and never glottalised. Getting rid of aspiration and glottalisation (see Section B2) is one of the most important problems the English-speaking learner has to face. Unlike NRP, French /r/ is typically sounded in all contexts; it is a totally different articulation from its English counterpart, being realised as a back tongue uvular approximant [ʁ]. English post-alveolar /r/ is completely unacceptable if transferred to French. If you want to sound even remotely authentic in French, uvular [ʁ] is the one essential consonant to master.

French /l/ is invariably clear – there is no dark *l* as in NRP and most types of English (modern English vocalised dark *l* may sound like a back vowel to French ears). Note that final **m** and **n** are not true consonants, but normally merely indicate that the preceding vowel is nasal (see below). The palatal nasal in *agneau* 'lamb' can nowadays safely be replaced by /nj/.

Description of vowels

All French vowels can vary in duration, for instance being longer in open syllables, but this vowel length is phonemically insignificant. Vowels are all steady-state, not diphthongs, and it is important not to diphthongise vowels such as /o/ in *beau* 'beautiful' and /e/ in *fée* 'fairy'. Two crucial features of the French sound system which you have to master are (1) front rounded vowels and (2) nasal vowels.

(1) Front rounded vowels are made with the front of the tongue raised but with rounded lips (see Section A6). They include /y/ as in *tu* 'you' (similar to a lip-rounded [i] vowel), and /ø/ in *peu* 'little' (similar to a lip-rounded [e]); a third vowel /œ/ (similar to a lip-rounded [ɛ]) occurs in closed syllables, e.g. *neuf* 'nine' /nœf/.

The vowel /y/, always spelt **u**, must be kept distinct from /u/, always spelt **ou** as in *tout* 'all'. There are many pairs where the meaning is dependent on this contrast. Make sure that French /u/ is a true back vowel (lots of young NRP speakers produce a front vowel for English /uː/). Many English speakers hear the vowels in *peu* and *neuf* in terms of the vowel in NURSE. The French vowels, although central, are strongly lip-rounded and this rounding must be imitated. Check by looking in a mirror.

(2) There are three nasal vowels in French, namely /ɛ̃/, as in *vin* 'wine' (similar to a nasalised English /æ/), /ã/, as in *banc* 'bench' (similar to an unrounded nasalised English /ɒ/), and /ɔ̃/ as in *bon* 'good' (similar to a fully rounded nasalised English /ɔː/). Note that it is essential to distinguish the vowels /ã/ and /ɔ̃/ (most English people don't!). On the other hand, the old /ɛ̃/ – /œ̃/ contrast, still taught in most British schools, is superfluous. As mentioned above, the vowel /œ̃/ is extinct in most standard modern French, having effectively been replaced by /ɛ̃/, e.g. /brɛ̃/ *brun*, 'brown', /lɛ̃di/ *lundi* 'Monday'. Note that many younger speakers use an open central vowel in between the two.

Nasal vowels are indicated in the spelling by syllable-final **n** or **m**. These orthographic consonants are not themselves sounded, which means, for example, that *conte* 'tale' and *compte* 'account, charge' sound exactly the same: /kɔ̃t/.

Spelling

The French spelling system is archaic and full of confusing complexities, but it is essential to take note of spelling–sound relationships. 'Silent consonants' abound; to give just a few examples: *h̲eure* 'hour', *ne̲z̲* 'nose', *tabac̲* 'tobacco', *banc̲* 'bench', *sirop̲* 'syrup', *so̲t̲* 'stupid', *respe̲c̲t̲* 'respect', *frai̲s̲* 'cold', *tar̲d̲* 'late'. A number of words show variation: *août* 'August' may be pronounced /ut/ or /u/; *tous* 'all' can be /tu/ or /tus/.

Silent consonants, especially in the commonest words, often return in connected speech as liaison forms. Compare:

vous /vu/ 'you'   *vous avez* /vuz ave/ 'you have'
vingt /vɛ̃/ 'twenty'   *vingt-et-un* /vɛ̃t e ɛ̃/ 'twenty-one'

Orthographic **e** (without any accent) is silent when word-final (e.g. *huile* 'oil' /ɥil/), and often when word-medial; see below.

There are frequently numerous ways of indicating the same sound. For instance, the words *tan* 'tan', *taon* 'horsefly', *tant* 'so much', *tend* 'stretch', *temps* 'time, weather' are all pronounced identically, i.e. as /tɑ̃/, despite the different spellings.

Note that two of the orthographic accents of French are in phonetic terms largely superfluous. The circumflex (ˆ) no longer serves any phonetic purpose, and in reality there is no longer any consistent difference between **è** (*accent grave*) and **é** (*accent aigu* or 'acute'). However, the acute itself still has a very important function: **é** indicates that the vowel is fully sounded and not reduced to [ə] or elided, cf. *ménage* /menaʒ/ 'household' and *menace* /m(ə)nas/ 'threat'.

Stress ☺ Track 68

Stress is not essential to the phonological structure of the word in French. This makes French very different from English (or indeed most European languages) where the correct placement of stress is crucial for the recognition of polysyllabic words. See also Section B5.

In French, stress is predictable, falling on the final syllable of any word or phrase if pronounced in isolation, or on the final syllable of each intonation group in connected speech. (English-speaking learners of French are usually totally unaware of this important basic principle.) For example:

é 'tat | 'state'
les Etats-U 'nis | 'the United States'
Je voudrais par'tir | pour les Etats-U'nis | de'main.| 'I'd like to go to the United States tomorrow.'

Furthermore, French is syllable-timed, which implies that one needs to pronounce all syllables with roughly equal force and length. An important extra complication – especially in terms of listening comprehension – is that syllables spelt with unaccented **e** (1) reduce to /ə/ and (2) are almost invariably elided, e.g. *demi* 'half' /dəmi/ → /dmi/, *petit* 'small' /pəti/ → /pti/, *boulevard* /buləvar/ → /bulvar/. ☺ Track 69

German ☺ Track 70

Model

The model usually chosen for non-native learners is educated northern German, as heard on TV and radio. Regional and national varieties of German differ widely, especially in Bavaria, Austria and Switzerland. Swiss German, in its spoken form, is effectively a different language.

German consonant system

p	*Punkt*	/pʊŋkt/
b	*Bild*	/bɪlt/
t	*tot*	/toːt/
d	*dick*	/dɪk/
k	*Kopf*	/kɔpf/
g	*gelb*	/gɛlp/
f	*falsch*	/falʃ/
v	*voll*	/fɔl/
s	*es*	/ɛs/
z	*Sohn*	/zoːn/
ʃ	*schade*	/ʃɑːdə/
ʒ	*Passage*	/pɑˈsaːʒə/
ç	*nicht*	/nɪçt/
x	*Nacht*	/naxt/
h	*Hund*	/hʊnt/
l	*Leid*	/laɪt/
j	*ja*	/jɑː/
r	*rot*	/roɪt/
m	*Mensch*	/mɛnʃ/
n	*nein*	/naɪn/
ŋ	*Ring*	/rɪŋ/

German vowel system

iː	*tief*	/tiːf/
ɪ	*Schiff*	/ʃɪf/
eː	*See, Käse*[1]	/zeː ˈkeːzə/
ɛ	*Bett, Hände*	/bɛt ˈhɛndə/
a	*acht*	/axt/
aː	*Bahn*	/baːn/
ɔ	*Gott*	/gɔt/
oː	*so*	/zoː/
ʊ	*Bund*	/bʊnt/
uː	*Schuh*	/ʃuː/
ə	*Geschichte*	/gəˈʃɪçtə/
ər [ɐ]	*Fischer*[2]	/ˈfɪʃər/ [ˈfɪʃɐ]
yː	*grün*	/gryːn/
ʏ	*fünf*	/fʏnf/

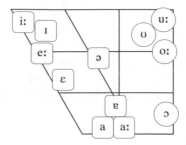

Figure C6.6　Basic German vowels

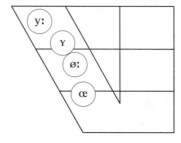

Figure C6.7　German front rounded vowels

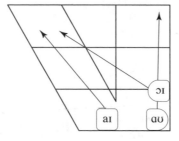

Figure C6.8　German diphthongs

øː	*schön*	/ʃøːn/
œ	*zwölf*	/tsvœlf/
aɪ	*Teil*	/taɪl/
aʊ	*Raum*	/raʊm/
ɔɪ	*neun*	/nɔɪn/

Notes

1 Some speakers, especially south Germans, have an additional vowel /ɛː/ represented by **ä**, e.g. *Käse*.

2 The more open /ɐ/ is the allophone before final /r/. Since most speakers of standard German only sound /r/ before vowels, it is only this more open allophone that provides a contrast in pairs such as: *Fische – Fischer*. It may be represented phonetically as [ɐ].

A reliable German pronunciation dictionary is *Der grosse Duden 6: Aussprachewörterbuch* (Mangold and Grebe 1990).

Description of consonants

Like its French counterpart, German /r/ is a back (uvular) approximant. However, unlike French, syllable-final **r** is normally unsounded. This means that German is effectively non-rhotic, but note that the orthographic final **r** does have an effect on the length or quality of the preceding vowel. German /l/ is clear in all contexts, and as a result many varieties of English dark *l* might sound vowel-like to German ears.

Apart from clear *l*, the velar fricative /x/, as in *acht* 'eight', *Buch* 'book', *rauchen* 'to smoke', and the palatal fricative /ç/, as in *nicht* 'not', *schlecht* 'bad', *durch* 'through', are the most difficult consonants. Both are spelt **ch**; they are in virtual allophonic relationship, /ç/ occurring after front vowels and also consonants, and /x/ elsewhere. Note that non-final orthographic **s** is pronounced /z/, as in *Seite* /ˈzaɪtə/ 'page'; orthographic **z** is an affricate /ts/, e.g. *Zeit* /ˈtsaɪt/ 'time'.

Description of vowels

Vowel length is important in German, which has a checked/free contrast similar to English. The greatest problem for most students are the front rounded vowels, two long and two short: /yː ʏ øː œ/, all indicated in the spelling by an *umlaut*, e.g. *grün* 'green' /gryːn/, *hübsch* 'pretty' /hʏpʃ/, *schön* 'beautiful' /ʃøːn/, *zwölf* 'twelve' /tsvœlf/. Vowels /eː oː/, e.g. *zehn* 'ten', *so* 'so' are steady-state. The close vowels /iː uː/ (e.g. *tief* 'deep' /tiːf/ and *Schuh* /ʃuː/ 'shoe') are peripheral and not diphthongised.

Spelling

Although not as efficient as that of Spanish, German orthography is much more reliable than that of English or French, with a good correspondence between sound and spelling. It is important to absorb the rules for vowel length; the most significant are perhaps that long vowels are shown with double vowel letters or **h**, e.g. *Saal* /zaːl/ 'hall', *Wahl* /vaːl/ 'choice', and short vowels are often followed by double consonant letters, e.g. *dann* /dan/ 'then'. Even so, there are exceptions.

Connected speech

Unlike Spanish and French, Standard German has clear word separation, and initial vowels are typically preceded by a glottal stop, e.g. *einundachtzig* 'eighty-one' [ˈʔaɪn ʔʊnt ʔaxtsɪç]. This is totally different from English, where the final consonants tend to be linked to the following word, e.g. *an apple* [ə næpl]. English students have to avoid using linking and intrusive *r*, e.g. in *aber ich* [ˈaːbɐ ʔɪç] 'but I' or *meine Absicht* [ˈmaɪnə ʔapzɪçt] 'my intention'.

Word stress

This has similarities to English, with each word having an obvious stressed syllable. There is considerable vowel reduction in unstressed syllables to /ə/, but generally affecting orthographic **e**, e.g. *Bekannte* 'acquaintance'. Rhythm, as in English, is stress-timed, i.e. it is essentially based on intervals between stresses.

Section D
EXTENSION

D1

**David
Abercrombie**

RP – R.I.P.?

David Abercrombie (reprinted from *Fifty Years in Phonetics* (1991), Edinburgh: Edinburgh University Press, pp. 48–53)

In this extract, written at the end of the twentieth century, Abercrombie discusses the changing status of traditional Received Pronunciation, making gloomy predictions for its future prospects. Much of what he forecast seems to be coming true!

RP today: its position and prospects

It is about thirty-five years since I last published anything on RP. The reason for this long gap in talking about such an interesting and controversial subject is that I have been away from England, except for occasional visits, during the whole of that time. Of course, there are many opportunities of hearing English people talk on the radio and on television, and I have been teaching at a university – Edinburgh – which attracts many English students. So I am able to say something about phonetic and phonological trends in present-day RP. My chief interest in the accent, though, has always been sociolinguistic, and it is more difficult to discover what is happening in the field from outside England. But let us first look at the phonetic/phonological aspects.

Naturally I do not believe RP has been *phonetically* stable since Daniel Jones described it sixty-five years ago; no-one would expect it to be. No accent or dialect remains static; linguistic change is always at work. I am sure, moreover, that RP has never been as homogeneous as Daniel Jones made it appear. It has always been subject to variations which are personal and idiosyncratic, and this apparently to a much greater extent than other accents of England. RP is therefore difficult, if not impossible, to define phonetically (though there is one feature always present – the extensive use of 'creaky voice'). In other words, it is not phoneticians who say who is an RP speaker and who is not; it is *socially* defined. My own definition (which some find irritating) of an RP speaker is 'someone who is recognised to be so by other RP speakers'.

It is difficult to find any phonetic variations becoming predominant. One may venture to suggest, however, some phonological trends which it seems may prevail. Most conspicuous of these, though it is not very common, is the replacement of the diphthong in, for example, *mouse* by the diphthong in, for example, *mice*. I have seen an RP-speaking character in a comic strip in a newspaper represented as saying 'ight of the hice' for 'out of the house'. The falling together of the two diphthongs does not seem to be known in any other accent of England. I know of only one regular broadcaster who does this, but it may be heard in the speech of certain members of the Royal Family. Other prevalent phonological developments are: the almost universality of 'intrusive' rs, as in *idea-r-of*, *law-r-and-order*, though it is as much reprobated as ever; the disappearance of [uə] and its replacement by [ɔː], as in *poor*, *sure*, *during*; and the replacement of [ou] by [ɜ] in many words, for example in *goal*. I have heard *floating* and *flirting* confused. All of these have been present in the speech of some RP speakers for many years.

David
Abercrombie

These observations are based largely on listening to speech on radio and television. Radio broadcasts, and much of television, are put out by the BBC, and at
this point a digression on RP and the BBC might be in order. It has popularly
been supposed that the BBC used to demand of its announcers that they speak
RP, whose use the BBC promoted. 'BBC English' has often been used as a syn-
onym for RP. All BBC announcers did speak RP, it is true, but in fact that was
an accidental by-product of another policy: that BBC employees – administrators
as well as announcers – should be of good social position, with appropriate interests and tastes. The BBC had an official whose business it was, by interview, to
ensure this (he was a high-ranking ex-naval officer). The question of accent never
arose; all suitable applicants naturally spoke RP. It is interesting, by the way, that
Sir John, later Lord, Reith, the head of the BBC, did not speak RP (he was a
Scot). There was an Advisory Committee on Spoken English to the BBC; not
all of its members were RP speakers. So it is difficult to make a case for the BBC
deliberately promoting RP.

With this digression we can leave the phonetic-phonological aspects of RP,
and turn to the sociolinguistic field.

Sociolinguistically speaking, RP is a very remarkable accent. It seems, in fact,
to be unique; I do not know of any accent like it anywhere else in the world.
There are, of course, accents of great prestige in many countries. These are all
regional accents, however; whereas RP is non-regional. It extends over the whole
of England, although only a minority of educated people speak it. But it gives this
minority privilege and power in many walks of life.

How does such a non-regional accent come to exist? An accent community is
normally geographically based. What can a non-regional accent be based on?

Just as RP is a unique accent, a unique institution provides its basis. This
institution is the English public school, curiously named because it is anything but
public: it is extremely private. There are a number of these schools. They are
boarding schools, attended by pupils from thirteen to eighteen or nineteen years
of age who, while at school, are isolated from their surroundings, though they
meet pupils of other public schools when playing against them at various sports.
These schools are very expensive. RP is never explicitly taught in them, but it is
acquired effortlessly from one's fellow pupils, most of whom will anyway already
have learnt RP from their families at home.

If children come from a non-RP-speaking family but their parents can afford
the expense, and consider it worth it, these children will still join the RP-speaking
community, even though their parents remain outside it.

The converse, incidentally, is also true. Some parents who are RP speakers
may prefer, for various reasons, not to send their children to a public school;
the children nevertheless will speak RP, and so will belong to the accent
community.

From this brief survey of the sociolinguistic background of RP, the crucial fact
about it cannot fail to emerge: it is a blatantly undemocratic institution. It is the
status symbol of an elite, an aristocracy neither of merit nor of birth, but one
whose power is fortuitously arrived at. People are evaluated, not according to
their achievements and abilities, but according to their accent.

**David
Abercrombie**

I have elsewhere claimed that in fact there is in England an 'accent bar', on one side of which are the RP speakers and on the other side the non-RP speakers. I coined the term on the model of the 'colour bar' which is, or has been, found in some societies, and to which an accent bar is in many ways analogous (though of course a colour bar is a much more serious matter). One respect in which they are different is that a colour bar usually has the majority of people on the 'right' side of the bar, whereas the accent bar has only a small minority on the 'right' side.

The consequences of the accent bar can be very varied. For example, the poet Tony Harrison recounts how, when he was a schoolboy (not at a public school), he was jeered at in class by his English teacher for reading poetry aloud in a local accent instead of in RP. Yet nowadays, with an unchanged local accent, he is considered to be an admirable radio broadcaster of his own poems. In one of his poems he writes 'RIP RP', which aptly sums up the outcome of the accent bar as far as he is concerned (and incidentally shows how the term 'RP' has spread in recent times).

I read in the press recently of a judge's decision concerning the future of a young girl, which provides another example. As the consequence of a divorce, the girl had gone to live with her father, while her brother and sister lived with the mother. The father sent the girl to an expensive school, the result being that she became an RP speaker. Her brother and sister continued to speak with their local accents. The judge, asked to decide on the girl's future, said he accepted that the girl now spoke 'posh' and had moved into a different social class. ('Speaking "posh"' is a popular expression for speaking RP.) She should therefore stay with her father so as not to have to mix with speakers of a socially inferior accent. The accent bar thus ran through the middle of a family.

RP is a much disliked accent in many parts of the world, particularly in Scotland and America. I am an RP speaker, so I speak from experience. It is disliked, as well as envied, by many people in England also. This dislike is becoming more common, and also more outspoken. There are signs that RP's prestige, privileges, and power are being eroded. One ought really to live in England to observe in detail changes which may be taking place, and I do not do so, as I have said; I live in Scotland. Still, much can be gleaned from television and the radio, on which many regular speakers – news readers, presenters, commentators, foreign correspondents, meteorologists – do not nowadays speak RP. In addition to local accents of England, many Scots and Irish accents can also be heard. A large number nowadays are women, moreover. So the public have become quite used to the absence of what used to be thought a necessity for an authority: a male, RP-speaking, voice.

The authority of prominent people in public life, such as Prime Ministers, has traditionally been associated with RP. Prime Ministers [in the twentieth] century, whatever their political party, unless they are not English (Lloyd George was Welsh and Ramsay MacDonald was Scottish), have until recently always been RP speakers. We have just seen, however, three successive Prime Ministers who spoke with English regional accents: Harold Wilson, James Callaghan, and Edward Heath. We have now an RP-speaking Prime Minister again in Mrs Thatcher, but if her successor were not, it would occasion no surprise. The tradition has been broken.

David
Abercrombie

Perhaps the most interesting developments are that some speakers of RP seem themselves to be turning against it; and that some young people have elected to speak with a local accent, even though their parents are RP speakers.

Signs of these developments are perceptible even to someone, like myself, living outside England. I have had, for example, at the University of Edinburgh, students from England whose background would lead one to expect them to be RP speakers, but who seem to be deliberately trying to modify their accent by adopting features of other accents, Scots for instance.

I am visited quite often by a number of young relatives of mine – two different families – who were brought up in London by parents one of whom was an RP speaker and whom in the past children would almost certainly have chosen to copy. In both families they have chosen to adopt a local London accent instead. Doubtless the choice was not consciously made; but it seems to reflect a prevailing climate of opinion.

One would really need to be on the spot to assess accurately how general these trends are. It would appear that not much hope can be expected from phoneticians, who seem not very concerned about possible changes in public attitudes to RP and its speakers. Many phoneticians nowadays, moreover, including the most productive and original, are themselves not RP speakers, which may be why they seem indifferent to problems which do not concern them personally.

There are an enormous number of people, all over the world, being taught English, and teaching requires a *pronunciation model* for the learner to emulate. English offers a wide choice of accents suitable as models, more perhaps than most other languages. One of these accents, of course, is RP. It is a very natural, not to say inevitable, choice of model for learners in Europe, and perhaps further afield. Its reputation as a prestige accent is widespread among educators, even if its ambiguous position is not fully realised. The teacher, moreover, has available a large number of pedagogical aids to its use, such as pronouncing dictionaries, disk and tape illustrative recordings, phonetic texts, treatments of special aspects such as intonation, and so on.

Nevertheless, RP has disadvantages as a model. It has a larger vowel system, with many diphthongs, than most accents of English; this can be a teaching problem. It has great prestige in some places, but it arouses hostility or dislike in others. In some parts of the English-speaking world it is not found very intelligible. These points have to be set against its advantages as a model.

RP is probably one of the most widely used models in the English-teaching world, the other being what is usually known as General American, which is really the accent of the Middle West. Although many Europeans mix more with Americans than with British, no one has advocated General American as a model for Europe; indeed there is a widespread feeling that there is something undesirable about an American accent, which is a very old-fashioned attitude. In fact it is a very good model.

Another possible model would be a Scottish accent. It is admired everywhere, is highly intelligible, and phonetically offers a minimum of problems. If provided with pedagogical aids, it would provide an excellent model. But that is another story.

**David
Abercrombie**

Another possible model would be based on the learners' own mother tongue. Such a model has already appeared in India, Egypt, and West Africa, as I have seen for myself. The advocacy of such a model has been called by an American writer 'the British heresy'. A French expert on language teaching has recently put forward such a model for French learners of English, and presumably this would apply to other European languages. But that, too, is another story.

The position and prospects of RP today, then, it seems to me are not very bright. If I may venture a prophecy, RP is slowly but surely on its way out.

Questions, suggestions and issues to consider

1   From your observations, or perhaps even your personal experience, would you agree that the status of traditional RP has changed in recent years? What evidence is there for or against? If you think change has taken place, do you think it's stopped, or is it still going on?

2   Abercrombie comments on the speech of British prime ministers up to Margaret Thatcher. What can you say about the speech of those who have followed her (John Major and Tony Blair)?

3   Some people are noted for having changed their speech from traditional RP (or something very close to it) to a regional accent variety. Three examples commonly mentioned are the DJ and radio personality John Peel, the rock star Mick Jagger and the classical violinist Nigel Kennedy. What do you think might be their various motivations in making this change?

4   What kind of English accent would you yourself recommend as a pronunciation model to foreign learners of English? Would your answer vary depending on what part of the world they lived in? Re-read Sections A1 and C6 in the light of what Abercrombie suggests.

5   An idea is presently current which takes up Abercrombie's suggestion of basing a learner's pronunciation model on his/her own language (see Jenkins 2000 for the best known presentation of this type of argument). What would be the advantages to such an approach? Could you foresee any possible disadvantages?

D2   ## ATTITUDES TO ACCENTS

**Daniel
Jones**

Daniel Jones (originally entitled 'Speech training: the phonetic aspect' (1935). Reprinted from *British Journal of Educational Psychology* 5: 27–30)

Daniel Jones is generally considered to be the greatest British phonetician of the twentieth century and the man who laid the foundations world-wide for phonetics as we know it today. Although one of his important contributions was his detailed description of English pronunciation on the basis of traditional RP, he was perhaps the first linguist to set down clearly his opposition to prescriptivism in speech training and to advocate respect for native accents of all kinds.

Daniel Jones

Aim and methods of phonetics

The aim of the phonetician is twofold: (1) to determine with precision the movements made by the tongue and other parts of the organs of speech in pro-nouncing words and sentences, (2) to cause his pupils to perform unaccustomed movements with their organs of speech; in other words, to pronounce new sounds or new combinations of sounds.

The processes of phonetics can be applied in various ways. For instance, it is possible by means of them to teach an apt pupil to pronounce a foreign language in a manner almost indistinguishable from a native, whether that language is one such as French, which has certain affinities with English, or whether it is an absolutely remote one such as Chinese or Zulu. It is also possible to teach a pupil to make changes in his pronunciation of his mother tongue; and it is this aspect of phonetic work in which this [paper] is chiefly interested.

It should be explained here that phonetic work is not concerned with voice-production. The phonetician is concerned with tongue articulations, etc.; we leave the manner of producing the voice to those who are specialists in that subject. These two branches of speech training should, in my view, be kept distinct; any *pronunciation* can be combined with either good or bad *voice-production*. There are plenty of people, for instance, who speak what is called 'good' English but use bad voice-production. And conversely one not unfrequently hears good voice-production combined with quite incorrect pronunciation; this may be observed notably when good singers sing foreign songs.

'Good' and 'bad' pronunciation

Another point to be noted is that the phonetician concerns himself with the recording of facts, and his teaching is based on such records; he does not (or at any rate it is better that he should not) concern himself with what is 'good' or 'bad' in pronunciation, or with what is 'right' or 'wrong' or with the 'prettiness' or 'ugliness' of sounds.

In fact, it is his function to take up a rather detached attitude in regard to such questions. By doing so he finds that much of what is sometimes called 'beautiful' or 'ugly' in speech is not intrinsic beauty or ugliness at all, but is merely convention. The use of a certain sound recalls an unpleasant circumstance or reminds us of somebody we do not like or whom we despise, and (often with-out realizing the connexion) we attribute ugliness to the *sound* instead of to the circumstances recalled by it.

To give an example: many people think it ugly to pronounce *face* as [fais]. But if you come to think of it there is nothing intrinsically ugly about this syl-lable or about any parts of it; we use the vowel-sound [ai] in *nice*, *twice*, and *ice* without thinking it ugly, and the sound cannot become ugly simply because some-one puts an *f* in front of it. In fact, I can imagine that if we are thinking of snow and ice or skating, many people might consider the sound of the word *ice* rather pretty. But if I were to make exactly the same sound [ais] in speaking of the '[aɪs] of clubs,' some of those people might regard that same sound as being ugly. This instance shows that we are not dealing with intrinsic prettiness or ugliness: the sound [aɪs] cannot vary its inherent prettiness according as a person uses it to denote frozen water or a certain card in a pack.

The real reason why people who pronounce [feɪs] do not like the sound of [faɪs] is that they connect the variant [faɪs] with Cockneys and slums and what they call 'vulgarity,' while they connect by a convention [feɪs] with gentility or elegance or culture. (Incidentally, it may be remarked that [feɪs] and [faɪs] may both be said with either good or bad voice-production.)

This detached attitude of merely regarding sounds as sounds (apart from any inherent beauty they may possess, if any), of examining them as we find them, of analysing their mode of formation and noting who are the people who use them, leads to very useful results. When we come to study pronunciation with this attitude of mind, we make many interesting discoveries, some of which may cause surprise. One discovery which the observer of phonetic phenomena makes at quite an early stage of his studies is that he finds he actually uses a great many pronunciations which at first he might have been tempted to condemn. Another is that when you listen carefully to the speech of those who condemn particular forms of pronunciation, you will often hear them use the very pronunciations they are condemning. It is also interesting to find out the effect which one's own pronunciation has on different people; my pronunciation was, for instance, once described by a teacher of some position as 'the speech of costermongers and servant girls,' and on another occasion by a provincial amateur philologist as a 'nauseating London simper.'

We learn from such experiences to be very tolerant about other people's pronunciation; and that tolerance greatly facilitates the task of practical teaching. If one is trying, for instance, to teach the sort of English I am now using to a class of Cockney schoolboys, and if one is intolerant about their speech and tells them that their way is 'wrong' or 'bad' or 'ugly,' it simply antagonizes them. They do not like being told that the kind of English they have always used and which is used by their parents, their brothers and sisters and friends, is 'bad.' But if the teacher takes up a more tolerant attitude and explains that they have a language which serves its purpose well for home use, but that there exist many other ways of talking; that some of these ways are only understood well in restricted areas, say London, or South Lancashire, or the neighbourhood of Dundee, while others are readily understood over much wider areas – some, in fact, over the whole of the English-speaking world; that it often comes in very usefully if a man can talk a kind of English which is easily understood everywhere, and that is why a special kind of English is taught in school; then the teacher can get the boys on his side, and they become willing to learn the school pronunciation instead of thinking it silly and affected.

As to details of the methods of applying phonetics in the teaching of speech, I could, of course, give many examples to show what can be done, but it is hardly necessary to do so here, since most if not all of [ʌs] are familiar with modern methods of teaching pronunciation. But I should like to emphasize one thing, namely, that phonetic methods deal not only with the articulations of consonants but also with the more difficult problem of the utterance of vowels. It is a relatively easy thing to teach a child to say *butter* when his home pronunciation is to use what we call the 'glottal stop' instead of the *t*, or to say *getting* when his home pronunciation is *gettin*; and it is generally not difficult (provided you can induce the pupil to co-operate willingly) to cure lisping and other individual mispronunciations of consonants. But it is a good deal more difficult, though none the less feasible, to teach the so-called 'cultured' pronunciation of *face*, *tea*, and *two* to pupils accustomed to say [fais], [tʰəi], [tʰəu]. Such things are mainly a matter of directing the pupils to put their tongues and lips into certain positions, and helping them by suitable dictation exercises to discriminate by ear between different shades of sound-quality.

Conclusions

Any pronunciation can be combined with either good or bad voice-production.

Much of what is sometimes called 'beautiful' or 'ugly' in speech is merely convention. The beauty or ugliness applies to certain environments, and we are apt to attribute beauty or ugliness to sounds which remind us of those environments.

A study of phonetics often reveals that we ourselves use pronunciations which at first sight we might be tempted to condemn. We thus learn to become very tolerant of other people's pronunciation; this tolerance on the part of a teacher of speech makes him more efficient.

Questions, suggestions and issues to consider

1 We have included this extract because it is one of the very first examples of what might be termed a liberal approach to social variation in speech. What do you think might have been the reactions to this paper in the Britain of the 1930s? What might be the reactions in Britain today?

2 Are there nowadays any reasons for teaching children to change their natural speech? Do Jones's arguments that people should be encouraged to speak in a manner which is widely intelligible still hold?

3 Would you agree that it is easier to change the pronunciation of consonants than that of vowels? Go back to Sections A5 and A6 for help in this discussion.

4 Do you consider that there are such things as 'ugly' or 'pretty' speech sounds? Would you agree with Jones that 'much of what is called "beautiful" or "ugly" ... is merely convention'? Or do you think aesthetic criteria can indeed be applied to pronunciation?

5 From what you have learned of phonetics so far, do you find that you actually use pronunciations which at one time you might have been tempted to condemn? If so, draw up a list. Talk to other members of the class and exchange your views on this matter.

PRONUNCIATION WORRIES

David Crystal (reprinted from *The English Language* (1988), Harmondsworth: Penguin, pp. 57–61)

In this extract, the linguist, writer and broadcaster David Crystal discusses some of the most frequent pronunciation complaints heard from BBC listeners. He points out that what is often regarded as 'sloppy' speech is in fact characteristic of everyday usage for most speakers. Crystal also provides a list of words which have alternative pronunciations in British English.

[G]enerally actors try to pronounce words clearly, paying special attention to their endings, and without rushing weak syllables. In this way, the words can be heard more clearly at the back of the theatre. But their speech is much slower than normal conversation as a result. In three renditions of Hamlet's 'To be, or not to be' speech by different actors, the speeds ranged from 130 to 190 spm [syllables per minute] – on average, half the speed of normal conversation.

The same point applies to other professional voice users, such as news broadcasters, radio announcers, priests, judges, and politicians. These people all have to speak in abnormal conditions – from a pulpit, in front of a crowd, into a microphone. In most cases, the listeners cannot see the speaker's face clearly enough (or see it at all, in the case of radio) to enable them to get clues from the movement of the lips, or from the facial expression, as to what is being said. To be sure that their speech stands the best chance of being understood by all, then, professional speakers know that they must speak relatively slowly and distinctly. If they do not, they risk criticism of being unintelligible, or of being too informal, casual, or 'sloppy'.

Enter the radio listeners, for the most common of all complaints to the BBC concerns the topic of pronunciation. And sloppy speech is the charge most often cited. The irony, of course, is that in almost every case the words called sloppy are in fact perfectly normal pronunciations in everyday speech, and everyone uses them. They include such forms as *Feb'ry* for *February*, *lib'ry* for *library*, *Antar'tic* for *Antarctic*, *as'matic* for *asthmatic*, *twel'ths* for *twelfths*, *patien's* for *patients*, *reco'nize* for *recognize*, and so on. It's very difficult in fact to say some of these words in their 'full' form – try pronouncing the second **t** in *patients*, for example. But many listeners, it seems, expect such precise articulation over the air, and are ready to demand it in writing, to the tune of thousands of letters each year.

Most listeners give just one reason for their complaint: a letter is there in the spelling, and so it should be pronounced. This is another example of the widespread belief that speech is a poor relation of writing. We always need to remind ourselves that speech came first, in the history of our species, and that we all learn to speak before we learn to write. To be worried about our pronunciation because it does not match the spelling is a strange reversal of priorities. We also need to remember that pronunciation patterns have changed radically since the days when the spelling system was laid down. English spelling hasn't been a good guide to pronunciation for hundreds of years.

But despite all this, many people do act very angry when sounds are left out that they think ought to be there, or sounds are put in which they think ought not to be. Probably the most famous case of this last point is the use of an 'intrusive r' by speakers of Received Pronunciation: the insertion of an /r/ between vowels, when there is no *r* in the spelling. The most well-known instance, because of its frequency in the news, is *law and order* – widely known as 'Laura Norder'.

One listener sent in a collection of over 100 intrusive *r*s which he had heard in one day's listening. He included examples like *Shah (r) of Persia, draw(r)ing*, and *awe(r)-inspiring*. These are the noticeable ones, because the /r/ stands out clearly after the *ah/aw* vowels, which are said with the mouth quite widely open. It's much more difficult to hear this kind of /r/ when it occurs after the less sonorous /ə/ vowel – the vowel that we use at the end of words like *sofa* or *Persia*. Unless Received Pronunciation speakers are taking extreme care, and speaking very self-consciously, they automatically put an /r/ into such phrases as *Africa(r) and Asia, an area(r) of disagreement*, and *drama(r) and music*. I have a tape recording of a critic vociferously condemning the intrusive *r* in *law and order*, in the course of which he said 'the idea of an intrusive *r* is obnoxious', putting in an /r/ at the end of *idea!*

Where does the intrusive *r* come from? It's the result of these speakers unconsciously extending a pattern already present in their accent, as found in the linking *r* sequence described above. It is important to notice that, although there are thousands of English words which end in the letter *r*, only four kinds of vowel are involved: /ɔː/ as in *four*, /ɑː/ as in *car*, /ɜː/ as in *fur*, and /ə/ as in *mother*. What has happened is that, over the years, the linking /r/ has been extended to *all* words ending in one of these four vowels, when they're followed by another vowel. The effect is most noticeable in words ending in /ɔː/, as in *law and order*, because there are in fact not very many such words in the language, so the usage tends to stand out.

Of course, explaining why a pronunciation has developed doesn't explain why some people have come to hate it. It's the same with other areas of usage. Why do some people hate *hopefully*? The reason is likely to be something to do with the way one social group, at some time in the past, adopted a usage in order to keep themselves apart from another social group which did not. In particular, an accent comes to be used like a badge, showing a person's social identity. At any one time, there are several pronunciation patterns which are 'loaded' in this way. Current examples include 'dropping the *h*' ('*ospital* for *hospital*) and 'dropping the *g*' (*walkin*' for *walking*). These days such forms are considered to be uneducated – though a century ago, they were often to be found in cultured speech (as in the upper-class use of *huntin', shootin'* and *fishin'*).

All of this presents radio managers with a problem, of course. Although only a minority of listeners are antagonized by such matters, none the less they are antagonized – and this is not what radio broadcasting is meant to be about. Announcers and presenters who are sensitive to these issues therefore often go out of their way to avoid using a pronunciation which they know will upset people. They may go through their scripts and underline problem cases. Far more than the intrusive *r* is involved, of course. The problems include changes in stress (e.g. **dis**pute vs

David
Crystal

dispute) and the pronunciation of individual words (e.g. saying *recognize* with or without the *g*). A selection of issues is [given below]. Foreign words pose special problems, as do the names of people and places. A Pronunciation Unit has long been established at the BBC to help answer queries about such matters. During the 1986 World Cup matches, the Unit had to issue guidelines to its commentators about the players, referees, linesmen, managers, and others involved – it took twenty-seven pages.

Controversies of the 1980s

The following list includes many of the words which have alternative pronunciations in current English. The asterisk indicates the pronunciation recommended in the 1981 BBC guide compiled by Robert Burchfield.

adversary	stress on *1st or 2nd syllable
apartheid	vowel in 3rd syllable as in *height* or *hate*
apparatus	vowel in 3rd syllable as in *car* or *fate*
applicable	stress on *1st or 2nd syllable
ate	vowel as in *set or *late*
centenary	vowel in 2nd syllable as in *ten* or *teen*
centrifugal	stress on *2nd or 3rd syllable
comparable	stress on *1st or 2nd syllable
contribute	stress on 1st or *2nd syllable
controversy	stress on *1st or 2nd syllable
deity	vowel in 1st syllable as in *say* or *see*
derisive	*s* in 2nd syllable as in *rice* or *rise*
dilemma	vowel in 1st syllable as in *did* or *die*
diphtheria	*ph* as */f/ or /p/
dispute	stress on 1st or *2nd syllable
economic	vowel in 1st syllable as in *met* or *me* (both accepted)
envelope	vowel in 1st syllable as in *den* or *don*
furore	said as *3 syllables or 2
homosexual	vowel in 1st syllable as in *hot* or *home*
inherent	vowel in 2nd syllable as in *see* or *set*
kilometre	stress on *1st or 2nd syllable
longitude	*ng* as in *range* or *long*
medicine	said as *2 syllables or 3
migraine	vowel in 1st syllable as in *me* or *my*
pejorative	stress on 1st or *2nd syllable
plastic	vowel in 1st syllable as in *cat* or *car*
primarily	stress on *1st or 2nd syllable
privacy	vowel in 1st syllable as in *sit* or *sigh*
sheikh	vowel as in *see* or *say*
Soviet	vowel in 1st syllable as in *so* or *cot*
status	vowel in 1st syllable as in *sat* or *state*
subsidence	vowel in 2nd syllable as in *Sid* or *side*
trait	final t *silent or sounded

David Crystal

The problem becomes particularly acute if a radio channel decides to adopt a policy of friendliness or informality in response to listener demand. To make speech come across in a normally informal way, it is necessary to speed it up, and to introduce assimilations and elisions. If these are not introduced, either because they lessen the clarity of what is said or because they attract listener criticism, the speech will inevitably sound formal, clipped, and controlled. But listeners cannot have it both ways. If they want their announcers to sound friendly, they must expect a chatty style, with all the consequences that has for pronunciation.

As long as society contains divisions, there will always be differences in pronunciation, and, as a consequence, arguments about which form is best and which accent is most acceptable. The arguments can be healthy and informative, or nasty and intolerant. They are usually the latter. BBC announcers with accents other than Received Pronunciation regularly receive hate mail. And when I present *English Now* on Radio 4, my own accent – a mixture of Wales, Liverpool, and southern England – is often criticized. The letter-writers usually ask for the removal, forthwith, of the offending parties.

Getting the sack because of your speech isn't unknown. I know of two cases – one in an estate agent's, the other in a hairdresser's – where assistants have had to leave because their accents were felt to be inappropriate. And in 1970 there was a much-publicized case of a blacksmith who committed suicide because he could not cope with the ridicule levelled at his accent when he moved from Yorkshire to the South of England. Remembering such stories, a tiny plea for tolerance would seem a reasonable way to end this section.

Questions, suggestions and issues to consider

1   Find further examples to support David Crystal's rejection of the listeners' claims that 'a letter is there in the spelling, and so it should be pronounced'.
2   Do you think you use intrusive *r*? If you think you do not, then is this because you come from a region where rhotic English is spoken (e.g. Scotland, the West Country, most of the USA)? Or are you a non-rhotic speaker who has made a conscious effort to eliminate it from your speech?
3   Look at the list of 1980s controversies. Do you think your own pronunciation follows the 1981 BBC recommended (starred) form or not? Try saying each word in both ways mentioned. Decide which of the two forms you think is more up to date (ask your parents or grandparents and see what they say). Do any of the starred forms seem inappropriate or out of date to you?
4   At the moment (2003) British radio and television has newsreaders with modified Scottish and Welsh accents on their national services. Is this in your view a good idea? Should it be extended and include, say, Geordie, Scouse or Birmingham? Or would you agree with the letter writers who ask for such announcers to be sacked?
5   Have you any personal experience of problems relating to regional accents? Or do you know of anyone in your family, or amongst your friends, who has suffered because of his or her regional speech? Exchange your experiences with others in the class.

D4

PHONETICS APPLIED TO TEACHING THE DEAF

Dennis Fry

Dennis Fry (reprinted from *Homo Loquens* (1977), Cambridge: Cambridge University Press, pp. 139–43)

Dennis Fry was a phonetician who took a particular interest in the problems of the deaf and in discovering the best ways to help people with speech and hearing problems. Here he pleads for the early diagnosis of profoundly deaf babies.

A severe loss of hearing, from whatever cause, will interfere with the natural and spontaneous development of the capacity to speak and to take in speech, for it will mean that the sounds of speech arriving at the baby's ears will not be loud enough to provide the basis for learning unless some special steps are taken. One of the hazards of deafness is that the defect is not a visible one. Obvious abnormalities are readily recognized at birth or soon afterwards; even blindness reveals itself at an early stage, but loss of hearing may be undetected for a long time and this has serious consequences as far as the development of speech is concerned. Mothers very often notice something strange in the early behaviour of a baby who is deaf, especially if they have already had a child with normal hearing. One mother, for example, realized that her baby was deaf at the age of twenty-seven days because it did not react in the way an elder sister had done, but usually it takes much longer than this before anyone even suspects that a baby's hearing is not normal.

Discovering at the earliest possible moment if a child has a hearing loss is vitally important for speech, for a number of reasons. For the ordinary person the word 'deaf' tends to have an all-or-none character; if you are deaf you cannot hear anything and if you are not, you can hear everything. The true state of affairs is not this at all and this is why those who are professionally concerned in the matter tend to talk more about hearing loss than about deafness. If you are sitting about three feet away from someone who is talking in an ordinary tone of voice, the sounds are reaching you at a level of about 60 db.[1] and they will be loud enough for you to carry on a conversation quite comfortably. You might, however, happen to be slightly deaf so that the sounds were considerably fainter, let us say about as loud as if they reached you at a level of 40 db. In that case your hearing loss for speech is 20 db. If you were much deafer than this, the sounds of speech might be quite inaudible to you even at three feet and then your hearing loss for speech is at least 60 db. and may be more. Deafness is therefore a graded effect which can be measured in decibels and most commonly the degree of hearing loss varies with frequency, that is to say a person may be particularly deaf to high frequencies, to mid-frequencies or to low frequencies, or he may be more or less equally deaf all over the frequency range. A baby who is born with a hearing loss may have any degree of loss and in any part of the range. One fact that is not generally appreciated is that it is very rare indeed for a child to be born without any capacity at all for perceiving sound; in practically every case, if enough acoustic energy is supplied to the ears, the child will experience some sensation of sound, if only within a narrow band of frequencies.

Dennis Fry

The sounds of speech as they leave the speaker's lips will not provide enough energy to be of use to a baby with a considerable hearing loss but this energy can be magnified and brought up to a useful level by means of amplifiers in the form of hearing-aids. These devices may have a number of very sophisticated features but their essential purpose is to magnify the intensity of any sounds which they transmit and so to compensate as far as possible for a hearing loss. In order that speech may develop naturally in a deaf child it is important that suitable amplification should be provided during the first year of life. It is an interesting fact that while everyone understands the need for supplying prostheses[2] to, say, a thalidomide baby[3] at the earliest possible stage, it is very difficult even for those closely concerned to see the importance of fitting hearing-aids to a deaf baby. The matter is of course bound up with the early detection of a hearing loss, which must be ultimately the task of a suitable clinic, but once the presence of deafness is established or even strongly suspected, it is perfectly possible for a baby of eight or nine months to be equipped with hearing-aids.

The reason why this is so important will be clear from all that has been said about the development of speech. It is a well-established fact that deaf babies babble just like hearing babies and the sounds they produce are not noticeably different. A critical moment comes, however, when in the ordinary way the sound of adult speech would act as a trigger for the child's babbling. Time after time it is reported by mothers that a deaf baby babbled up to a certain time and that then the babbling faded; this is because the sound of other people's speech is just not audible or not audible enough to the baby to continue the normal process of development. One thing that contributes to the breakdown is the fact that it is just about this time that a child begins to crawl so that it tends to move farther away from its mother. While it is in the mother's arms or on her knee a good deal of the time, her voice may be audible despite the baby's hearing loss, but when it becomes mobile, the added distance reduces the loudness of the voice. The deaf child who is fitted with hearing-aids continues to hear his mother's speech and there is a good chance that his progress will follow that of the hearing child at this vital point. There are literary hundreds of children with a severe hearing loss which has been discovered early who have acquired speech that is very little different from that of hearing people. This is because the mother in each case has realized the nature of the problem and has taken the necessary steps to see that the child was continually hearing speech despite his deafness. In more than one case this has been done in the early stages without any hearing-aids simply by the mother's talking all the time right into the child's ear. One of the most tragic things that can happen, and it still does so all too frequently, is that the mother is told either 'We cannot be sure whether your child is deaf, so please bring him back in two or three years' time and then we may be able to tell you' or else 'I am sorry to tell you that your child is very deaf, so it will not be much good trying to talk to him'. But the first months and years are of vital consequence for the acquiring of speech and language and the plain fact is that even a child with perfectly normal hearing would not learn to talk if he did not hear speech all the time. A child with a hearing loss needs to hear speech much more than a hearing child and not less; his mother needs to accompany every action and every event with speech so that the baby's brain may have the best chance of developing for itself the immense store of information which we have seen to be necessary. This is a tremendous task for any mother but if it is successfully accomplished, it is a very rewarding one since it reduces dramatically the handicap under which the child labours for the rest of its life.

It is perhaps not easy to see how, even when these steps are taken, the child can possibly work anything like normally with speech. His deafness not only makes the sounds of speech faint or inaudible, it also distorts them because it changes the relations of high, middle and low frequencies. Even with the best of hearing-aids, the deaf ear cannot hear speech as the normal ear hears it. The clue is to be found in the functioning of acoustic cues. Each individual brain evolves for itself a system of cues which works for all the distinctions that have to be made. In doing so it is in any case relying on the entirely private version of speech sounds which the ears are relaying to the brain. There is no reason at all why English listeners should all use the same acoustic cues and we can be pretty sure that they do not. What is necessary is that, whatever cues they use in a given case, they should come out with the right answer, that is to say they should recognize correctly what phoneme is represented in the string. The deaf child can do exactly the same thing provided he hears speech loud enough and often enough. His ears are supplying him with different acoustic information and with less information than normal ears, but his brain will use this to arrive at cues which work. Let us take the example of the difference between /s/ and /ʃ/ in English which for most of us depends on a higher pitched and a lower pitched noise. To many deaf ears these actual noises must be indistinguishable, but we noticed that the sounds are accompanied by different formant transitions and these provide a cue which is available even to most deaf ears, as long as speech is made audible. It is again the parallel of the colour blind person who judges traffic lights by their position and not by their colour. Once the whole system is established, the deaf listener may have to rely somewhat more heavily on redundancy[4] than the normally hearing person, just as we do when there is distortion in the communication channel, and as far as his own speech is concerned, he will like the rest of us apply his acoustic cues to his own speech production, shaping his own sounds to the best of his ability until they make a match with those he hears from other people.

None of this should be taken to mean that deafness of any degree is other than a very grave disability when it is present at birth or very soon afterwards. It is a fact, however, that if deafness is discovered early enough, if proper advice is available and suitable hearing-aids are fitted and if the parents, especially the mother, are able to apply themselves to the arduous task involved, it is possible to go a very long way towards overcoming the obstacle which deafness presents to the normal acquisition of speech and language.

Notes

1   *decibel* (abbr. *db. or dB*): a standard unit used for expressing the intensity of sound (related to what the human ear perceives as loudness).
2   *prosthesis*: any artificial replacement for a part of the body, e.g. an artificial leg, breast implant, etc.

3   *thalidomide baby*: this refers to children born in the 1960s whose limbs were misformed or absent as the result of the mother taking the sedative thalidomide during pregnancy. The drug was later withdrawn from the market.

4   *redundancy*: referring to the way in which language provides more information than is basically needed. If any of the message is lost or not understood, this extra information will allow the receiver to interpret the message correctly.

Questions, suggestions and issues to consider

1   What does Fry mean when he states that 'for the ordinary person the word "deaf" tends to have an all-or-none character'? What is the reality of the situation?

2   Discuss the significance of 'babbling'. See if you can get access to a recording of a young baby babbling – or, even better, try to make such a recording yourself.

3   Which sounds do you think partially deaf people will normally have most difficulty with – vowels or consonants? Why?

4   If you know a person who uses a hearing aid, ask them (tactfully) to explain to you how it improves their life. Try also to discover what they feel its limitations to be.

5   By the age of twenty most people have begun to lose the top frequency range of their hearing. Can you hear the high-pitched whistle emitted by a TV set? If you can, you can be pretty confident that you have maintained good high-frequency hearing. Ask how many of the class are still able to hear it. If one can't detect the TV whistle, do you think this degree of hearing loss would impede one's understanding of speech? If not, why not?

MAKING COMPUTERS TALK

Peter Ladefoged (reprinted from *Vowels and Consonants: An Introduction to the Sounds of Language* (2001), Oxford: Blackwell, pp. 68–73)

There are many problems involved in the process of making machines talk – in producing what is known technically as 'synthetic speech'. In this extract, the phonetician Peter Ladefoged summarises some of the difficulties and indicates how phoneticians and computer scientists attempt to solve them.

How writing must be pronounced

How do we get a computer to talk? My mother-in-law was nearly blind for many years at the end of her life. What she needed was a way of turning anything that could be written into good spoken English. She wanted to be able to put a book in front of a computer, sit back, and enjoy it. (How the computer was going to turn the pages was not her concern.)

Peter Ladefoged

Computers have been able to synthesize speech for many years [and] make sounds like English sentences. But the quality of most synthetic speech is still not high enough to make enjoyable listening. One might think that all we need are the values of the formant[1] frequencies and amplitudes,[2] [etc.]. But there are many steps in this process that are still not fully understood. So let us see why computers don't yet sound like you and me.

We want to have a system that will turn any kind of written text into synthesized speech, forming what is called a Text-To-Speech (TTS) system. The first step in turning a text into speech is to find all the abbreviations and symbols. They have to be converted into their full forms. Abbreviations have to be distinguished so that the sentence 'Dr. Smith lives at 10 Sunset Dr.' is pronounced as *Doctor Smith lives at ten Sunset Drive*, and 'St. Paul's church is on Church St.' as *Saint Paul's church is on Church Street*. Symbols have to be interpreted so that '$14.22' becomes *Fourteen dollars and twenty-two cents*, and '£1.40' becomes *One pound forty*. Most good TTS systems can deal with all these examples.

We also have to deal with acronyms, spelling out 'TTS' as *text to speech* and turning 'HE' into *His Excellency* or *high explosive*, whichever seems more suitable in the context. Some acronyms are normally not spelled out, but are pronounced just as a sequence of letters (like USA or UK). Others are pronounced as if they were words (like UNESCO). New acronyms (like TTS) are continually being devised, making this a difficult problem.

Numbers are pronounced in several different ways. Think how you would say *The year 1999* as compared with *1999 cars*. If you are talking about the year it has to be *nineteen ninety nine* or *nineteen hundred and ninety nine*, but the number of cars could be *one thousand nine hundred and ninety nine*. Telephone numbers are pronounced in different ways in different countries. Americans might pronounce 404 5911 as *Four zero four, five nine one one*, whereas British speakers might say *Four nought four, five nine double one*.

Once we have a text that contains only words, we have to take the written words and change them so that they are spelled phonetically. This may be quite straightforward. A written sentence like 'Black cats bring good luck' becomes, in a phonetic transcription, **blæk kæts brɪŋ gud lʌk**. Even if you don't remember the phonetic symbols for the vowels, you can still see the relationship between the letters and the phonetic symbols. But that was an easy sentence. We all know how difficult it is to spell some English words. The computer has similar difficulties in turning written English into a phonetic transcription. We will consider how it does this first for consonants and then for vowels.

Consonants are fairly easy to deal with. Each letter often corresponds to a phonetic symbol, as in the sentence 'Black cats bring good luck'. In this sentence, the only consonants that have to be changed from two letters into one symbol are the 'ck' at the end of 'black' and 'luck' and the 'ng' at the end of 'bring'. A general rule changing 'ng' at the end of a word into the phonetic symbol ŋ will work very well. Another example of a combination of letters that has to be regarded as a single sound is 'sh'. The computer has to know that this is not a sequence of the sound s followed by h, but a single sound of the kind that we earlier called a fricative. It gets a little more complicated in the case of the

Peter
Ladefoged

letters 'th', which can stand for either the fricative in *thin* or the one in *this*, in which the fricative noise is accompanied by vocal fold vibrations. A rough rule is that if the word is a noun, adjective, or adverb, then 'th' represents the voiceless sound in *thin*, otherwise it represents a voiced sound, as in words such as *the*, *this*, and *that*. Similarly, the computer has to have a general rule making 'ph' into the phonetic symbol **f** in words such as *photo* and *siphon*. Of course all the rules have problems and don't always work. When the computer comes to 'haphazard' it has to know that this word is an exception to the rule, and is not pronounced as if it were *hafazard*.

Vowels are a little more complex. When you were learning to read you had to deal with the problem of the silent 'e' at the ends of words. Each vowel letter can have at least two pronunciations. For example, the vowel 'o' is pronounced as a so-called long vowel[3] when it is followed by a silent 'e' as in *note*, or when it is separated by a single consonant from another vowel in the same word, as in *notable*. It has a so-called short vowel sound when there are two or more consonants after it as in *bottle*, or when there is a single consonant and a word boundary after it, as in *not*. But these rules are far from foolproof. The first vowel in *nothing* has neither the sound of *not* nor that of *note*. We simply have to regard this and many other words as exceptions to the rules. Computer systems working only in terms of spelling rules with no exceptions soon get into difficulties. They cannot deal with the six different pronunciations of 'ough' in American English: *tough, though, bought, bough, cough, through* – to which the British add a seventh: *thorough*, which has ə in the last syllable.

If we have a computer with a large enough memory, we do not have to bother so much with spelling rules. We can store a large dictionary so that every word can be changed into its phonetic form simply by looking it up. The only problem with this form of synthesis is that it fails completely whenever it comes to a new word that is not in its dictionary, such as the previously little-used name *Clinton*. Most text-to-speech systems now rely on a mixed system, using a dictionary lookup for many words, but having spelling rules available for new words.

Phonetic rules and dictionaries will not be enough in some cases. In the sentence *The dog's lead was made of lead*, only a very smart computer could tell that the two forms of *lead* should be pronounced differently. A sophisticated speech synthesizer could manage by understanding the sentence in much the same way as we do. We know that the spelling 'l e a d' represents two different words. We also know that dogs have leads, and that they can be made of metal. In this way we know that the first 'lead' refers to the one word, and the second to the other. A human like you reading this page can appreciate the difference simply from the information in the text. A sufficiently powerful computer could do the same.

But the main problem remains. Computers reading long passages nearly always sound very machine-like because they can't get the correct intonation. They don't know which words should be emphasized and how the different tunes should be produced. They can handle simple sentences, and even use the punctuation to produce the intonation difference between 'He likes cats – and dogs with long hair', and 'He likes cats and dogs with long hair'. But other differences in phrasing are more subtle. When we speak, we know where to put the emphasis because we know the meaning and the grammatical structure of different sentences. If I asked you to name some liquids, you might say *Water is a liquid*, with the emphasis on *Water*. But if I asked you to name some properties of water, you might say *Water is a liquid*, with the emphasis on *liquid*. It is simple for you to make these differences. But computers have to learn a lot about language before they can manage such subtleties.

Early speech synthesis systems could say simple sentences, and distinguish between statements and questions appropriately. Now they are able to produce a wider variety of intonations, and they are very good at conveying straight-forward information. But they use smoother pitch changes without the small ups and downs that occur in the real human intonation curves. Nor do they have the variety of intonations that any of us produce in everyday conversations. And when it comes to reading anything dramatic, they fail hopelessly. It will be a long time before a computer can give a good performance of *Hamlet* that my mother-in-law would have enjoyed.

Words and sounds in sentences

In discussing the problems of synthesizing speech, we have so far skipped over one point that deserves a section all to itself. When we talk we do not say each word separately. There are no pauses between the words in a phrase. That's why there is virtually no difference between phrases like *A name* and *An aim*.

One result of running the words together is that the pronunciation shown in the dictionary is seldom the way many common words are pronounced in a sentence. The end of one word will be changed because of the influence of the following word. When you talk about a hand gun you may well pronounce it as something like *hang gun*, without the **d** being fully formed. If a hand gun ever becomes an everyday item (what an awful thought) it will certainly be pronounced as if it began with *hang*, just as has happened in the case of the familiar word 'handkerchief'.

Combinations of words are continually changing so that they are easier to pronounce. Sometimes there are even semi-recognized spellings such as 'gonna' and 'wanna' for 'going to' and 'want to'. But the effects of talking in a standard colloquial style are not limited to just a few words. I've often heard a phrase like 'this shop' pronounced as *thish shop*, and 'in play' as *im play*.

Some people think that those who say things like this are not talking as precisely as they should. They consider such pronunciations to be sloppy speech. But this is something that everybody does. If you try to pronounce each word separately and distinctly, you will sound most unnatural. When somebody tells you that you should say *going to* instead of *gonna*, just tell them that you are talking more efficiently. You are conveying the same meaning with less effort.

Some speech synthesizers sound unnatural because they produce sentences that are too stilted. They do not take sufficient account of the way words run into one another. Sometimes they also fail because they do not allow for the ways in which many of the little words in speech become much abbreviated. When said in isolation the words *two* and *to* are the same. But they differ in the sentences *I have two fish* and *I have to fish*. The same is true for *but* and *butt* in *The goat will*

Peter
Ladefoged

butt you, but it won't hurt much. Nearly all the small grammatical words such as *but, and, for, to, from, a, the* are pronounced in a very reduced form in conversational speech. Speech synthesizers normally get most of these words right because they typically use the reduced forms. Problems arise in the failure to use the full form when it is required, as in a sentence like *He went to and from London.* In this sentence, the words *to* and *from* are pronounced in their full forms, and not in the reduced forms that occur in a sentence such as *He went to London from Paris.*

Although there are no pauses between most words in a spoken phrase, the white spaces between the words on a page certainly affect the way a phrase is pronounced. We can all hear the difference between *a stray tissue* and a *straight issue*, even though the sequence of phonetic symbols in a transcription is exactly the same. This is because when a **t** occurs at the beginning of a word (as in *tissue*) it has a burst of noise followed by a short period during which the vocal folds are not vibrating. During this period there is a semi-random noise centered at the frequencies of the formants. At the end of a word there is usually no burst of noise, and the clue to the presence of a **t** is in the vowel before it, and the movements of the formants as the **t** is formed. In addition, a word such as *straight* with a **t** at the end has a much shorter vowel than a word such as *stray* with no final consonant. We will return to this point below.

Similar differences are shown by the white spaces in the sentences *I'm gonna get my lamp repaired* and *I'm gonna get my lamb prepared.* When a computer makes a phonetic transcription of these two sentences, the sequence of sounds is the same in both. But when you say them they are easily distinguishable. This is because a **p** (like a **t**) has a burst of noise when it occurs at the beginning of a word such as *prepared*, but not when it occurs at the end of *lamp.* The burst of noise may be sufficient to cover up much of the *re* in *pre(pared).* In each case the sound can be transcribed as a **p**. But a speech synthesizer needs to know that it has to produce a different waveform for a **p** or a **t** when it occurs at the beginning of a word as opposed to the end. In addition, as in the case of *straight issue* as compared with *stray tissue*, it has to know that the sequence *am* in *lamp* is shorter than the corresponding sequence in *lamb.*

There are differences between virtually all initial and final consonants. Sometimes they are only small differences in length, as in the case of **m** in *mum.* When this word is said in isolation, the final **m** is much longer than the initial **m**. Sometimes there are more distinct changes in quality, as in the case of **l** in *leaf* and *feel.* You can hear these differences more plainly when you listen to a recording played in reverse. You might expect *leaf* played backwards would sound like *feel.* But [in fact] it does not.

A number of other variants of sounds have to be taken into account in speech synthesis (or, indeed, on any occasion when we require a full account of the way a language is pronounced). Many sounds have different forms when they occur in different circumstances. For example, **t** is not only different when it occurs at the end as opposed to the beginning of a word. In American English it is very different when it occurs within a word, before an unstressed vowel as in *pretty* or *better.* In these words it sounds more like a very short **d**. In these circumstances **t** is often called a voiced flap[4] – a sound in which the tongue tip flaps very quickly

Peter
Ladefoged

against the roof of the mouth, rather than making full contact as in the pronunciation of word-initial **t**.

The sound **t** has at least one other variant that is important for high-quality speech synthesis. In a word such as *button* it is replaced by a glottal stop in most varieties of both British and American English. A glottal stop is the sound (or lack of it) caused by bringing the vocal folds tightly together, cutting off all air from the lungs. The phonetic symbol for a glottal stop is **ʔ**, so *button* can be transcribed as **bʌʔn**. You make a glottal stop when you cough or hold your breath. British English speakers (particularly those from big cities) tend to use glottal stops instead of **t** after a vowel. Cockney speakers are well known for pronouncing *butter* as **bʌʔə**.

Finally in this section, there is the matter of the length of each sound, which we mentioned briefly in comparing the words *stray* and *straight*, and *lamb* and *lamp*. The length of a vowel depends on a number of things. Firstly, each vowel has its own natural length; for example, the vowel **i** as in *heed* is longer than the vowel **ɪ** as in *hid*. Next, there is the question of whether the vowel is stressed or not. The first vowel in *personal* is stressed and is longer than the corresponding vowel in *personify*, which is unstressed. Third, vowel length depends on the number of syllables in a word. The vowel in *wit* is longer than the vowel in the first syllable of *witty*, and this in turn is longer than the vowel in the first syllable of *wittily*. Fourth, the length is very much affected by the way the syllable ends. We noted that the vowel in *stray* was longer than that in *straight*. The vowel in *strayed* is intermediate between these two. Long, medium, and short vowel lengths occur in *sigh, side, sight*, and in *Ben, bend, bent*. All these variations in vowel length can be described in terms of rules that a synthesizer can use. There are also similar complex rules governing consonant length that must be included in any high-quality synthesis system.

Variations in vowel and consonant length affect the rhythm of a sentence. Because speech synthesizers seldom pay sufficient attention to the small adjustments in length that are needed, they produce speech that is distinctly inhuman. We have already noted how the failure to produce natural pitch changes makes synthesized speech sound artificial. Mistakes in rhythm are equally responsible for the unnatural quality of synthetic speech.

Notes

1 *formant*: a concentration of energy around certain frequencies. Combinations of formants form distinctive patterns for different vowel sounds.
2 *amplitude*: The maximum extent of a sound wave determining intensity, and related to what the human ear perceives as loudness.
3 *long and short vowels*: Ladefoged uses these terms as labels for the classes we call the free/checked vowels.
4 *flap*: here used as an equivalent to tap (see Section A5).

Questions, suggestions and issues to consider

1 At one time it was thought that it would be extremely difficult for computers to cope with English spelling. Why has this in fact turned out not to be true? Is it an argument against the spelling reform which some people advocate?

D

2   Does Ladefoged's 'rough rule' for **th** actually work? Consider words like 'to think', 'to throw'. Can you improve on it?

3   What is likely to make synthesised speech sound 'inhuman' – and what can be done to avoid this?

4   Why would *leaf* played backwards not sound the same as *feel*? Specify the differences in (1) /l/ and (2) vowel length. (See Sections A5, B2 and B3 respectively.)

5   Is completely realistic synthetic speech a worthwhile goal? Give arguments for and against.

6   What kind of English accent would you yourself prefer to hear a computer using? Would you consider any pronunciation varieties to be completely unsuitable? Are your statements based on linguistic factors, social factors or commercial considerations – or just personal preference? (See Sections A1, C1–C4.)

Peter
Ladefoged

SECRETS OF SPEECH SOUNDS

D6

Steven Pinker (reprinted from *The Language Instinct* (1994), London: Penguin, pp. 166–70)

Steven
Pinker

Stephen Pinker, one of the world's leading experts on the psychology of language, discusses here the mysterious attributes which some speech sounds appear to possess, and in so doing provides his own 'guided tour up the vocal tract'.

The tongue is the most important of the speech organs, making language truly the 'gift of tongues.'[1] Actually, the tongue is three organs in one: the hump or body, the tip, and the root (the muscles that anchor it to the jaw). Pronounce the vowels in *bet* and *butt* repeatedly, *e–uh*, *e–uh*, *e–uh*. You should feel the body of your tongue moving forwards and backwards (if you put a finger between your teeth, you can feel it with the finger). When your tongue is in the front of your mouth, it lengthens the air chamber behind it in your throat and shortens the one in front of it in your mouth, altering one of the resonances: for the *bet* vowel, the mouth amplifies sounds near 600 and 1800 cps;[2] for the *butt* vowel, it amplifies sounds near 600 and 1200. Now pronounce the vowels in *beet* and *bat* alternately. The body of your tongue will jump up and down, at right angles to the *bet–butt* motion; you can even feel your jaw move to help it. This, too, alters the shapes of the throat and mouth chambers, and hence their resonances. The brain interprets the different patterns of amplification and filtering as different vowels.

The link between the postures of the tongue and the vowels it sculpts gives rise to a quaint curiosity of English and many other languages called phonetic symbolism. When the tongue is high and at the front of the mouth, it makes a small resonant cavity there that amplifies some higher frequencies, and the resulting vowels like *ee* and *i* (as in *bit*) remind people of little things. When the tongue is low and

**Steven
Pinker**

to the back, it makes a large resonant cavity that amplifies some lower frequencies, and the resulting vowels like *a* in *father* and *o* in *core* and in *cot* remind people of large things. Thus mice are t*ee*ny and squ*eak*, but elephants are hum*o*ngous and r*oa*r. Audio speakers have small tw*ee*ters for the high sounds and large w*oo*fers for the low ones. English speakers correctly guess that in Chinese *ch'ing* means light and *ch'ung* means heavy. (In controlled studies with large numbers of foreign words, the hit rate is statistically above chance, though just barely.) When I questioned our local computer wizard about what she meant when she said she was going to *frob* my workstation, she gave me this tutorial on hackerese. When you get a brand-new graphic equalizer for your stereo and aimlessly slide the knobs up and down to hear the effects, that is *frobbing*. When you move the knobs by medium-sized amounts to get the sound to your general liking, that is *twiddling*. When you make the final small adjustments to get it perfect, that is *tweaking*. The *ob*, *id*, and *eak* sounds perfectly follow the large-to-small continuum of phonetic symbolism.

And at the risk of sounding like Andy Rooney[3] on *Sixty Minutes*, have you ever wondered why we say *fiddle-faddle* and not *faddle-fiddle*? Why is it *ping-pong* and *pitter-patter* rather than *pong-ping* and *patter-pitter*? Why *dribs and drabs*, rather than vice versa? Why can't a kitchen be *span and spic*? Whence *riff-raff*, *mish-mash*, *flim-flam*, *chit-chat*, *tit for tat*, *knick-knack*, *zig-zag*, *sing-song*, *ding-dong*, *King Kong*, *criss-cross*, *shilly-shally*, *see-saw*, *hee-haw*, *flip-flop*, *hippity-hop*, *tick-tock*, *tic-tac-toe*, *eeny-meeny-miney-moe*, *bric-a-brac*, *clickety-clack*, *hickory-dickory-dock*, *kit and kaboodle*, and *bibbity-bobbity-boo*? The answer is that the vowels for which the tongue is high and in the front always come before the vowels for which the tongue is low and in the back. No one knows why they are aligned in this order, but it seems to be a kind of syllogism from two other oddities. The first is that words that connote me-here-now tend to have higher and fronter vowels than [words] that connote distance from 'me': *me* versus *you*, *here* versus *there*, *this* versus *that*. The second is that words that connote me-here-now tend to come before words that connote literal or metaphorical distance from 'me' (or a prototypical generic speaker): *here and there* (not *there and here*), *this and that*, *now and then*, *father and son*, *man and machine*, *friend or foe*, the *Harvard–Yale* game (among Harvard students), the *Yale–Harvard* game (among Yalies), *Serbo-Croatian* (among Serbs), *Croat-Serbian* (among Croats). The syllogism seems to be: 'me' = high front vowel; me first; therefore, high front vowel first. It is as if the mind just cannot bring itself to flip a coin in ordering words; if meaning does not determine the order, sound is brought to bear, and the rationale is based on how the tongue produces the vowels.

Let's look at the other speech organs. Pay attention to your lips when you alternate between the vowels in *boot* and *book*. For *boot*, you round the lips and protrude them. This adds an air chamber, with its own resonances, to the front of the vocal tract, amplifying and filtering other sets of frequencies and thus defining other vowel contrasts. Because of the acoustic effects of the lips, when we talk to a happy person over the phone, we can literally hear the smile.

Remember your grade-school teacher telling you that the vowel sounds in *bat*, *bet*, *bit*, *bottle*, and *butt* were 'short,' and the vowel sounds in *bait*, *beet*, *bite*, *boat*, and *boot* were 'long'? And you didn't know what she was talking about? Well, forget it; her information is five hundred years out of date. Older stages

Steven
Pinker

of English differentiated words by whether their vowels were pronounced quickly or were drawn out, a bit like the modern distinction between *bad* meaning 'bad' and *baaad* meaning 'good.'[4] But in the fifteenth century English pronunciation underwent a convulsion called the Great Vowel Shift. The vowels that had simply been pronounced longer now became 'tense': by advancing the tongue root (the muscles attaching the tongue to the jaw), the tongue becomes tense and humped rather than lax and flat, and the hump narrows the air chamber in the mouth above it, changing the resonances. Also, some tense vowels in modern English, like in *bite* and *brow*, are 'diphthongs,' two vowels pronounced in quick succession as if they were one: ba-eet, bra-oh.

You can hear the effects of the fifth speech organ by drawing out the vowel in *Sam* and *sat*, postponing the final consonant indefinitely. In most dialects of English, the vowels will be different: the vowel in *Sam* will have a twangy, nasal sound. That is because the soft palate or velum (the fleshy flap at the back of the hard palate) is opened, allowing air to flow out through the nose as well as through the mouth. The nose is another resonant chamber, and when vibrating air flows through it, yet another set of frequencies gets amplified and filtered. English does not differentiate words by whether their vowels are nasal or not, but many languages, like French, Polish, and Portuguese, do. English speakers who open their soft palate even when pronouncing *sat* are said to have a 'nasal' voice. When you have a cold and your nose is blocked, opening the soft palate makes no difference, and your voice is the opposite of nasal.

So far we have just discussed the vowels – sounds where the air has clear passage from the larynx to the world. When some barrier is put in the way, one gets a consonant. Pronounce *ssssss*. The tip of your tongue – the sixth speech organ – is brought up almost against the gum ridge, leaving a small opening. When you force a stream of air through the opening, the air breaks apart turbulently, creating noise. Depending on the size of the opening and the length of the resonant cavities in front of it, the noise will have some of its frequencies louder than others, and the peak and range of frequencies define the sound we hear as *s*. This noise-making comes from the friction of moving air, so this kind of sound is called a fricative. When rushing air is squeezed between the tongue and palate, we get *sh*; between the tongue and teeth, *th*; and between the lower lip and teeth, *f*. The body of the tongue, or the vocal folds of the larynx, can also be positioned to create turbulence, defining the various 'ch' sounds in languages like German, Hebrew, and Arabic (*Bach, Chanukah*,[5] and so on).

Now pronounce a *t*. The tip of the tongue gets in the way of the airstream, but this time it does not merely impede the flow; it stops it entirely. When the pressure builds up, you release the tip of the tongue, allowing the air to pop out (flutists use this motion to demarcate musical notes). Other 'stop' consonants can be formed by the lips (*p*), by the body of the tongue pressed against the palate (*k*), and by the larynx (in the 'glottal' consonants in *uh-oh*). What a listener hears when you produce a stop consonant is the following. First, nothing, as the air is dammed up behind the stoppage: stop consonants are the sounds of silence. Then, a brief burst of noise as the air is released; its frequency depends on the size of the opening and the resonant cavities in front of it. Finally, a smoothly changing resonance, as voicing fades in while the tongue is gliding into the position of whatever vowel comes next. As we shall see, this hop-skip-and-jump makes life miserable for speech engineers.

Finally, pronounce *m*. Your lips are sealed, just like for *p*. But this time the air does not back up silently; you can say *mmmmm* until you are out of breath. That is because you have also opened your soft palate, allowing all of the air to escape through your nose. The voicing sound is now amplified at the resonant frequencies of the nose and of the part of the mouth behind the blockage. Releasing the lips causes a sliding resonance similar in shape to what we heard for the release in *p*, except without the silence, noise burst, and fade-in. The sound *n* works similarly to *m*, except that the blockage is created by the tip of the tongue, the same organ used for *d* and *s*. So does the *ng* in *sing*, except that the body of the tongue does the job.

Why do we say *razzle-dazzle* instead of *dazzle-razzle*? Why *super-duper*, *helter-skelter*, *harum-scarum*, *hocus-pocus*, *willy-nilly*, *hully-gully*, *roly-poly*, *holy moly*, *herky-jerky*, *walkie-talkie*, *namby-pamby*, *mumbo-jumbo*, *loosey-goosey*, *wing-ding*, *wham-bam*, *hobnob*, *razzamatazz*, and *rub-a-dub-dub*? I thought you'd never ask. Consonants differ in 'obstruency' – the degree to which they impede the flow of air, ranging from merely making it resonate, to forcing it noisily past an obstruction, to stopping it up altogether. The word beginning with the less obstruent consonant always comes before the word beginning with the more obstruent consonant. Why ask why?

Notes

1   *the gift of tongues*: the ability to speak in many languages. This is a biblical reference to the miracle described in Acts ii 4.

2   *cps* ('cycles per second'): a measurement of frequency. The more normal term nowadays is Hertz (abbr. Hz).

3   *Andy Rooney (1919–)*: well-known American news correspondent on CBS who since the late 1970s has appeared on the news programme *60 Minutes*.

4   *baaad*: a way of expressing approval. Equivalent in American English to British 'wicked'.

5   *Chanukah* /xænəkə/: Jewish feast of lights.

Questions, suggestions and issues to consider

1   Think of more examples of close vowel vs. open vowel alternations. Make a list – get your class colleagues to join you in the quest.

2   If you speak a language other than English, or have a knowledge of another language, can you find any words or phrases to support Pinker's assertions on the close vs. open vowel sounds? Now do the same for the consonant examples (e.g. fricative – plosive).

3   Can you think of any other examples of 'phonetic symbolism'?

4   Dogs in English-speaking countries go *bow-wow*, but in France *ouah-ouah*. Can you find out from friends or relatives who speak other languages what imitative sequence they use, and whether any of these fit the patterns described by Pinker? (Bow-wow doesn't!) Do the same for imitative expressions for the noises made by: cats, chickens, cows, bells, and any other such examples you can think of.

USING PHONETICS IN CRIMINAL INVESTIGATIONS

Maurice Varney (originally entitled 'Forensic linguistics' (1997). Reprinted from *English Today* 52, 13.4: 42–4, 46–7)

In recent years, linguists (and in particular phoneticians) have been greatly in demand to assist in crime detection. Maurice Varney discusses the reasons for the increasing importance of forensic linguistics (as this branch of the science is called) and points out a few of the difficulties sometimes encountered. In the original article, Varney discussed three branches, namely handwriting; phonetics and phonology; discourse analysis, but in this extract we have selected only the second of these.

Forensic phonetics: a new, varied and very practical application of linguistic science

The term *forensic linguistics*, by analogy with forensic science and forensic medicine, where scientists and pathologists use their skills in connection with problems involved in both criminal and civil law cases, simply means that linguists act as expert witnesses in legal cases where some aspect of written and/or spoken language seems to be significant. Forensic linguistics, though its practitioners are still a small and select group of experts, now stands equally as an accepted branch of linguistics, alongside psycholinguistics, sociolinguistics, etc., and also alongside its older partners forensic medicine, forensic dentistry, forensic chemistry, etc. The speed at which forensic linguistics has been accepted by lawyers, judges and juries is somewhat surprising given that at least one of its branches, discourse analysis, is often rather subjective. Perhaps it is because the application of forensic linguistic techniques has led to swift and apparently reliable solutions to legal questions that the subject has acquired a respectable legitimacy which other branches of linguistics took decades to achieve.

There are three branches: handwriting; phonetics and phonology; and discourse analysis.

[. . .]

Phonetics and phonology

The expert in pronunciation and other features of speech appeared in literature and folklore, long before the notion of forensic phonetics and phonology developed. George Bernard Shaw, in 1912, in his play *Pygmalion* (later even more famous as the musical *My Fair Lady*) satirises Professor Henry Higgins, an expert teacher and student of speech. Higgins was almost certainly based on the phonetician Daniel Jones, who established Received Pronunciation as the English pronunciation standard for use by phoneticians and phonologists.

Jones and his immediate followers were primarily concerned with articulatory phonetics, describing and cataloguing how human speech is produced. Today, the main interest of most career phoneticians is acoustic phonetics, studying and interpreting the physics features of the sounds that human beings emit. Spectrographs and other equipment are used to produce visual analysis of speech to a depth of great sensitivity.

Maurice Varney

The notion of the 'voiceprint' has been put forward, analogous to that of 'fingerprints'. There is considerable evidence to suggest that no two people, living or dead, will ever have the same acoustic features of voice and that, no matter how well a person disguises the voice superficially, sensitive equipment will be able to show the base features of the original voice, and phoneticians will be able to interpret these.

Voiceprint analysis is used in a great range of legal cases, including blackmail, kidnapping, nuisance calls, confessions, telephone bomb threats, conspiracy, and hoaxes. Of course, the spoken message needs to be recorded before it can be examined and analysed, but this is often easy to do. Voiceprint comparison can only be done if there is a bank of recorded voices similar to fingerprint records. Such banks are being built up from cases where the criminals are apprehended and, as many perpetrators of crimes involving spoken messages reoffend, acoustic features of voices are recognised in the same way as fingerprints. An electronic programme has now been developed called Forensic Speaker Identification (SID) which conducts a 'voice line-up' identity parade and acoustically compares the voice patterns of suspects with that of the recorded message.

The Yorkshire Ripper case in northern England in the 1970s and 1980s involved phonetic and phonological analysis in a dramatic way. After a series of murders of women throughout Yorkshire, letters were sent to the detective in charge of the case, mocking him and his investigation and purporting to be from the Ripper himself. The letters were followed by a tape-recording, and it was confirmed that the hand-writing of the letters and that on the parcel containing the tape were the same.

The detective in charge was convinced that the tape was genuine, and he called in specialists from the University of Leeds, the dialectologist Stanley Ellis and the phonetician J. Windsor Lewis. They successfully and accurately identified the voice and speech patterns as coming from County Durham, farther north than Yorkshire. A village was pinpointed and the police investigation resources were turned to this area, every man who lived there being interviewed.

Ellis and Windsor Lewis were right in identifying the geographical features of the voice on the tape, but the tape was a hoax. The Ripper killed again and, when he was eventually caught, he was found to come from South Yorkshire. The sender of the hoax letters and tape was never found. The detectives and forensic linguists in this case were vilified and accused of making mistakes which cost more lives and millions of pounds, but the criticism is unjust. In the circumstances of the time, the linguistic evidence appeared genuine and the experts followed the only road open to them.

Apart from recognition of regional features and voiceprint acoustic features, forensic phoneticians are often called on to make educated guesses about the back-ground, age, education, etc., of the people whose voices they have on tape. This is a tricky process involving much subjectivity, but the track record has been good, and experience and case studies enable practitioners to deduce much from an anonymous voice. Linguistic background, possible profession, and even age can be assessed and often checked by parallel analysis of the vocabulary and sentence structure used.

All phonological features are considered by the forensic phonetician: pronuncia-tion, intonation, stress, pace, etc. In one case, a New Yorker living in California was arrested and indicted for making threatening calls to Pan American Airlines. His defence attorneys called in a voiceprint expert and the dialect expert William Labov, and together they proved the intonation of the anonymous caller was Bostonian and not New York. The suspect was acquitted (Labov 1988: 170–81).

Questions, suggestions and issues to consider

1 Find a copy of *Pygmalion* and read through those scenes where the legendary phonetic powers of Professor Higgins are portrayed. Are his talents in any way believable?

2 Do you yourself know from radio, television or newspaper reports of recent cases where forensic linguistics has had a role to play in solving a crime? Discuss these in class.

3 Some linguists disapprove of forensic phonetics on principle, believing that it is wrong for practitioners of an academic discipline to meddle with criminals and the law. Would you agree with that point of view?

4 Do you think it is realistic to expect linguists to deduce not only regional characteristics of speech but also features such as 'background, age and education'? What do you think might be the problems involved?

5 Make some recordings (either live or from the radio or TV) and play them to a group of classmates and/or friends. Ask them to judge such matters as regional accent, age, education, profession, etc. See if a knowledge of phonetics (no matter how slight) aids people in making their 'educated guesses'.

THE RISE OF 'UPSPEAK'

Barbara Bradford (originally entitled 'Upspeak in British English' (1997). Reprinted from *English Today* 51, 13.3: 33–6)

In this extract, Barbara Bradford discusses the nature and possible origins of an intonation pattern which appears to be increasingly common in the speech of many native English speakers, especially those of the younger generation. What she terms 'upspeak' has attracted much comment in recent years – not all of it favourable.

Upspeak in British English
An examination of a novel UK rising tone, with reference to its use in some other Anglophone countries

This article reports on a small-scale study of the use of a particular intonational feature, sometimes referred to as 'upspeak', by speakers of British English. The term *upspeak* is used here to refer to the use of a rising tone in the final tone

Barbara
Bradford

unit of a declarative clause where in RP a falling tone would be used. Its use seems to extend across geographical areas, social classes, the gender boundary and, to some extent, chronological boundaries, although it occurs most commonly in the conversations of those in their upper teens, twenties and thirties.

The article is based on observations of the occurrence of upspeak among British speakers in the mid-1990s and refers to speech data of a group of female RP speakers in their late teens and early twenties. The article suggests that upspeak has two main communicative functions and focuses on the interpersonal and situational factors which predispose speakers to use it.

Similar phenomena to upspeak have been documented in other areas of the English-speaking world in the last 35 years: New Zealand, Australia, Canada and the USA: see Britain (1992) on the occurrence of High Rising Terminal contours in New Zealand English, and references therein to research in other geographical areas. The present study provides independent confirmation of the existence and diffusion of this intonational feature in British English.

. . . The use of a final rising tone where a falling tone would be expected in RP is an established and well documented prosodic[1] feature not only of upspeak but also of non-standard accents in some regions of Britain, e.g. in Wales and Northern Ireland and in the English cities of Bristol, Liverpool, and Newcastle, and the county of Norfolk. It is also characteristic of regional accents in other traditional English-speaking countries, as well as Caribbean, Indian and some other varieties of English. (See Cruttenden, 1986, p. 137 ff.) What is important here is that the distribution of the rises is more *systematic* in regional and varietal accents of English than it is in upspeak. The upspeak rule is applied *non-systematically*, i.e. upspeakers do not convert *all* RP falling tones to rising tones, even where the structural conditions for the operation of the rule are fulfilled.

An explanation frequently offered for any change in language use is that young people are influenced in their way of speaking, particularly in interaction with their peer group, by the accents of role-model characters in films, advertisements and television programmes made in Australia, USA and dialectal areas of the UK. In the case of the appearance of upspeak, the Australian soap operas 'Home and Away' and 'Neighbours' and the Merseyside soap 'Brookside' are suggested as the initiators, since both Australian and Liverpool accents are perceived as demonstrating frequent rising tones. Such influences cannot be totally ruled out as it is likely that many of those in the age group now using upspeak will have watched these soaps. It is suggested here, however, that if it is the case that Australian soap operas have played a part in the initiation of upspeak in British English, it is because British youngsters have viewed characters in the programmes using the equivalent of upspeak in Australian English. What could have been spread in this way would, therefore, not be an aspect of General Australian pronunciation as such, but an international feature of the intonation of young people.

However, there are at least two counterarguments to this TV influence theory. Firstly, the fact that from the full set of phonetic features which make up any regional accent *only* the steep final rises in pitch have been adopted by the upspeakers is problematical. The main difference between the Australian accent and RP is the vowel sounds and so one might have expected to detect evidence

Barbara Bradford

of, at least, some vocalic adaptations. Secondly, I have personal experience of a 23 year old who is not a current viewer of any of the TV programmes which have been blamed for the use of upspeak but who started to use it in 1996 after returning from four months living and working abroad with a group of young British people. The key point here, though, is that she watched both of the Australian soaps avidly during her teenage years but neither she nor her peers used upspeak at that time. None of this is conclusive evidence to disprove the Australian soap influence theory, but it does suggest that an investigation of interpersonal and social factors may yield more productive findings.

Discourse intonation

A description of intonation which in sociolinguistic terms identifies and character-izes the meaning contrasts conveyed by intonation features was developed in the 1970s from original work being done in discourse analysis (Coulthard, 1977). Previous approaches had described intonation in terms of a range of attitudinal significances (O'Connor & Arnold, 1973) or in terms of grammar (Halliday, 1967). The theory of discourse intonation (Brazil, Coulthard & Johns, 1980; Brazil, 1985) describes the forms and functions of English intonation in terms of the discourse context and with reference to the social setting. It describes and explains the communicative value of intonation by focusing on the decisions a speaker makes at each point in the developing conversation. These are subconscious decisions about prominent syllables, tone and pitch levels.

According to this model, tones (i.e., major pitch movements) can, in simple terms, be divided into two categories: those which finally fall (fall and rise-fall), classified as *proclaiming*, and those which finally rise (rise and fall-rise), classified as *referring*. The two types of tone can be seen to relate to a contrast in meaning. In general terms, the rising tone can be said to be used by a speaker for that part of an utterance which s/he perceives or presents as existing common ground between him/herself and the hearer(s) at that point in the conversation, whereas the falling tone is used for that part of an utterance which the speaker perceives or presents as new to the hearer(s). The speaker's perspective on an idea, whether it is an idea already in play or whether it is a new contribution to the developing conversation will determine tone choice. This short sentence: 'I'm going to the theatre on Saturday', illustrates the meaning contrast of the finally falling and finally rising tones:

(i) // ↘ I'm going to the THEatre//↗ on SATurday//

or

(ii) //↗ I'm going to the THEatre// ↘ on SATurday //

(after Bradford, 1988)

In (i) the fall-rise tone comes in the tone unit containing *Saturday* which signifies that Saturday is discourse-old at this point in the conversation, so this sentence would be a suitable response to 'Would you like to go out to dinner on Saturday?' The falling tone is used for the part of the utterance which contains 'new' information for the hearer, i.e. *going to the theatre*. In (ii) the fall-rise tone comes in the tone unit

Barbara
Bradford

containing *going to the theatre* which signifies that this is information already activated at that point in the conversation so this sentence would be a suitable response to 'Would you like to go to the theatre on Friday?' The falling tone is used for the part of the utterance which contains the 'new' information for the hearer, i.e. *on Saturday*.

From this we can see that *tone* functions in discourse as a means by which participants indicate how they perceive the status of the information they are conveying in relation to the state of convergence between themselves. The finally-rising tone functions to increase the area of convergence and to lessen the conversational distance between them.

Affective and referential functions of upspeak

Upspeak is an intonational device used by speakers for two main communicative purposes.

First, it has an affective[2] dimension, acting as a bonding technique to promote a sense of solidarity and empathy between speakers and hearers. (See also Britain, 1992, and references therein.) An upspeaker seeks to reduce the social distance between him/herself and the hearer(s) by exploiting the rising tone, conventionally reserved to convey the idea of common ground and shared experience, and uses it as an intonational strategy to present hearer-new information and simultaneously to project or expand the state of convergence between them. This exploitation of the intonation system has the psycho-social effect of making the speaker sound less assertive or authoritative.

Second, upspeak has an important referential component, acting as a means of signalling salient chunks of information, and thus encouraging the hearer's continued involvement in the discourse. By presenting 'new' information as if it were part of 'common ground', a speaker indicates that the content of that part of the discourse is perceived to be of intrinsic or assumed mutual interest.

In this way, the speaker is able to provide cognitive stepping stones in the unfolding discourse to enable the hearer(s) to negotiate the stream of speech. This 'directing to a focus of interest' function may explain why upspeak occurs so frequently in narrative.

As a device for ensuring the hearer(s)' continued involvement and interest in the narrative, the use of upspeak may be similar in effect to the use of fillers such as 'Right?' or 'You know what I mean?', which are used by speakers to check that their listeners are keeping abreast of the information flow or are sympathetic to what is being said. They are in use in many varieties of English; for example, 'yeah?' and 'OK?' are used in the USA and extensively elsewhere, Canadian English speakers often add an 'eh?', and there is a tendency in South African English to use 'ya?'. Such fillers are pronounced with a steeply rising pitch movement and are located at the end of a falling-tone declarative, the declarative–filler combination producing a fall-rise contour which terminates with a steep and high rise. This leads us to conclude that the phonological form of upspeak, described earlier as a fall-rise with a steep and usually high terminating rise, is the conflation of a standard falling tone with the steep rise of a filler of the 'Right?' kind. In this way, the communicative force of the interrogative filler is intonationally incorporated into the declarative, making the filler itself redundant and reducing syntactic complexity.

Social factors

Barbara
Bradford

Although upspeak in British English appears to cut across gender, the available evidence indicates that it is most prevalent among and first displayed in the speech of young females. It permeates the speech of young males only after becoming well established among females. Assuming that upspeak can in part be explained as an emotive bonding technique, this initial resistance on the part of males might be construed as an exponent of the assertive masculine psyche with its inclination to retain authority and control – in this instance by not exploiting upspeak to reduce speaker–hearer distance. In contrast, the females' inclination to use it can be seen as a linguistic reflex of the female wish to appear approachable. It follows, then, that if a female is in a position of higher status than her interlocutor(s), or in a dominant role, but wishes her feminine identity to be taken into account, she would be inclined to use an intonational device which increased the area of convergence between them. One example of this affective function is the nurturing, non-authoritative speech of mothers to very young children, where the use of rising intonation patterns is well documented (Garnica, 1977; Ogle & Maidment, 1993). Upspeak does become a feature of the speech of some males once it is well integrated among the females in a community. Males may consciously or subconsciously choose to use this intonational device in situations where they wish to appear non-assertive and when they wish their contributions to be perceived as conciliatory rather than aggressive.

It appears that upspeakers are able to code-switch,[5] using upspeak in one context but not in another, according to situational factors. Upspeak is initially a peer group activity, creating a speech community among the young. Its use is reinforced by the acceptance it brings, signalling in-group solidarity, a wish both to include and to be included. Speakers switch between their normal intonation and upspeak, according to their perception of the setting, using upspeak in situations where they sense or desire social cohesion and hearer empathy.

The fact that upspeak has an irritating impact on many people in Britain, particularly those of the older generation, may be caused, at least in part, by a misjudgement of the social situation on the part of the upspeaker and a misconstrual of the upspeaker motivations on the part of the hearer(s). If a psychological signal for social bonding is given by the speaker where a distance is required by the hearer, it can be perceived as out of place and even disrespectful. The negative reaction on the part of the hearer could also relate to confusion caused by the incompatibility of a declarative statement containing an interrogative intonational component. The fact that a young speaker may use upspeak for a length of time when living or operating in one social context and then discontinue when in another was stated earlier as a personal observation. This suggests that upspeak is transient in nature, a phase through which some young people pass.

However, just as upspeak crosses the gender boundary once it has become established in a community, it seems also to cross chronological boundaries. In the USA and the Antipodes where it is well established it has spread through the age groups and is no longer used exclusively by the young. The factors governing its use can be seen not to be exclusively age-related, then, but to be motivated by the social and interpersonal conditions of the speech situation.

Barbara
Bradford

Conclusion

Upspeak has been heralded by the British media as a recent aspect of language change possibly triggered by the influence of Australian soap operas on teenage viewers. It has been suggested here that it has been in existence in many parts of the English-speaking world, including the United Kingdom, for at least 30 years. Whether the geographically disparate occurrences of upspeak are totally independent developments or the result of contact-induced spread is an open but interesting question. Either way, the communicative functions of upspeak can be explained by reference to interpersonal factors and the convergence or divergence of conversational distance, and its expansion seems to have been conditioned in all cases by sociolinguistic determinants.

Notes

1   *prosodic*: another term for supra-segmental, referring to phonetic features such as intonation, stress and rhythm.
2   *affective*: relating to moods, feelings and attitudes.
3   *code-switch*: the process of changing from one language or language variety to another.

Questions, suggestions and issues to consider

1   Do you think you use upspeak yourself? Do your friends? Watch an American, an Australian and an English soap and sample five minutes of dialogue from each. Is there any difference in the frequency of occurrence of upspeak?
2   Do you think that your pronunciation is more like that of your parents, or more like the speech of friends of your generation? Provide some examples to illustrate your answer.
3   Listen to the samples of speech varieties on your CD. Can you hear any examples of upspeak on any of them? Do this as a class exercise and compare notes.
4   Another explanation suggested for language change is the influence of films, advertisements and television programmes. What is your opinion on this? Can you think of any linguistic features you may have copied from any of these sources? If you have taken over any features from television, is there any specific variety of English which you are more likely to copy than another?
5   Upspeak is often said to be associated with narrative and, as Bradford points out, with younger-generation female speech. Let's see if these claims are true. Using a small selection of informants (your classmates or friends), ask them to make a 3–5 minute audio recording describing an interesting experience which they have had in the last six months. Listen to the recording and note instances of upspeak. Is there any difference between men and women informants? Are the upspeakers characterised by any other features (regional origins, social background, etc.)? If you have the opportunity, record some members of the older generation in the same way and see if any instances of upspeak occur with these informants.

D

HOW CHILDREN LEARN THE MEANING OF INTONATION

D9

David
Crystal

David Crystal (reprinted from *Listen to Your Child* (1986), Harmondsworth: Penguin, pp. 193–7)

In this extract David Crystal explains how experimentation has shown that children acquire their knowledge of intonation as part of a gradual process. It isn't as straightforward as adults might think.

Intonation – the melody of language – is one of the first features to be heard in the emerging speech of a child towards the end of the first year. But when children start using intonation to express their meaning, they don't learn all the possible tones of voice immediately. In fact, 10 years later they're still trying to sort out all the different nuances of meaning conveyed by the adult voice.

One of the first studies to show this was published by Alan Cruttenden in 1974. He started with the well-known melodic differences which can be heard whenever radio or TV announcers read the results of a football match. The way British announcers do it, it's quite possible to predict the result before the second score is read out – whether it will be a draw, a home win or an away win.

In each case, the first team, and its score, is read out with a melody which rises to quite a high level. You can't predict anything at the point when the announcer says

Liverpool 3

But as soon as the name of the second team is read out, you know straight away what the result is, even though you haven't heard the score yet.

For a draw, the pitch of the voice usually falls from quite high up to quite low down in the voice range. The emphasis is on the team's name, and the actual score tags on at the end, also very low down in pitch, and not strongly stressed at all. It's as if the voice is saying: 'The second score doesn't do anything special – it's the same as the first – so I'm not going to draw special attention to it.' If we drew this on a kind of musical stave, it would look like this. (Each black dot marks a syllable, and the lines mark noticeable glides in pitch.)

```
High up    Liverpool   3    Everton   3
Low down    • • •      ✓      \  •     •
```

– A home win has a very different pattern. Here the second part of the result is usually uttered in a much lower tone, with the actual score being said more loudly. It looks like this:

```
Liverpool   3    Everton   2
 • • •      ✓     • • •      ↷
```

This time the voice is saying: 'There is a different score coming up, so I'll draw attention to it – but, sadly, it isn't as big as the first.'

David
Crystal

An away win presents yet another pattern. Here the second part of the result is usually said in a much higher tone than the first, with the score being quite strongly emphasized. It looks like this:

Liverpool   3   Everton   4

The voice is now saying: 'There's a new score coming, everyone, and wow, it's bigger than the first one.'

Cruttenden drew up a list of possible games, such as Forfar vs Stranraer. He chose Scottish teams because he was studying children from the Manchester area and he didn't want to use well-known English teams in case this influenced the children's judgements. Some children can't bear the thought of their favourite team losing, and that would mess up any experiment.

He recorded the results using a typical announcer intonation, but left the second score out – for instance,

Forfar   3   Stranraer

It must have sounded as if the announcer had been murdered at the crucial moment!

He then played the recording to a group of adults, all mother-tongue speakers of English, and asked them to guess the overall result – draw, home or away. They all predicted the result correctly.

Now the stage was set for the children. Cruttenden played the tape to 28 boys in the junior classes of a primary school. The children were aged between 7 and 11. He gave them a few practice examples first, to show them what they had to do, What were *their* guesses like?

Five of the children didn't seem to grasp the point of the experiment. In every case they gave the same result – all home wins or all away wins! Fortunately, the remainder were more cooperative!

There were three 7-year-olds in the group: they scored an average of 3 correct out of 7 results. There were twelve 8-year-olds: their score was an average of 3.2 correct. The ten 9-year-olds scored 4.1; and the two 10-year-olds scored 4.5. There was thus a clear development in the ability to interpret the intonation patterns.

But something else is more significant. Even at age 10, the children hadn't reached the level of competence shown by the adults. Only one child in the whole group got all seven results correct (he was 8;11). Only eight children scored over 4. Most of them did quite well in identifying draws (15 made no errors here), but the other patterns were quite erratic.

Cruttenden's children were all boys. I tried out the same experiment inform-ally on some girls once and the results were the same. No sexism here.

Nor does interest in football have anything to do with it. Cruttenden actually rated the children for their interest in football. Some were keen. Others weren't. There was a weak correlation: the more you're interested in football (and thus, presumably, listen to the scores on radio or TV), the better you'll do. But this

David
Crystal

doesn't explain all the results. In fact, the child who did best was rated as having no interest in football at all!

Now, if this experiment told us only about how children come to understand football results, it wouldn't be very interesting. But the patterns of intonation which the announcer uses in giving the results are found in everyday conversation as well. For instance, if someone says:

Has John bought a blue car or a red car?

the intonation bounces along just as it does in a score-draw result:

Has John bought a blue car or a red car?

The voice is saying: 'The second mention of the word *car* doesn't add any new information – it's the same as the first – so I'm not going to draw special attention to it. Pay attention to the colours instead.'

It very much looks, then, as if children are still sorting out the meanings of intonation patterns as late as 9 or 10 years of age, or even older. Other tests of intonation produce similar results. For instance, do you think that 10-year-olds would be able to tell the difference between the following pairs of sentences?

She dressed, and fed the baby (i.e. the mother got dressed, and then she fed the baby).
She dressed and fed the baby (i.e. the baby was dressed and fed).

In writing, you can make the difference by using a comma. In speech, the two sentences sound quite different. Say them aloud (unless you're reading this in a train, and can't!). In the first you'll pause at the comma and your voice will go up. In the second, you'll read straight through and your voice will go down.

In a 1985 study Cruttenden gave this pair of sentences to 20 adults and 20 children, showing them three pictures. In the first picture, a mother is putting her dress on, with a feeding bottle ready. In the second picture, she's dressing the baby, with the feeding bottle in the background. In the third picture (which was included as a distraction), she's feeding herself. Everyone had to point to one of the pictures when they heard each sentence.

Once again, the results were clear. On the second sentence, for instance, 19 out of 20 adults made the correct decision, whereas only 9 out of 20 children did. Several other sentences, showing other differences in intonation, were also tested, and the results were on similar lines. However, the adults themselves didn't always achieve good scores, suggesting that the task was quite a difficult one to grasp.

Here's an easy intonation contrast which you can try out for yourself. Find some 8-year-olds and say you're going to ask them a simple question after they hear some sentences. Give them an irrelevant question first, so that they get the idea (such as *Michael gave a pencil to Fred. Who gave the pencil to Fred?*). Then give them the first relevant sentence (saying it with a strong emphasis on the words in italics):

John gave a book to *Jim,* and he gave one to *Mary.*

**David
Crystal**

You then ask:

> Who gave the book to Mary?

And the children will reply 'John' – along with various expressions of contempt, that you should be asking such ridiculously simple questions.

Next, say the same sentence, but with a different emphasis (making sure the *he* is particularly well stressed):

> *John* gave a book to *Jim,* and *he* gave one to *Mary.*

Again you ask:

> Who gave the book to Mary?

This time, the answer should be 'Jim'. But you'll find that most 8-year-olds will still say 'John'. And even 9-year-olds can be caught out. They assume that the first person in the sentence is the one who does the action. They haven't learned to appreciate that a strong emphasis on some other word can change the meaning of a sentence quite dramatically.

There's no doubt that as children approach secondary school, they still have a lot to learn about the meanings conveyed by the inflection of the adult voice. I wonder if they pick up all the nuances in the speech of their teachers, for instance? If not, they could always be set some extra weekend homework: obligatory listening to the football results!

Questions, suggestions and issues to consider

1   Try repeating Cruttenden's football experiment with a group of adults and a group of children. Do your results correspond to his?

2   Listen to football results on an English-speaking radio programme or TV channel, and see if you can predict the outcomes in advance.

3   Now ask a non-native English speaker to do the same. Ask if similar patterning holds true for other languages.

4   Repeat Crystal's *John-Jim-Mary* experiment. Again try it out on adult non-native speakers of English.

GLOSSARY

There is a certain amount of flexibility in phonetic terminology. The meanings given here are naturally those we have used in this book but in a few cases we have added terms commonly employed by other writers. No attempt has been made to provide precise, elegant, formal definitions but rather to use language which is reasonably easy to understand. Words in bold are defined elsewhere in the glossary.

Many works on phonetics have a glossary similar to this. Two which provide much more coverage and detail are Trask's (1996) *Dictionary of Phonetics and Phonology* and Roach's (2002) *Little Encyclopaedia of Phonetics*.

accent	A pronunciation **variety** characteristic of the speech of a group of people. Cf. **dialect**.
acoustics	The scientific study of sound.
acrolectal	Associated with speakers of the most privileged socio-economic classes. Derived from the noun *acrolect*, meaning a **dialect** of this type.
active articulator	The **articulator** which moves in an **articulation**, e.g. the tip of the tongue for /t/.
advanced	Articulated more to the front. **Diacritic** [₊], e.g. /k/ in *keen* [ki̟ːn]. Opposed to **retracted**.
affricate	A **manner of articulation** involving a complete closure that is released slowly, thus producing **homorganic friction**, e.g. /tʃ dʒ/.
airstream	A flow of air typically outward from the lungs. An airstream of some sort (usually **pulmonic egressive**) is necessary to produce any speech sound.
allophone	A **realisation** of a **phoneme**.
alveolar	A **place of articulation** involving the tip/blade of the tongue (**active articulator**) and the alveolar ridge (**passive articulator**), e.g. English /t n s/.
antepenultimate	One before the last but one. Often used with reference to **stress**.
approach stage	The initial stage in the **articulation** of a **stop** when the **articulators** move towards each other.
approximant	A **manner of articulation** produced with the **articulators** sufficiently apart for there to be no audible **friction**, e.g. English /r j/. Approximants can be of two types, either central approximants (e.g. English /w r j/) or **lateral** (e.g. English /l/).

articulation	A movement made by the **organs of speech** in order to produce a speech sound. Adj.: *articulatory*.
articulator	Any organ or part of an organ in the vocal tract which is involved in the production of a speech sound.
articulatory system	Relating to the **articulators** found in the **supra-glottal** vocal tract (i.e. in the throat, mouth and nose).
aspiration	A delay in **voicing** after the **release** of a **voiceless stop**, often described as a brief 'puff of air' or [h]-like sound, e.g. *pie* [pʰaɪ].
assimilation	The replacement of one **phoneme** by another under the influence of a third as a result of **phonetic conditioning**, e.g. if *green bag* is said as /ˈɡriːm bæɡ/, then /n/ is said to assimilate to /m/ under the influence of the following /b/. Assimilation may be of different types: place, manner and energy.
auditory	Referring to any aspect of hearing.
back vowel	A **vowel** for which the back of the tongue is the highest part, e.g. /uː/.
backing diphthong	A **diphthong** involving tongue raising and backing to [ʊ] or /uː/.
basilectal	Associated with speakers of the least privileged socio-economic classes. Derived from the noun basilect, meaning a **dialect** of this type.
bilabial	A **place of articulation** involving both lips, e.g. /p b m/.
breathy voice	A **glottal setting** where the **vocal folds** vibrate as for **voice** but the arytenoids are apart so that air can escape through the gap at the rear of the **glottis**, e.g. Hindi [bʱ].
cardinal vowels	A set of reference **vowels**, independent of any language, widely used in linguistic description. The basic set are termed primary cardinal vowels. The secondary cardinal vowels have reverse lip shapes.
central	Referring to **vowels** pronounced with the centre of the tongue as the highest part, e.g. [ə]. Opposed to **peripheral**.
centring diphthong	A **diphthong** involving tongue movement to [ə].
checked vowels	A phonological class of **vowels** found in English, German and other related languages which in the same phonetic contexts are shorter than **free vowels**. (Also termed *short vowels*.)
citation form	The form of a word when pronounced in isolation.
clear [l]	A slightly **palatalised** [l], e.g. /l/ in *leaf*, /l/ in German *Wahl* 'choice'.
close (adj.)	A sound, often a vowel, articulated with the tongue raised close to the roof of the mouth.
closed syllable	A **syllable** ending in a **consonant**, e.g. *hot*.
closing diphthong	A **diphthong** involving the tongue rising closer to the roof of the mouth.

cluster	A sequence, within the same **syllable**, of a number of **consonants**, e.g. /gr/ and /spt/ in *grasped*.
coda	The final, consonantal element of the **syllable**. See also **rhyme**.
commencement	The first **stressed syllable** of the **head**. It is the second most prominent **syllable** in the **intonation group**.
complementary distribution	Where the **allophones** of a **phoneme** are predictable from phonetic context. Cf. **free variation**.
consonant	Sounds occurring at the margins of **syllables**.
content words	Words such as nouns, main verbs, adjectives, adverbs, which have a high information content. Also called *lexical words*. Cf. **function words**.
contracted form	A form derived from the combination of two **function words**, e.g. *will not → won't.* (Also termed *contraction*.)
contrastive analysis	The linguistic study of two languages side by side to establish points of difference and similarity.
creak	A **glottal setting** involving low **frequency** vibration of the front **vocal folds**. In language, generally found as part of **creaky voice** (see below).
creaky voice	A **glottal setting** where the front **vocal folds** vibrate slowly (as for **creak**) whilst the back vocal folds vibrate rapidly (as for **voice**).
dark [ɫ]	A **velarised** [l], e.g. English *fill*. Symbolised as [ɫ].
dental	A **place of articulation** involving the tip of the tongue and the front teeth, e.g. /θ ð/ in *thanks, those*, Spanish /t d n/ [t̪ d̪ n̪] in *tonto* 'fool', *donde* 'where'.
devoicing	When in a particular context a sound which is normally **voiced** is realised as partially or completely **voiceless**, e.g. /b/ and /d/ in *bad cough*.
diacritics	Marks added to phonetic symbols to supply extra information, e.g. [˜] added to a **vowel** [ε] shows it to be **nasalised** [ɛ̃].
dialect	A language **variety** of a group of people defined geographically and/or socially. Note that dialect applies to grammar and vocabulary only. Cf. **accent**.
diphthong	A **vowel** where there is an obvious change in tongue and/or lip shape. (Also termed *vowel glide*.)
discourse	Referring to the analysis of language in units larger than a single sentence, e.g. paragraphs, conversations.
distributional variation	Differences in language usage between **accents** dependent on the occurrence or non-occurrence of a **phoneme** in certain contexts. Such differences operate without exception, e.g. /r/ in **rhotic** vs. **non-rhotic** accents.
double articulation	A speech sound involving two **places of articulation**, e.g. English /w/.
duration	The amount of time taken up by a speech sound.
egressive	Outgoing. Opposed to **ingressive**.

elision	A process by which a **phoneme** is deleted, e.g. /t/ in English *last week* ['lɑːs 'wiːk].
energy of articulation	Another term to cover the **fortis/lenis** contrast.
epenthesis	Insertion of a **segment** into a word, e.g. Irish *film* [fɪləm]. Adj. *epenthetic*.
error analysis	A technique for predicting a language learner's potential errors by systematic analysis of errors already made.
Estuary English	A loose term for modern **varieties** of educated English, which while removed from **basilectal** London speech, nevertheless show many traces of London influence.
fortis	A phonological class of **voiceless obstruent consonants** with energetic **articulation**, e.g. English /k f s/. Opposed to **lenis**.
free variation	When the occurrence of a particular **allophone** cannot be predicted from phonetic context. Cf. **complementary distribution**.
free vowels	A **phonological** class of **vowels** found in English, German and related languages which includes all except the **checked vowels**. In similar phonetic contexts, the free vowels are longer than the checked. (Also termed *long vowels*.)
frequency	The number of vibrations per second. Used in **phonetics**, especially with reference to **vocal fold** vibration.
fricative	A **manner of articulation** which involves a narrowing in the **vocal tract** so that audible **friction** is produced, e.g. English /s z/.
friction	Hiss produced by air turbulence.
front vowel	A **vowel** articulated with the front of the tongue highest, e.g. English /iː/ in FLEECE.
fronting diphthong	A **diphthong** involving tongue raising and fronting to [ɪ] or [iː].
function words	Words such as prepositions, pronouns, conjunctions, articles, auxiliary verbs which structure the sentence, rather than passing on much information. (Also termed *grammatical words* or *form words*.) Opposed to **content words**.
General American	The **prestige accent** of the United States. (Also termed *Network American*.)
glide	See **diphthong**.
glottal	Referring to **articulations** involving the **glottis**, e.g. [h ʔ].
glottalisation	A **secondary articulation** involving the addition of **glottal stop** (normally in the **approach stage**), e.g. **syllable**-final English /t p tʃ/ in *that stopwatch* [ðæʔt 'stɒʔpwɒʔtʃ]. Adj. *glottalised*.
glottal replacement	Substitution of a **consonant** (most commonly /t/) by **glottal stop**. (Also termed *glottalling*.)

glottal setting	A number of ways in which the larynx can operate so as to produce different types of **voicing**, **creak**, etc.
glottal stop	Complete closure of the **vocal folds** followed by sudden release.
glottis	The space between the **vocal folds**.
grave	(Used with reference to **fricatives**.) Having mostly low-**frequency** hiss. Cf. **sharp**.
grooved	**Fricatives** involving the **airstream** being channelled through a groove formed along the mid-line of the tongue, e.g. [s z].
h-dropping	Referring to **accents** of English (including the majority of England's **basilectal** varieties) which lack consistent /h/ in **content words**, e.g. *high-handed* /aɪ 'ændɪd/.
head	The sequence of **stressed syllables** in an **intonation group** immediately preceding the (intonation) **nucleus**.
hierarchy of error	A ranking of the gravity of learners' errors in terms of their effect on **native speakers**.
hold stage	The second stage in the **articulation** of a **stop** when the **articulators** are held in contact so as to block the passage of the **airstream**.
homophones	Words of different meaning (spelt differently or similarly) that are pronounced in the same way, e.g. *scene – seen, seal* 'aquatic mammal' – *seal* 'to close firmly'.
homorganic	Having the same **place of articulation**, e.g. /n/ and /d/ in *trendy* /'trendi/.
idiolect	The speech of a single individual.
ingressive	Ingoing. Opposed to **egressive**.
intensity	The amount of energy in a sound wave perceived as loudness.
interlinear	**Intonation** marking which indicates **pitch** with dots and lines placed between a pair of horizontal lines.
in-text	**Intonation** marking which indicates **pitch** within the text itself by means of stylised marks (e.g. circles, angled marks).
intonation	The **pitch** patterns of speech.
intonation group	A group of words forming a complete **intonation** pattern. (Also termed *breath group, sense group, tone group*.)
intrusive *r*	A type of r **liaison**, similar to **linking *r***, but not traceable to any **r** in the spelling, e.g. *I saw it coming* /aɪ 'sɔːr ɪt 'kʌmɪŋ/.
L1, L2	Abbreviations for mother tongue (first language) and target language (second language).
labial	Referring to the lips.
labialisation	A **secondary articulation** involving the addition of lip-rounding, e.g. English [kʷ] in *quilt*.
labial-velar	A **double articulation** involving (1) the lips and (2) the back of the tongue against the velum, e.g. /w/ in *wise*.

labio-dental	A **place of articulation** involving the lower lip and the upper front teeth, e.g. /f v/ in *fine, vine.*
lagging assimilation	An **assimilation** in which one **phoneme** changes under the influence of a preceding phoneme, e.g. when *in the corner* is pronounced as /ɪn nə ˈkɔːnə/. (Also termed *perseverative* or *progressive.*)
language invariable stress	Languages where all words have the same **stress** pattern, e.g. French: final stress; Welsh: **penultimate** stress; Czech: initial word stress.
lateral	A **manner of articulation** in which the **airstream** escapes over the lowered sides of the tongue. The term includes lateral **approximants** (e.g. /l/ as in *little*), and also lateral **fricatives** (e.g. /ɬ/ as in Welsh *llyfr* 'book').
lateral release	The **release** of a **plosive** by means of lowering the sides of the tongue following a **homorganic stop**, e.g. English *bottle.*
leading assimilation	An **assimilation** in which one **phoneme** changes in advance of a following phoneme, e.g. *in Greece* pronounced as /ɪŋ ˈgriːs/. (Also termed *anticipatory* or *regressive.*)
lenis	A phonological class of **voiced obstruent consonants** articulated with relatively little energy and with potential **voice**, e.g. English /g v z/. Opposed to **fortis**.
lexical variation	Differences in language usage between **accents** dependent on the choice of one **phoneme** or another in a particular set of words, e.g. /æ/ or /ɑː/ in the BATH words.
lexically designated stress	Languages where **stress** can fall anywhere in the word but is fixed for each item, e.g. English, German and Portuguese.
liaison	The insertion of a **consonant** in order to facilitate the **articulation** of a word sequence, e.g. French *ces* /se/, *animaux* /animo/ but *ces animaux* /se z animo/.
lingual	Used in **phonetics** as an anatomical term referring to the tongue.
linking *r*	A frequent form of **liaison** in **non-rhotic accents** of English whereby silent word-final **orthographic r** is sounded if the following word begins with a **vowel**, e.g. *more* /mɔː/ but *more ice* /mɔː r ˈaɪs/. Cf. **intrusive *r***.
manner of articulation	How the **articulators** affect the **airstream** passing through the **vocal tract** so as to result in a **stricture** of either (1) complete closure, (2) narrowing or (3) open approximation.
marginal phoneme	A foreign **phoneme** found only within a restricted set of words such as loans or names, e.g. /x/ in English in words like *lo<u>ch</u>, Ba<u>ch</u>.*
minimal pair	A pair of words distinguished by a single **phoneme**, e.g. *bit – sit.*
minimal set	A set of words in a given language distinguished by a single **phoneme**, e.g. *bit – sit – pit – lit – nit.*

monosyllable	A word of one **syllable**, e.g. *bat.* Cf. **polysyllable**.
nasal	(1) Referring to the space inside the nose. (2) A **manner of articulation** involving the soft palate being lowered so that the **airstream** escapes via the **nasal cavity**, e.g. /m n ŋ/. Cf. **oral**.
nasal cavity	The space inside the nose.
nasal release	The release of a **plosive** by the lowering of the soft palate allowing the **airstream** to pass out through the nose.
nasal vowel	**Vowel** articulated with the soft palate lowered, thus adding the resonance of the **nasal** cavity, e.g. French /ɛ̃/ in *faim* 'hunger', Portuguese /ĩ/ in *vim* /vĩ]/ 'I came'.
nasalisation	A **secondary articulation** involving the addition of **nasal** resonance to an **oral** sound, e.g. the **vowel** in English *man* [mæ̃n].
native speaker	A person who speaks a language as his or her mother tongue.
neutralisation	See **phoneme neutralisation**.
non-native speaker	A person who has acquired a language in any way other than by speaking it from early childhood as a mother tongue. Cf. **native speaker**.
non-regional pronunciation (NRP)	A type of educated British English **accent**, employed typically by younger speakers, which is not localisable through specific regional characteristics. Cf. traditional **Received Pronunciation**.
non-rhotic	Those varieties of English where **orthographic r** is pronounced only before a **vowel**, e.g. most forms of English spoken in England and Wales (including **NRP**), Australian and South African. Cf. **rhotic**.
nuclear tone	The **pitch** pattern of the **nucleus** of an **intonation group**.
nucleus	Note that this term is used for two completely different concepts: (1) The most prominent **syllable** in an **intonation group**. (Also termed *tonic*.) (2) The most prominent element of a syllable. See **syllable nucleus**.
nucleus location	The placing of the **nucleus** within an **intonation group**.
obstruent	A term covering **stops** and **fricatives**. Cf. **sonorant**.
onset	The initial consonantal element of a **syllable**.
open	A sound (usually a **vowel**) which is articulated with considerable space between the upper surface of the tongue and the palate, e.g. /ɑː/ in *bar*, German /aː/ as in *Bahn* 'path'. Opposed to **close**.
open syllable	A **syllable** which does not end in a **consonant phoneme**, e.g. *see, boy*. Opposed to **closed syllable**.
oral	(1) Concerning the mouth. (2) Referring to **articulations** made with the soft palate raised so that air escapes via the mouth and not the nose; cf. **nasal**.
oral cavity	The space inside the mouth.
organs of speech	All organs involved in the speech process.

orthography	Another term for spelling. Adj. *orthographic*.
overlapping stops	A sequence of **stops** which involves one or more of their stages being inaudible.
palatal	A **place of articulation** involving the front of the tongue and the hard palate, e.g. /j/ in *yes*.
palatalisation	A **secondary articulation** involving the addition of front tongue raising towards the palate, e.g. *news* [nʲuːz].
palato-alveolar	A **place of articulation** involving the blade/front of the tongue and the rear of the alveolar ridge/front of the hard palate, e.g. /ʃ/ as in *shiver* and /dʒ/ in *jeans*.
paralinguistic	Referring to paralanguage, i.e. features of communication which are not part of language as such, e.g. gestures, facial expressions, tones of voice.
passive articulator	The **articulator** which does not move in the production of a speech sound, e.g. the alveolar ridge in /t/.
penultimate	One before the last. Often used with reference to **stress**.
peripheral	Referring to **vowels** produced at the edge of the **vowel diagram**. Opposed to **central**.
pharyngeal cavity	The space inside the pharynx. Also spelt 'pharyngal'.
phonation	The process by which the **vocal folds** are positioned so as to produce various **glottal settings**, e.g. **voiced**, **voiceless**, **creak**, etc.
phoneme	One of a set of abstract units which together form the sound system of a given language, and through which contrasts of meaning are produced.
phoneme neutralisation	In certain phonetic contexts, it may not be possible to allocate an **allophone** to one **phoneme** category rather than another. The phonemic opposition is thus neutralised; e.g. the final **vowel** in *happʏ* [i] could be regarded as either /ɪ/ or /iː/, as its **realisation** shares features of both these phonemes.
phonemic inventory	The complete set of **phonemes** in a language.
phonemic transcription	An alphabetic system for showing the sounds of a language, which allots one symbol to each **phoneme**. Phonemic transcription uses relatively simple letter shapes and is placed between slant brackets / /.
phonetic conditioning	A term used to cover any way in which speech sounds are influenced by adjacent (or near-adjacent) **segments**.
phonetic transcription	Transcription which shows articulatory detail by means of representing the **allophones** of **phonemes**. Phonetic transcription is detailed and placed between square brackets [ ].
phonetics	The scientific study of speech sounds.
phonology	The branch of linguistics that deals with the system and patterning of sounds in a language. Adj. *phonological*.

pitch	The property of a sound (related to **frequency**) which enables a listener to perceive it as high or low. In rough terms, the higher the frequency, the higher the pitch.
place of articulation	The point in the **vocal tract** at which a sound is made.
plosion	The noisy release of air in the final stage of a **stop**.
plosive	A **manner of articulation** which involves a complete closure in the **vocal tract** followed by a rapid release of the **airstream**, e.g. /p b/ in *pie, buy*.
polysyllable	A word of more than one **syllable**, e.g. *bicycle*. Cf. **monosyllable**.
post-vocalic	In a context following a **vowel**.
pre-glottalisation	A stop **consonant** incorporating a **glottal stop** occurring in the **approach stage**. Also termed *glottal reinforcement*.
prestige accent	A social **accent** associated with high status.
pre-vocalic	In a context before a **vowel**.
prominence	A combination of properties such as **stress**, **pitch**, **duration** and loudness which together make a sound stand out from others.
pulmonic	Involving the lungs.
r-colouring	The addition of a **retroflex** quality to **vowels**, e.g. American *bird, car*, etc.
realisation	The process by which the abstract phonemic unit becomes physical reality in the form of sound. Loosely, the way in which a particular **phoneme** is said on a given occasion.
realisational variation	Differences in language usage between **accents** dependent on the **realisation** of a particular **phoneme**.
Received Pronunciation (RP)	The term which has been used since the 1920s for the traditional **prestige accent** of British English. Usually abbreviated to RP. Sometimes called *BBC English*. Cf. **non-regional pronunciation** (NRP).
reciprocal assimilation	Two-way assimilation whereby two phonemes are simultaneously changed, e.g. /s/ and /j/ in *Bless you* /ˈbleʃ ʃuː/.
regional variation	Variation in speech which differs from one geographical area to another. (Also termed *areal variation*.) Cf. **social variation**.
release stage	The final stage in the **articulation** of a **stop** in which the **articulators** part and the **airstream** is allowed to escape with **plosion**.
retracted	Articulated further **back**. **Diacritic** [ˍ], e.g. English /k/ in *cork* [kɔːk]. Opposed to **advanced**.
retroflex	A **place of articulation** which involves the tongue-tip being curled back to articulate with the rear of the alveolar ridge, e.g. [ʈ ɖ ɳ] in Indian languages (e.g. Hindi). The tongue-bunching characteristic of many types of American /r/ is also often loosely referred to as retroflex.

rhotic	Those varieties of English where **orthographic r** is pronounced wherever it occurs, e.g. most forms of American English, Scottish and Irish English. Cf. **non-rhotic**.
rhyme	A term to cover the **nucleus** and **coda** elements in the **syllable**.
rhythm	Patterns of the timing of **syllables** in speech, in some way similar to rhythmic patterns in music.
salient	A conspicuous feature of a language **variety**, especially something which is popularly regarded as being characteristic of the **accent** concerned, e.g. **uvular** [ʁ] in Geordie.
schwa	The **central vowel** /ə/ as in *about*, *better*, French *atelier* 'studio', German *Bekannte* 'acquaintance'. Derived from Hebrew for the sound in that language.
secondary articulation	A modification applied to the main **articulation** of a speech sound. Secondary articulations comprise **palatalisation**, **velarisation**, **labialisation**, **glottalisation**, **nasalisation**.
segment	Individual speech sounds, i.e. **consonants** and **vowels**, that can be represented by means of the symbols of a phonetic alphabet. Adj. *segmental*.
segmentation	The process of dividing up the flow of speech into individual speech sounds (or **segments**).
sentence stress	Used loosely to refer to the stress patterns of connected speech.
setting, articulatory	A term used to cover the way in which the **organs of speech** are held throughout the speech process. Setting varies from one language to another and, within languages, from one **accent** to another.
sharp	(Used with reference to **fricatives**.) Having mostly high-**frequency** hiss. Cf. **grave**.
smoothing	An effect whereby in a **vowel sequence** one element is partly or totally lost, e.g. *tyre* /taɪə/ realised as [taə] or even [taː].
social variation	Differences in language usage which are dependent on factors such as social class, age, religion, etc. Cf. **regional variation**.
sonorant	A term covering **nasals**, **approximants** (**central** and **lateral**) and **vowels**. Cf. **obstruent**.
sonority	The relative loudness or carrying power of a sound compared to that of other sounds which have similar **pitch**, **stress** and **duration**, etc. Adj. *sonorous*.
speech mechanism	Another term for the **organs of speech**.
steady-state vowel	A **vowel** articulated with tongue and the lips held in one position. (Also termed *monophthong* and *pure vowel*.) Cf. **diphthong**.

stigmatised	Used with reference to **accent** features which invoke social disapproval of various kinds, e.g. ridicule, correction.
stop	A term covering **plosives** and **affricates**, involving a complete closure in the **vocal tract** with the soft palate raised.
stress	The combination of features (loudness, **pitch**, **vowel duration** and **vowel quality**) which make certain **syllables** seem more prominent than others. Primary stress refers to the most prominent syllable in a word; secondary stress to the second most prominent.
stress-timed	A type of speech **rhythm** which gives the impression of regular intervals between stressed **syllables**, e.g. English, Dutch and German. Cf. **syllable-timed**.
stricture	A narrowing of a part of the **vocal tract** made by the actions of the **articulators**.
strong form	The form which certain **function words** have when pronounced **stressed** or in isolation. Opposed to **weak form**.
supra-glottal	Referring to parts of the **speech mechanism** situated above the larynx, i.e. the pharynx, mouth and nose.
supra-segmental	Phonetic phenomena which cover an extent greater than the individual **segment**, e.g. **pitch**, **stress**. Cf. **segment**.
syllabic consonant	A **consonant** which functions as a **syllable nucleus**, e.g. English /n̩/ in *hidden* /ˈhɪdn̩/.
syllable	A linguistic unit larger than the **phoneme** and smaller than the word, usually containing a vowel as its **nucleus**.
syllable nucleus	The most prominent, **sonorous** element of a **syllable**.
syllable-timed	A type of speech **rhythm** which gives the impression of **syllables** occupying roughly equal amounts of time, e.g. French, Yoruba. Cf. **stress-timed**.
systemic variation	Differences in language usage between **accents** dependent on variations in the number of phonemes in the phoneme system.
t-voicing	A **voiced realisation** of /t/, symbolised as 't̬', e.g. American English *sitting, matter*.
tag-question	A structure, consisting of an auxiliary verb and pronoun, attached to the end of a statement for confirmation, e.g. *Andrew lives in Birmingham, doesn't he?*
tag-type response	Brief questions similar in structure to a **tag-question**. Tag-type responses are used as a rejoinder in **discourse**, e.g. *He's selling his bike. – Is he?*
tap	A **manner of articulation** where the **active articulator** strikes the **passive articulator** with a single rapid, percussive movement, e.g. Spanish *para* 'for' [ˈpaɾa].
(lexical) tone	**Pitch** movements that in a **tone language** (e.g. Chinese, Ewe, Korean) are capable of distinguishing word meaning.
tone language	A language which utilises **tones** as **phonemes**.

tongue arch	The hump formed by the tongue for a **vowel articulation**.
tongue height	The degree to which the tongue approaches the roof of the mouth.
trill	A **manner of articulation** where the **active articulator** strikes the **passive articulator** with a number of rapid, percussive movements, e.g. Spanish *parra* 'grapevine' ['para]. (Also termed *roll*.)
upspeak	The tendency for speech of younger persons to include a preponderance of terminal rising tones for statements (as opposed to the falling patterns to be found in traditional RP), especially in narrative.
utterance	A term used to refer to any stretch of speech.
uvular	A **place of articulation** involving the uvula and the back of the tongue, e.g. French *rire* [ʁiːʁ] 'to laugh'.
variety	A term covering both **accent** and **dialect**, referring to variation in language usage between various groups of people.
velar	A **place of articulation** involving the velum and the back of the tongue, e.g. /k/ in *kick*.
velarisation	A **secondary articulation** involving the addition of tongue back raising towards the velum, e.g. **dark** [ɫ] in *build*.
velic closure	A closure made between the soft palate and the pharynx wall during the **articulation** of non-**nasal** sounds.
vocal folds	The two folds of ligament contained in the larynx that by vibration produce **voice**. (Also termed *vocal cords*.)
vocal tract	The passageways above the larynx used in speech, i.e. the **nasal**, **oral** and **pharyngeal** cavities.
voice	A **glottal setting** involving rapid vibration of the **vocal folds**, producing a 'buzz' which accompanies almost all **vowel** sounds and **voiced consonants**.
voiced	Referring to a sound articulated with **voice**, e.g. all **vowels** and **consonants** such as [m z g ð]. Opposed to **voiceless**.
voiceless	A sound articulated without **voice**, e.g. [s k θ]. Opposed to **voiced**.
vowel	A sound formed with a **stricture** of open approximation which acts as a **syllable nucleus**.
vowel diagram	A stylised figure used to represent **vowel qualities** based on apparent **tongue height**.
(vowel) glide	See **diphthong**.
vowel quality	The **acoustic** nature of a **vowel** sound as perceived by the human ear.
vowel reduction	An effect found in most forms of native-speaker English, whereby **peripheral vowel phonemes** are replaced in unstressed **syllables** by /ə ɪ ʊ/ or a **syllabic consonant**.

vowel sequence	A sequence of **vowels** within a single **syllable**. Used in descriptions of English particularly to refer to the sequences /aɪə aʊə/.
weak form	The reduced forms of unstressed **function words**, e.g. *are* /ə/, *and* /n̩/. Opposed to **strong form**.
whisper	A **glottal setting** in which a **pulmonic airstream** is forced through a gap between the arytenoid cartilages.
word stress	Used to refer to the **stress** characteristics of individual words. Cf. **sentence stress**.

FURTHER READING

Books

Ashby, P. (1995) *Speech Sounds*, London: Routledge. [A clearly written introduction to the basics of general phonetics with many examples and numerous practical exercises.]

Avery, P. and Ehrlich, S. (1992) *Teaching American English Pronunciation*, Oxford: Oxford University Press. [Perhaps the best simple description of General American. Aimed at non-natives.]

Bauer, L. (1994) *Watching English Change: An Introduction to the Study of Linguistic Change in Standard Englishes in the Twentieth Century*, London & New York: Longman. [A discussion, with many examples, of present-day language change.]

Bauer, L. (2002) *An Introduction to International Varieties of English*, Edinburgh: Edinburgh University Press. [An excellent introduction to native-speaker varieties of English, covering pronunciation, grammar, vocabulary and spelling. Interesting material on colonial Englishes.]

Brown, G. (1990) *Listening to Spoken English*, 2nd edn, London: Longman. [The most accessible discussion of features of connected speech.]

Carr, P. (1999) *English Phonetics and Phonology*, Oxford: Blackwell. [A good brief introduction to phonetics with a more detailed examination of phonological theory. Examples include many from Scottish English.]

Cruttenden, A. (1997) *Intonation*, 2nd edn, Cambridge: Cambridge University Press. [A comprehensive introduction to the topic of intonation. Obtain the revised second edition.]

Cruttenden, A. (ed.) (2001) *Gimson's Pronunciation of English*, 6th edn, London: Arnold. [The standard work in the subject of present-day English pronunciation. Recently revamped and brought up-to-date. Comprehensive, but not always easy to read.]

Crystal, D. (ed.) (1995) *The Cambridge Encyclopedia of the English Language*, Cambridge: Cambridge University Press. [Similar to Crystal (1997) below but concentrating on the English language. Has interesting sections on previous states of the language and present-day language varieties. The book is packed with photographs and illustrative diagrams, and in all ways a good lead-in to the subject.]

Crystal, D. (ed.) (1997) *The Cambridge Encyclopedia of Language*, Cambridge: Cambridge University Press. [Fascinating collection of over 60 sections covering a huge range of linguistic topics of wide interest. Much of the book is devoted to speech. Has many excellent diagrams and photographs. One of the best sources of background to many aspects of linguistics (including phonetics). Very up-to-date.]

Dalton, C. and Seidlhofer, B. (1994) *Pronunciation*, Oxford: Oxford University Press. [A very useful practical work, which aims at making teachers of English as a foreign language aware of aspects of phonetics relating to pronunciation training and how to apply these in the classroom.]

Denes, P. B. and Pinson, E. N. (1993) *The Speech Chain: The Physics and Biology of Spoken Language*, 2nd edn, New York: Freeman. [A classic work on the physics and biology of speech which is the best introduction for the non-specialist.]

Deterding, D. H. and Poedjosoedarmo, G. R. (1998) *The Sounds of English*, Singapore: Prentice Hall. [A good general introduction to the phonetics of English but especially useful because of the information it contains on the phonetic/phonological systems of the languages of the Far East.]

Ewen, C. J. and van der Hulst, H. (2001) *The Phonological Structure of Words: An Introduction*, Cambridge: Cambridge University Press. [A more advanced treatment of theoretical phonology, discussing several modern approaches, with particular reference to the level of the word.]

Foulkes, P. and Docherty, G. (1999) *Urban Voices: Accent Studies in the British Isles*, London: Arnold. [A collection of research papers covering a wide range of topics in Irish and British urban accents.]

Fry, D. B. (1979) *The Physics of Speech*, Cambridge: Cambridge University Press. [A lucid introduction to what is admittedly a difficult area.]

García Lecumberri, M. L. and Maidment, J. A. (2000) *English Transcription Course*, London: Arnold. [The best book available for people wanting to get thorough practice in transcription of British English.]

Handke, J. (2000) *The Mouton Interactive Introduction to Phonetics and Phonology*, Berlin & New York: Mouton de Gruyter. [An innovative introductory survey of general phonetics and phonology presented in the form of a CD-ROM. It is particularly valuable for its many examples of different types of speech sound and numerous animations illustrating features of articulation, etc.]

Hughes, A. and Trudgill, P. (1996) *English Accents and Dialects*, 3rd edn, London: Arnold. [A very popular introduction to the subject which includes information on pronunciation, grammar and vocabulary. Quite easy to read and has useful back-up audio material.]

International Phonetic Association (1999) *Handbook of the International Phonetic Association*, Cambridge: Cambridge University Press. [Gives brief descriptions of the phonetic/phonological systems of 29 languages from all over the world (including European languages such as German, French, Dutch, Swedish, Portuguese). It also includes a useful introductory section on basic phonetic concepts and an appendix on the history of the IPA.]

Jenkins, J. (2000) *The Phonology of English as an International Language*, Oxford: Oxford University Press. [A polemic aimed at simplifying traditional treatment of pronunciation teaching and calling for tolerance of non-native varieties. Has stirred up debate.]

Jenkins, J. (2003) *World Englishes*, London: Routledge. [A book in the same series as the present volume, and in a sense complementary to it inasmuch as it discusses world varieties of English in greater detail.]

Kreidler, C. W. (1997) *Describing Spoken English*, London: Routledge. [Concentrates on phonology, examining the main varieties of English worldwide.]

Ladefoged, P. (2001) *A Course in Phonetics*, 4th edn, New York: Harcourt Brace Jovanovich. [Widely acknowledged as an excellent introductory course to general phonetics. Many examples from a wide range of languages.]

Ladefoged, P. (2001) *Vowels and Consonants: An Introduction to the Sounds of Language*, Oxford: Blackwell. [An interesting book on segments. It turns cutting-edge research on areas like synthetic speech and speech recognition into attractive reading for the non-specialist.]

Lass, R. (1987) *The Shape of English: Structure and History*, London: Dent. [An introduction to English language which contains much interesting material on the history of English pronunciation and also on present-day language varieties.]

MacCarthy, P. (1975) *The Pronunciation of French*, London: Oxford University Press. [See below.]

MacCarthy, P. (1975) *The Pronunciation of German*, London: Oxford University Press. [Although in some areas outdated, these two books are among the few available which explain the phonetics of these foreign languages in relatively simple terms to speakers with a British English background.]

McArthur, T. (ed.) (1992) *The Oxford Companion to the English Language*, Oxford: Oxford University Press. [Contains a large number of articles on all aspects of English, including many dealing with pronunciation and language varieties.]

McMahon, A. (2001) *An Introduction to English Phonology*, Edinburgh: Edinburgh University Press. [A very well organised and lucidly presented introduction to phonetics and phonology aimed at the complete beginner.]

Pinker, S. (1994) *The Language Instinct*, Harmondsworth: Penguin. [A well-written introduction to several aspects of modern linguistics in which many areas of phonetics and phonology are explained in an easily understood way. The emphasis is on psycholinguistics.]

Roach, P. (2001) *English Phonetics and Phonology: A Practical Course*, 3rd edn, Cambridge: Cambridge University Press. [A very popular course covering as it does the basics of these subjects.]

Roach, P. (2001) *Phonetics*, Oxford: Oxford University Press. [A brief introduction to general phonetics aimed at the complete beginner.]

Stockwell, P. (2002) *Sociolinguistics: A Resource Book for Students*, London & New York: Routledge. [In the same series as the present volume. Provides a comprehensive introduction to sociolinguistic concepts and devotes considerable space to social variation in pronunciation.]

Tench, P. (1996) *Intonation Systems of English*, London: Cassell. [A book which covers a wide area of a complex field. It aims to explain difficult ideas in as simple a manner as possible. Has excellent examples throughout.]

Tranel, B. (1987) *The Sounds of French*, Cambridge: Cambridge University Press. [Useful textbook which combines a theoretical introduction with many practical hints to the learner.]

Trask, R. L. (1996) *A Dictionary of Phonetics and Phonology*, London & New York: Routledge. [By far the best book available for the authoritative explanation of phonetic/phonological terminology in straightforward language. Many examples from a wide range of languages and varieties.]

Trudgill, P. and Hannah, J. (2002) *International English: A Guide to Varieties of Standard English*, 4th edn, London: Arnold. [A popular introduction to varieties of English worldwide covering pronunciation, grammar and vocabulary.

Wells, J. C. (1982) *Accents of English* (3 vols), Cambridge: Cambridge University Press. [The standard work on accent varieties. One of the three volumes is devoted exclusively to the British Isles.]

Wells, J. C. (2000) *Longman Pronunciation Dictionary*, 2nd edn, Harlow: Pearson Education. [The best reference work of this kind available. Apart from indicating the pronunciation of over 75,000 words, it provides much information on matters such as sound/spelling relationships, pronunciation change in progress, and explanation of technical terms.]

Journals

Many of the journals in the fields of phonetics and phonology, although containing excellent scholarly work, are somewhat forbidding to the non-specialist. Two exceptions, concentrating on present-day language usage and world varieties, are *English Today* and *English World-Wide*.

English Today has a wide variety of lively articles aimed at a general audience and many of these deal with pronunciation matters. *English World-Wide* is more academic in its approach but often has readable descriptions of research into many aspects of English pronunciation, with an emphasis on accent variation.

One other journal which may prove of interest is *English Language Teaching*, which offers useful advice and reports of linguistic research aimed at those teaching English to non-native speakers. The material is wide ranging, dealing with all aspects of English including pronunciation training.

Websites

We list here just a very small selection of the best of the numerous websites now available on the Internet. By visiting these, you can gain access to an enormous amount of background information on phonetics, phonology, acoustics, accents and dialects, and much more. You may be interested in experimenting with speech analysis programs such as WASP. These will enable you, for example, to discover the nature of your intonation patterns, and then allow you to synthesise new speech melodies and superimpose them on your original utterances. You can also go to sites on Estuary English, read a wide selection of articles on pronunciation that have appeared in the press, and find recordings of the cardinal vowels and photographs of the vocal folds in action.

http://www.phon.ucl.ac.uk/ (WASP, Estuary English, *Longman Pronunciation Dictionary*, accents)

http://www.humnet.ucla.edu/humnet/linguistics/faciliti/uclaplab.html (demos and illustrations)

http://hctv.humnet.ucla.edu/departments/linguistics/VowelsandConsonants/course/contents.html (click and listen IPA chart)

http://www.fon.hum.uva.nl/praat/ (speech analysis program)

http://www.cf.ac.uk/encap/staff/tench/tswords.html (transcribing English words)

http://www.let.uu.nl/~Rene.Kager/personal/TV1/Pho_tools.htm (interactive exercises, demos, tools) and http://www-uilots.let.uu.nl/~Rene.Kager/personal/TV2/accents.htm (accents)

http://www-uilots.let.uu.nl/~audiufon/data/e_cardinal_vowels.html (cardinal vowels)

REFERENCES

Abercrombie, D. (1991) *Fifty Years in Phonetics*, Edinburgh: Edinburgh University Press.

Bradford, B. (1988) *Intonation in Context*, Cambridge: Cambridge University Press.

Bradford, B. (1997) 'Upspeak in British English', *English Today* 51, 13.3: 29–36.

Brazil, D. (1985) *The Communicative Value of Intonation*. Discourse Analysis Monograph No. 8. Birmingham: University of Birmingham English Language Research.

Brazil, D., Coulthard, M. and Johns, C. (1980) *Discourse Intonation and Language Teaching*, London: Longman.

Britain, D. (1992) 'Linguistic change in intonation: the use of high rising terminals in New Zealand English', *Language Variation and Change* 4.1: 77–104.

Burchfield, R. (1981) *The Spoken Word: A BBC Guide*, London: BBC Publications.

Catford, J. C. (1988) *A Practical Introduction to Phonetics*, Oxford: Oxford University Press.

Coulthard, M. (1977) *An Introduction to Discourse Analysis*, London: Longman.

Cruttenden, A. (1974) 'An experiment involving comprehension of intonation in children from 7 to 10', *Journal of Child Language* 1: 221–32.

Cruttenden, A. (1985) 'Intonation comprehension in ten-year-olds', *Journal of Child Language* 12: 543–86.

Cruttenden, A. (1986) *Intonation* (2nd edn, 1997), Cambridge: Cambridge University Press.

Cruttenden, A. (1994) *Gimson's Pronunciation of English*, 4th edn, London: Arnold.

Crystal, D. (1986) *Listen to Your Child*, Harmondsworth: Penguin.

Crystal, D. (1988) *The English Language*, Harmondsworth: Penguin.

Crystal, D. (ed.) (1997) *The Cambridge Encyclopedia of Language*, Cambridge: Cambridge University Press.

Ewen, C. J. and van der Hulst, H. (2001) *The Phonological Structure of Words: An Introduction*, Cambridge: Cambridge University Press.

Fougeron, C. and Smith, C. L. (1999) 'French', in IPA (1999) *Handbook*, 78–81.

Fry, D. B. (1977) *Homo Loquens*, Cambridge: Cambridge University Press.

Fry, S. (2001) *The Stars' Tennis Balls*, 2nd edn, London: Arrow.

Garnica, O. K. (1977) 'Some prosodic and paralinguistic features of speech to young children', in C. E. Snow and C. A. Ferguson (eds) *Talking to Children: Language Input and Acquisition*, 63–88, Cambridge: Cambridge University Press.

Halliday, M. (1967) *Intonation and Grammar in British English*, The Hague: Mouton.

Hughes, A. and Trudgill, P. (1996) *English Accents and Dialects*, 3rd edn, London: Arnold.

IPA (1999) *Handbook of the International Phonetic Association*, Cambridge: Cambridge University Press.

Jenkins, H. (ed.) (1982) *The Arden Shakespeare: Hamlet*, London and New York: Methuen.

THE INTERNATIONAL PHONETIC ALPHABET (revised to 1993, corrected 1996)

CONSONANTS (PULMONIC)

	Bilabial	Labiodental	Dental	Alveolar	Postalveolar	Retroflex	Palatal	Velar	Uvular	Pharyngeal	Glottal
Plosive	p b			t d		ʈ ɖ	c ɟ	k ɡ	q ɢ		ʔ
Nasal	m	ɱ		n		ɳ	ɲ	ŋ	N		
Trill	ʙ			r					R		
Tap or Flap				ɾ		ɽ					
Fricative	ɸ β	f v	θ ð	s z	ʃ ʒ	ʂ ʐ	ç ʝ	x ɣ	χ ʁ	ħ ʕ	h ɦ
Lateral fricative				ɬ ɮ							
Approximant		ʋ		ɹ		ɻ	j	ɰ			
Lateral approximant				l		ɭ	ʎ	L			

Where symbols appear in pairs, the one to the right represents a voiced consonant. Shaded areas denote articulations judged impossible.

CONSONANTS (NON-PULMONIC)

Clicks		Voiced implosives		Ejectives	
ʘ	Bilabial	ɓ	Bilabial	ʼ	Examples:
ǀ	Dental	ɗ	Dental/alveolar	pʼ	Bilabial
ǃ	(Post)alveolar	ʄ	Palatal	tʼ	Dental/alveolar
ǂ	Palatoalveolar	ɠ	Velar	kʼ	Velar
ǁ	Alveolar lateral	ʛ	Uvular	sʼ	Alveolar fricative

OTHER SYMBOLS

ʍ Voiceless labial-velar fricative
w Voiced labial-velar approximant
ɥ Voiced labial-palatal approximant
ʜ Voiceless epiglottal fricative
ʢ Voiced epiglottal fricative
ʡ Epiglottal plosive

ɕ ʑ Alveolo-palatal fricatives
ɺ Alveolar lateral flap
ɧ Simultaneous ʃ and x

Affricates and double articulations can be represented by two symbols joined by a tie bar if necessary.   k͡p   t͡s

VOWELS

	Front	Central	Back

Where symbols appear in pairs, the one to the right represents a rounded vowel.

SUPRASEGMENTALS

ˈ Primary stress
ˌ Secondary stress
ˌfoʊnəˈtɪʃən
ː Long eː
ˑ Half-long eˑ
˘ Extra-short ĕ
| Minor (foot) group
‖ Major (intonation) group
. Syllable break ɹi.ækt
‿ Linking (absence of a break)

DIACRITICS

Diacritics may be placed above a symbol with a descender, e.g. ŋ̊

̥ Voiceless	n̥ d̥	̤ Breathy voiced	b̤ a̤	̪ Dental	t̪ d̪
̬ Voiced	s̬ t̬	̰ Creaky voiced	b̰ a̰	̺ Apical	t̺ d̺
ʰ Aspirated	tʰ dʰ	̼ Linguolabial	t̼ d̼	̻ Laminal	t̻ d̻
̹ More rounded	ɔ̹	ʷ Labialized	tʷ dʷ	̃ Nasalized	ẽ
̜ Less rounded	ɔ̜	ʲ Palatalized	tʲ dʲ	ⁿ Nasal release	dⁿ
̟ Advanced	u̟	ˠ Velarized	tˠ dˠ	ˡ Lateral release	dˡ
̠ Retracted	e̠	ˤ Pharyngealized	tˤ dˤ	̚ No audible release	d̚
̈ Centralized	ë	̴ Velarized or pharyngealized ɫ			
̽ Mid-centralized	ě	̝ Raised	e̝	(ɹ̝ = voiced alveolar fricative)	
̩ Syllabic	n̩	̞ Lowered	e̞	(β̞ = voiced bilabial approximant)	
̯ Non-syllabic	e̯	̘ Advanced Tongue Root	e̘		
˞ Rhoticity	ɚ a˞	̙ Retracted Tongue Root	e̙		

TONES AND WORD ACCENTS

LEVEL			CONTOUR		
e̋ or	˥ Extra high	ě or	˩˥ Rising		
é	˦ High	ê	˥˩ Falling		
ē	˧ Mid	e̋	˦˥ High rising		
è	˨ Low	ȅ	˩˨ Low rising		
ȅ	˩ Extra low	e̋	˧˩˧ Rising-falling		
↓ Downstep			↗ Global rise		
↑ Upstep			↘ Global fall		

Jenkins, J. (2000) *The Phonology of English as an International Language*, Oxford: Oxford University Press.

Johnson, S. (1755) *A Dictionary of the English Language*, London: Strahan.

Jones, D. (1935) 'Speech training: the phonetic aspect', *British Journal of Educational Psychology* 5: 27–30.

Jones, D. (1956) *The Pronunciation of English*, 4th edn, Cambridge: Cambridge University Press.

Jones, D. (1962) *An Outline of English Pronunciation*, 9th edn, Cambridge: Heffer.

Kohler, K. (1999) 'German', in IPA (1999) *Handbook*, 86–9.

Labov, W. (1988) 'The judicial testing of linguistic theory', in D. Tannen (ed.) *Linguistics in Context: Connecting Observation and Understanding*, 159–82, Norwood, NJ: Ablex.

Ladefoged, P. (2001) *Vowels and Consonants: An Introduction to the Sounds of Language*, Oxford: Blackwell.

Ladefoged, P. and Maddieson, I. (1996) *The Sounds of the World's Languages*, Oxford: Blackwell.

Lerond, A. (ed.) (1980) *Dictionnaire de la prononciation*, Paris: Larousse.

Maddieson, I. (1984) *Patterns of Sounds*, Cambridge: Cambridge University Press.

Mangold, M. and Grebe, P. (eds) (1990) *Der grosse Duden 6: Aussprachewörterbuch*, 2nd edn, Mannheim: Dudenverlag.

O'Connor, J. D. and Arnold, G. F. (1973) *Intonation of Colloquial English*, 2nd edn, London: Longman.

Ogle, S. A. and Maidment, J. A. (1993) 'Laryngographic analysis of child directed speech', *European Journal of Disorders of Communication* 28.3: 289–97.

Pinker, S. (1994) *The Language Instinct*, Harmondsworth: Penguin.

Roach, P. (2002) *A Little Encyclopaedia of Phonetics*, http://www.linguistics.reading.ac.uk/staff/Peter Roach

Rosewarne, D. (1984) 'Estuary English', *Times Educational Supplement*, 19 September 1984.

Salesbury, W. (1550) *A Playne and Familiar Introduction*, 2nd edn (1557), rpt. in A. J. Ellis (1869) *On Early English Pronunciation*, vol. 3, 743–94.

Trask, R. L. (1996) *A Dictionary of Phonetics and Phonology*, London & New York: Routledge.

Varney, Maurice (1997) 'Forensic linguistics', *English Today* 52, 13.4: 42–7.

Wells, J. C. (1982) *Accents of English* (3 vols), Cambridge: Cambridge University Press.

Wells, J. C. (2000) *Longman Pronunciation Dictionary*, Harlow: Pearson Education.

Windsor Lewis, J. (1969) *A Guide to English Pronunciation*, Oslo: Universitetsforlaget.

INDEX

Most significant sections for topics are shown in **bold**.